Saving Grace at Guantanamo Bay

Guantanamo Bay

A Memoir of a Citizen Warrior

Montgomery J. Granger

Major (Ret.), Medical Service Corps, United States Army Reserve
Joint Detention Operations Group (JDOG) Medical Service Officer

Strategic Book Publishing and Rights Co.

Strategic Book Publishing and Rights Co.
12620 FM 1960, Suite A4-507
Houston TX 77065
www.sbpra.com

Hardcover version published in 2010.
Softcover version published in 2012.

ISBN: 978-1-61897-963-6

Typography and page composition by J. K. Eckert & Company, Inc.

The Real Story of Detention and Medical Duty with
Joint Task Force 160 U.S. Naval Station,
Guantanamo Bay, Cuba,
During Operation Enduring Freedom and the Global War
on Terrorism (GWOT, as known within military circles)

8 February–26 June 2002

To my wife Sandra, my sons Benjamin, Harrison, Theodore, and Hamilton, and my daughter Hermione, and to all those who truly supported us during my deployments and beyond: Robert and Lillian Spears, Diane and Steve Domke, Karen and Tom Furgal, Elliott and Brenda Strobin, Anthony Perna, Tom Cassese, Richard Hyman, William Groth, Jerry Maxim, John Sexton, and Robert DelRosso. Thomas Fuller said, "If you have one true friend you have more than your share," and that is why I feel truly blessed by those who stood by us in our times of need.

Sandra, more than any other person, has survived and maintained her love for me and our children for too many deployments, too many sleepless nights, and too much uncertainty. No one should have to endure what she has, and yet many do, over and over again. I am unfathomably in her debt, and am more grateful than words could ever describe for her nurturing, healing, and fierce love and loyalty.

Contents

Acknowledgments

I would like to acknowledge the support and confidence of Mr. Andrew Carroll, editor, friend, and true patriot. Your wisdom, faith, character, and amazing work ethic are truly awe-inspiring.

I would like to thank Dr. Lee Harford, Jr., Director, U.S. Army Reserve Office of History, and his colleague, Jason Wetzel, Field Historian, for their review and constructive comments and opinions on this work. I am very grateful for their time and kind consideration.

I would like to acknowledge the confidence and support of Strategic Book Publishing and the many people there who made this book possible. To Joanne and Georgie for their limitless patience, gentle guidance, and kind attention to my needs, to Jenn for her kind, efficient, and professional work and especially to Cindi, for her soothing, rational guidance, and calm reassurance.

Prologue

"One hundred victories in one hundred battles is not the most skillful. Subduing the other's military without battle is the most skillful."

—Sun Tzu

I became interested in prisoner of war operations as a teenager, when my mother introduced me to a friend of hers who had been a POW during World War II. Horst (his first name), a Scoutmaster nearly sixty years old, was a retired naturalized citizen of the United States of America when I met him. He had been a lieutenant in the German Wehrmacht, and was captured during the Battle of the Bulge by members of Patton's 3rd Army. Horst told me his platoon was full of "old men and boys, and some *taube* (deaf)." They had no ammunition, no food, and no hope. Their supplies had been cut off for days, and they had no communication with their superiors. He said they woke up one snowy morning in the early winter of 1944 to find themselves surrounded by American Sherman tanks. He said a lone American noncommissioned officer (NCO), a *schwartze* (black), walked unarmed to the center of a clearing in front of their position and motioned for someone to come out. The American soldier, Horst told me, had a white cloth attached to a stick. Horst went out and was able to communicate terms with the NCO. Horst and his platoon should walk out to the clearing, deposit their weapons in a pile, and surrender. Horst said he did so, without dissent amongst his charges, and they were taken away in Army trucks to "God knows where. We thought we would be killed because we had heard of SS killing American prisoners. But we were well cared for." Horst said that at every turn he was treated with dignity and respect. He said they were immediately given wool blankets, and when they got to a holding area they

1

were given hot food and coffee. He said eventually he was taken to the United States to an internment facility. Horst claimed to still own the wool coat he was given as a prisoner of war. This story struck me as amazing, although it probably shouldn't have. I was proud of the fact that our troops treated him so well. I was proud to be an American, and I wanted right then to know more about this subject to see if Horst's treatment was the norm.

Of course, like most young boys growing up in the 1960s and early 1970s, I was aware of the Vietnam War, but don't remember hearing much about prisoners in that conflict until I was a bit older. I read about South Vietnamese interrogators taking suspected Viet Cong prisoners up in helicopters in pairs, tossing one out, and then not being able to shut the other one up as he gave every piece of information he could think of to save his own life. Eventually I read about our captured pilots at the Hanoi Hilton in North Vietnam. I began to see the difference between how the U.S. treated prisoners and how other countries did it.

I remember watching the TV sitcom *Hogan's Heroes,* which was about an eclectic group of WWII Allied prisoners of war incarcerated almost of their own free will by a bunch of bungling German soldiers who themselves were harassed by the SS. I remember thinking this couldn't possibly be an accurate depiction of what it was like, but it was fun to watch and very interesting, this idea of treating an enemy, someone who before they were captured was trying to kill you, with respect and dignity.

I discovered later in my independent studies that the truth was that the Law of War dictated how POWs should legally be treated, but it was really up to the countries at war how they decided to treat their captives, and many countries operated quite chivalrously. There was a pecking order of how you were treated based on your rank and even branch of service. For example, German WWII prisoner of war camps for enemy pilots (*Stalag Luft*) were the best places to be held, unless you were Jewish, in which case you would have been segregated and treated less well. Our own rules for actual POWs are similar to this day, with enlisted enemy prisoners of war employed in work details (payment must be offered), enemy non-commissioned officers employed as supervisors, and enemy officers not having to work at all, but receiving a stipend to spend at a prison camp store (called a canteen), also run by POWs. This however, is predicated on the status of the captive as a legal or illegal combatant. And POWs in American camps aren't treated differently based on religion, ethnicity, or country of origin.

One of the first things done when U.S. forces capture a combatant is determine their legal status. If the combatant conforms to the Law of War for example, and is uniformed, carries his or her weapon(s) openly, and whose nationality is among those listed as legal combatant state opposed to us, chances are that the captive is a legal combatant. However, if the combatant is not uniformed, conceals his weapon(s), and is not of a nationality among those on a list of countries officially opposed to us in the conflict, chances are he's an illegal combatant. For an illegal combatant captured by United States forces, one of his first opportunities at receiving justice is a tribunal of military officers to determine his legal status if it is in doubt. The facts are presented in a court-like atmosphere and the alleged illegal combatant is given certain cursory legal rights with which they can plead their case.

I have been a part of mock tribunals of this nature in my training with Military Police Enemy Prisoner of War (EPW) units. The standard of guilt or innocence is similar to that of the U.S. justice system grand jury indictment: If the preponderance of credible evidence presented would lead a reasonable person to conclude that it is more likely than not that the person is guilty of the offense, then the conclusion is the finding of a "true bill" of indictment. This is the 51 percent rule. The scale of justice needs tip only ever so slightly in one direction, but tip it must, or a finding of "no true bill" is declared and the defendant goes free.

If it is determined that a combatant is illegal, according to the Law of War and other rules, regulations, and procedures governing their treatment, things go very differently for the detainee. But that doesn't mean, in the U.S. military system, that he is condemned to abuse and torture—quite the contrary. Military forces of the United States are trained to conform to moral standards of conduct, and are trained to care for any captive with dignity and respect, regardless of legal status.

As I grew older and more curious I read more and more about wartime treatment of prisoners. I read about the British prison ships of our Revolutionary War, where more Americans died on these floating cemeteries in New York Harbor than were killed on the battlefield. I read about the Confederate Civil War prison at Andersonville, Georgia, where Union inmates preyed on each other amidst unimaginable conditions that slowly and wretchedly claimed over twelve thousand lives. The National Prisoner of War Museum, grown out of legislation that created the Andersonville National Historic Site in 1970, is located in Andersonville and opened in 1998 to "interpret the role of prisoner of war camps in history" and "to commemorate the sacrifice of Americans who lost their lives in such camps."

I learned of the tragic story of our own internment camps of Americans of Japanese and German descent. And although many of us might question the necessity of this action today, at the time our government deemed it necessary. Individuals were not tortured or abused, but many of their rights were abridged or denied, and their lives were turned upside down. Many lost property and jobs, and all lost a measure of dignity.

I read about the Bataan Death March at the beginning of World War II, the forcible transfer of over seventy-five thousand U.S. and Filipino prisoners of war by the Imperial Japanese Army over the distance of sixty miles through brutally hot tropical terrain without food, water, or mercy—other than at the business end of a bayonet.

In college I studied contemporary Russian/Soviet history as an elective, which cannot be properly understood unless one gains a working knowledge of the Gulag (Soviet political prison), so much a part of the Soviet-era Russian gestalt of refined misery. I learned from reading first-person accounts that Russian POW camps during WWII were notoriously harsh and tortuous.

The loneliness, the despair, and the nearly immeasurable human suffering numbering in the tens of millions of deaths, from the West African slave trade and the Holocaust, to the political prisons of Fidel Castro and the torture chambers of Saddam Hussein, can send one spiraling into nihilistic oblivion. Friedrich Nietzsche saw in his philosophical crystal ball the absolutely limitless black hole of mankind's potential evil, and it has manifested itself in the jailers and murderers of the prisons of the world.

Perhaps one of the most disturbing depictions of a foreign prison was that of the Turkish prison detailed in the 1978 film *Midnight Express,* which told of an American drug smuggler's nightmarish experience at the hands of sadistic and cruel guards. Billy Hayes, the American whose experience is the basis for the film, said after it was made that the depiction of the guards was not totally accurate, but the conditions depicted were. The organization Amnesty International, which is the world's prison and human rights police, said in a 2002 report that "the practice of torture is widespread and typical of treatment in most prisons throughout the world."

With that said, torture and abuse are decidedly *not* typical in U.S. Army prisons, either in the United States or out of it. Torture is not condoned in U.S. Army detention facilities that I have observed or even heard about in nearly ten years of service and two detention mission deployments—one to Guantanamo Bay, Cuba, and one to Iraq—with Army EPW units. The mere suggestion of torture would be tantamount to "fighting words" in the circles that I ran in because of the serious personal and professional commitment to the principle of fair treatment—with dignity and respect—which we held in highest regard for all captured combatants.

All of today's military personnel are *volunteers,* and many of us who serve in detention operations, especially those in the Reserves, are in the law enforcement and incarceration professions in their U.S. civilian jobs, which is a great advantage over our Active Duty (AD) component comrades who more times than not have only book knowledge of the incarceration of EPW and detained persons, or have only brig or Fort Leavenworth experience, and who more often than not are put in charge of us Reservists once we deploy. And yes, there is discrimination towards Reserve units by their Active Duty Army counterparts—sometimes subtle, sometimes overt. And *no,* that is not to say there is never confusion or misinterpretation, especially by those in charge, whether Active Duty or Reserve. There are those in the EPW business, Reservists, who have confused the detainee incarceration mission with civilian-style corrections or work camps. Detention facilities for illegal combatants are decidedly not correction or rehabilitation facilities, and do not operate with a work camp mentality. But even these confusions have not led, in my experience, to institutionalized torture or abuse.

The definition of torture has gone through significant changes since 9/11. The "Bybee Memo" of 1 August 2002, sent from Assistant Attorney General Jay S. Bybee to Alberto R. Gonzales, counsel to the president, amended the language of a 1994 statute that ratified the United Nations Convention against Torture and made the commitment of torture a crime. To be torture, the memo concluded, physical pain must be "equivalent in intensity to the pain accompanying serious physical injury, such as organ failure, impairment of bodily function, or even death." And inflicting that severe pain, according to the memo, must have been the "specific intent" of the defendant to amount to a violation of the statute. Human rights groups reacted with horror when the Bybee memo was leaked to the press in June 2004, and it was quietly rescinded by the Justice Department on 30 December 2004.

The current definition of torture is from the U.S. Department of State's Second Periodic Report of the United States of America to the Committee Against Torture, 6 May 2005:

"For an act to constitute 'torture' it must satisfy each of the following five elements in the definition of torture set forth at 8 C.F.R. § 208.18(a): (1) the act must cause severe physical or mental pain or suffering; (2) the act must be intentionally inflicted; (3) the act must be inflicted for a proscribed purpose; (4) the act must be inflicted by or at the instigation of or with the consent or acquiescence of a public official who has custody or physical control of the victim; and (5) the act cannot arise from lawful sanctions."

The following is the definition of torture via the Code of Federal Regulations referenced above.

"8 CFR 208.18

§ 208.18 Implementation of the Convention Against Torture.

(a) Definitions. The definitions in this subsection incorporate the definition of torture contained in Article 1 of the Convention Against Torture, subject to the reservations, understandings, declarations, and provisos contained in the United States Senate resolution of ratification of the Convention.

> (1) Torture is defined as any act by which severe pain or suffering, whether physical or mental, is intentionally inflicted on a person for such purposes as obtaining from him or her or a third person information or a confession, punishing him or her for an act he or she or a third person has committed or is suspected of having committed, or intimidating or coercing him or her or a third person, or for any reason based on discrimination of any kind, when such pain or suffering is inflicted by or at the instigation of or with the consent or acquiescence of a public official or other person acting in an official capacity.

> (2) Torture is an extreme form of cruel and inhuman treatment and does not include lesser forms of cruel, inhuman, or degrading treatment or punishment that do not amount to torture.

> (3) Torture does not include pain or suffering arising only from, inherent in or incidental to lawful sanctions. Lawful sanctions include judicially imposed sanctions and other enforcement actions

authorized by law, including the death penalty, but do not include sanctions that defeat the object and purpose of the Convention Against Torture to prohibit torture.

(4) In order to constitute torture, mental pain or suffering must be prolonged mental harm caused by or resulting from:

(i) The intentional infliction or threatened infliction of severe physical pain or suffering;

(ii) The administration or application, or threatened administration or application, of mind altering substances or other procedures calculated to disrupt profoundly the senses or the personality;

(iii) The threat of imminent death; or

(iv) The threat that another person will imminently be subjected to death, severe physical pain or suffering, or the administration or application of mind altering substances or other procedures calculated to disrupt profoundly the sense or personality.

(5) In order to constitute torture, an act must be specifically intended to inflict severe physical or mental pain or suffering. An act that results in unanticipated or unintended severity of pain and suffering is not torture.

(6) In order to constitute torture an act must be directed against a person in the offender's custody or physical control.

(7) Acquiescence of a public official requires that the public official, prior to the activity constituting torture, have awareness of such activity and thereafter breach his or her legal responsibility to intervene to prevent such activity.

(8) Noncompliance with applicable legal procedural standards does not per se constitute torture."

No definition of torture was ever discussed in any of my training as a Medical Service officer serving with U.S. Army Enemy Prisoner of War units, or in my studies leading up to completing my Military Police officer advanced training, nor in any briefing, seminar, or talk. It was never addressed because it was understood that we, as keepers of the American flame of Loyalty, Duty, Respect, Selfless Service, Honor, Integrity and Personal Courage (the Army Values), do not harm, humiliate, torture, or abuse those entrusted to our care. I do not know what U.S. military interrogators are told or trained on in this regard, and the CIA is absolutely not included in this caveat.

Some countries respect the Law of War, and some do not, and, according to the International Committee of the Red Cross (ICRC) representatives I have spoken with since 2002, most do not. But, also according to the ICRC, "nobody does [detention operations] better than Americans." An ICRC Group leader said this to me while I was stationed at Abu Ghraib prison, west of Baghdad, Iraq, about a year after the infamous abuse scandal there, and while the Iraqi government ran a small prison within a prison (called the "Hard Site") for common Iraqi criminals at Abu Ghraib, aided by U.S. penitentiary experts. I escorted the ICRC during their visit to the prison in-processing station, but they were much more interested in how the Iraqis were doing at the "Hard Site" than they were about our operations at Camp Redemption, the tent prison just inside the walls of Abu Ghraib in which we held detainees.

Unlike my conversations with ICRC physicians at Guantanamo Bay in 2002, the conversations at Abu Ghraib were not focused on how Americans treat their prisoners—or in this case, "detainees." "You do it so much better than everyone else," I was told. "We're not really here to see what *you're* doing," they said. We briefed them, and I took them through the in-processing station at Abu, but they were noticeably impatient to get to the Hard Site. They had heard of abuses there—not by the American advisors, but by the Iraqi guards. They were concerned about security, retaliations, and brutality of Iraqis on Iraqis.

I have read the accounts about the mistreatment of detainees at Abu Ghraib, and I have seen the photographs, and more than that, I have heard the firsthand stories of those who were there in 2004, because they were my colleagues in the 800th Military Police Brigade. I did not go with the Brigade to Iraq in the late winter of 2003. I was slated to travel with Task Force Iron Horse and the Fourth Infantry Division through Turkey into Northern Iraq to help set up and run EPW operations in the north, but the Turkish Parliament voted not to let U.S. troops through their country, so my unit, the 455th Military Police Detachment (Brigade Liaison Detachment, or "BLD"), stayed at Fort Dix, New Jersey, training and then waiting for deployment orders for nearly six months; meanwhile my brigade colleagues entered into a heart of darkness none of them could have imagined, and without us. Orders for the 455th never came that year.

These 800th MP Brigade colleagues of mine are good, honest, hard-working, and loyal Americans who went to Iraq to prove they were the best at what they did. Veterans of Vietnam, the Gulf War, Panama, Grenada, Kosovo and other conflicts and operations; all volunteers, all professional soldiers, all willing to give the last full measure of their lives for the good of our country, yet something did go terribly wrong.

The abuse at Abu Ghraib in 2004 was an aberration, and I think most reasonable people understand that, but has anyone really explained why? General Janis Karpinski made a good attempt in her book, *One Woman's Army* (published by Miramax in 2005), as she explains her role and that of the 800th MP BDE, and insists the unit was stretched too thin and was never given adequate resources to accomplish its mission. She claimed that her gender was a factor in how she (and, by association, the unit) was treated and supported. She also believed the fact that the unit was a Reserve unit and not a regular army unit, played a part in how she and the 800th were treated. Her most convincing observation was in pointing out that the ultimate failure leading up to the abuse was the fact that certain procedures were put in place by the general in charge at the time, Major General Geoffrey D. Miller, which forbade the Military Police command and staff from oversight of escort guard personnel while they were in the intelligence portion of the prison. Typically, escort guards simply escort detainees from point "A" to point "B" and don't get involved in "softening up" the detainees.

Miller, who was the commander of JTF Gitmo from November 2002 to July 2003, was then sent to Iraq and became the overall commander of all incarcerated persons under U.S. control there in August of 2003. In one of her many interviews in an attempt to clear her name, Karpinski said that Miller had told her to treat the detainees "like dogs." Miller denied this, but he set the tone and the command emphasis for how the intelligence officers handled the detainees in interrogations. He allowed the interrogators to direct prison guards to do what they did, including the abuse. Janice Karpinski may have had her problems, but she was decidedly not in charge of the interrogation section of Abu Ghraib, and she did not have command and control over what happened in that section of the prison. Based on what I've learned since then in conversations with members of her staff, I'd say this was almost an understatement.

General Karpinski's assertions are consistent with my observations at Guantanamo Bay: that the detention mission always plays second fiddle to the interrogation mission. Of course this is natural, as the whole purpose of detaining illegal combatants during wartime is to hopefully obtain valuable information that could possibly save lives and prevent destruction of property. But how that is accomplished is a sometimes messy and imperfect process.

When I was at Abu Ghraib in 2004 to 2005, I noticed many differences in how an interview (we weren't allowed to even utter the term "interrogation") was conducted. There was a transparency there in that where I worked—the in-processing section of Abu—the interviews took place in a section of the same semi-hard building just around the corner from the main hall, which housed the incoming detainees and housed all other aspects of the in-processing operation, including medical. Since there were no glass windows or insulation in any of the buildings—just plywood covering the window openings—one would be able to hear any screaming or loud abuse, including slaps or things falling to the floor. No such sounds were ever heard. Furthermore, the detainees were taken directly from the main holding area (one large room) to the interview rooms in plain sight, and then brought straight back after the interview, also in plain sight. Guards had to sign these detainees in and out of the holding area and were trained to observe them for signs of abuse and report anything out of the ordinary. In the Army, just the *appearance* of impropriety can sometimes be a serious violation of the Uniform Code of Military Justice. Everyone was minding their Ps and Qs, at least when I was there.

In his 2005 Xulon Press account, then 800th MP BDE Chaplain Michael Cannon, Jr., wrote about in his book, *Abu Ghraib: Reflections in the Looking Glass,* the juxtaposition between the expected standard of behavior from extremely young, under-trained National Guard troops—operating at the direction of still mostly un-prosecuted intelligence service personnel, in a mission they weren't supposed to be involved in ("prepping" detainees for interrogation), therefore abhorrently abusing detainees—and the ultra-violence-loving American public, evidenced by our lusty consumption of horror films, video games, and open brutality and graphic violence on prime time television, and a general acceptance of violence over, say, love, beauty, and caring. I would recommend this book as required reading for any American who has the courage to look in the mirror and reflect on their opinions of what happened at Abu Ghraib. And no, not to excuse anything that went on there, but to truly appreciate the *American* element involved. These young people whose lives were turned upside down are a reflection in the looking glass of who we all are as Americans, for good or ill, whether we like it or not. If we choose to look at the horrific photos taken during the abuse, we should also be willing to look at our own "ugly American" face in the process. Understanding *why* is essential if we are to prevent such things in the future.

Unfortunately, we did not learn all the lessons we could have from that experience, but many of those things have more to do with leadership and logistics than they do with upholding good moral, ethical, and legal standards. The priority of resources in a war will always be the most important factor in deciding which elements of the battle will probably be the most successful. The overall commander and his or her immediate subordinates must decide how small to cut the pie slices for each aspect of the fight. Resources are not infinite in an American war. Politicians, generals, and soldiers all have a role to play in exacting the just right balance of how much of the pie to give to combat arms (infantry, artillery, armor), combat support (security, engineering, intelligence, communications, military police), and combat service support (supply, maintenance, transportation, medical services, military police). At the planning level we call this the principle of "economy of force." Notice however, that Military Police are mentioned in both combat support and combat service support operations. The Military Police Corps of the United States Army is perhaps the most diversified and flexible corps in our military. It provides twenty-three different and distinct functions within the framework of the following five major areas: Police Intelligence Operations, Law and Order, Area Security, Maneuver and Mobility Support, and Internment/Resettlement. The latter area of responsibility includes: Detainee Operations, Dislocated Civilians, Populace and Resource Control, and U.S. Military Prisoner Handling. It is unique to the Army. No other branch of the military are trained or equipped to handle large numbers of EPW or detainees.

A wartime commander must decide how much support and resources to pour into each area. Nearly all of the Army's combat service support units are Reserve units. Many combat support units are Reserve units as well, and some of the combat arms units are National Guard.

In peacetime one does not need a lot of medical, maintenance, supply, transportation, or detainee support. In wartime these units stand up, but are not necessarily included fully in the brotherhood of the Active Duty Army plans and operations, and—as happened to the 800th Military Police Brigade, a Reserve Unit out of Uniondale, New

York, leading up to the disgrace at Abu Ghraib—they were not taken seriously with regard to their requests for necessary resources for the mission. The resource of competent and effective leadership should not to be overlooked as an essential element here. Janice Karpinski was taken from without the 800th MP BDE world of leadership, which had served amazingly well in the Gulf War. Colonel Alan Ecke served as the Deputy Commander for the 800th MP BDE and was in position to competently and expertly take over the command of the unit as then-commander Brigadier General Paul Hill was retiring at the end of the unit's initial tour in Iraq, which saw the unit stand up detainee operations there. The unit was given an extended tour and its mission expanded to include running the "new" detention operations at Abu Ghraib. Janice Karpinski was taken from outside the unit as the bright shining female star of the MP Corps. Karpinski didn't know a soul in the 800th prior to coming to Iraq to be its new leader. The unit was decimated with morale problems after learning of its untimely extension. The recipe for disaster had just been concocted.

The operation at Guantanamo Bay at this moment (and since November of 2002) is a combined Joint Task Force Guantanamo. Back when the mission was in its first nine months or so there were actually two Joint Task Forces there. One was my Joint Task Force, JTF 160, which did the detention mission, led by Marine Brigadier General (one star) Michael Lehnert, and the other was JTF 170, which did the interrogation mission, led by Army Major General (two stars) Michael Dunleavy. Don't think for a minute that JTF 160 had priority over the mission. Again, the whole purpose of the mission was to obtain information from detainees in order to win the Global War on Terror.

U. S. President Barack Hussein Obama has signed an executive order to close the detention facility at Gitmo no later than 22 January 2010, but without detailing whether, where, or how many of the detainees are to be held or prosecuted. The Supreme Court of the United States has several times overturned presidential decisions to try the detainees according to the Uniform Code of Military Justice (UCMJ) or modifications thereof, also authorized by Congress, asserting that (even though there is no legal historical precedence to support its ruling) detainees at Guantanamo Bay, Cuba (decidedly foreign soil), are entitled to the protections of habeas corpus. These protections have been denied to previous war criminals, even those who committed war crimes on U.S. soil. Such was the case during World War II, when eight captured German saboteurs were tried by a military commission after President Franklin Delano Roosevelt asked the opinion of the Supreme Court as to the legality of such a trial and received the court's endorsement based on the belief that only citizens of the United States were entitled to its protections during wartime.

Where will these few hundred prisoners go if detention operations cease at Gitmo? What rules will apply to them, and based on what rationale or laws? Are we so desperate to join the world of political correctness that we would jeopardize our own sovereign right to hold and prosecute those illegal combatants who would destroy us? The current recidivism rate of one in seven released Gitmo detainees would suggest it would be unwise to simply close the place and set the detainees free.

Most people don't realize that in time of war the Army (the official jailer of Enemy Prisoners of War, Civilian Internees, Protected Persons, and Detainees for the U.S. Military) employs trained Military Police and other branch officers, NCOs, and enlisted soldiers to identify, capture, process, intern, hear, try, dispense with, and release retained persons in an efficient, legal, moral, ethical, and professional manner. We do not train to torture or abuse. We do not condone mistreatment or torture of retained persons, no matter their status.

We are trained to use prison psychology on detainees in order to keep them fat and happy, as they are more likely then to be reliable intelligence assets, and are also therefore less likely to be dangerous to themselves, other detainees, and the guard force. Remember too, that wartime captives are trained on our detention operations and how to disrupt them. Every released detainee is a cache of valuable details on how best to resist and disrupt U.S. detention operations if he or his ilk should be captured in the future.

This journal expresses the raw, sometimes hideous side of human incarceration, but it also exposes the politically less correct reality that soldiers who care for detained persons act humanely, even though they are sometimes conflicted and confused, and that they can act honorably and with integrity within the mission of the Enemy Prisoner of War unit despite great hardship and phenomenal stress.

Hopefully, through the lens of my journal as the Joint Detainee Operations Group (JDOG) Medical Service Officer for Joint Task Force (JTF 160) at the U.S. Naval Station at Guantanamo Bay, Cuba, from February to June 2002, you will be able to appreciate the complex and emotionally demanding job of caring for detainees with dignity and respect, while simultaneously hating them for making your life a miserable living hell.

Call to Duty

"If there must be trouble, let it be in my day, that my child
may have peace."

—Thomas Paine

On Thursday, 20 December 2001, the commander of my U.S. Army Reserve unit, the 455th Military Police Detachment (Brigade Liaison Detachment), Lieutenant Colonel (LTC) Robert T. Hendricks, phoned me and the members of my unit about the possibility of being deployed in support of Operation Enduring Freedom and the Global War On Terror that had been declared following the terrorist attacks on the Twin Towers of the World Trade Center in Manhattan, New York, and the Pentagon in Alexandria, Virginia.

Not since 1990, during Operation Desert Shield, as a member of the 102nd Medical Battalion (BN), Lexington Avenue Armory, 42nd (Rainbow) Infantry Division (New York Army National Guard), had I received such information regarding actual deployment. The ground war in the Gulf War was anticipated to be bloody and long. We were stepping up our training and getting our vehicles painted desert cammo and getting our uniform sizes taken for the tan uniforms of the desert, also known as DCUs, or Desert Camouflage Uniforms. Then, just as quickly as Operation Desert Storm had started it seemed, it was over. A quick end-run around stagnant Iraqi troops defeated the ill-prepared and weakened enemy in just ten days.

Our plans for the Gulf War were based on a Cold War model of a World War II scenario. The Iraqis had dug in and fortified their locations along several fronts. They held their best troops, the Republican Guard, in reserve. These troops were held back to prevent or defeat an attempt by us to strike behind their lines, both from the sea with

15

Marines and from the air with paratroopers. Holding back their best forces also protected these troops against a first wave frontal assault by us, and gave them the advantage of a potentially punishing counter attack should we break through the lines of the regular Iraqi army. But the Republican Guard were never seriously employed, and our decisive air and artillery assaults, followed by swift armored attacks, outmatched the malnourished and somewhat abandoned and scared regular Iraqi troops along the trench lines. Once the heavy fighting started they began to surrender in droves.

The 800th Military Police Brigade, an Army Reserve Enemy Prisoner of War (EPW) Brigade, also known as an Internment/Resettlement (I/R) Brigade, had been deployed to the Gulf region in support of Operation Desert Storm, and based their approach on a conventional war scenario that would see front line troops taking prisoners and then funneling them back to a central location where incarceration facilities would be constructed. This plan flew out the window when then Commander of U.S. Central Command, General H. Norman Schwarzkopf's Hail Mary Pass or End Run around the right flank of the massed Iraqi troops took place, reminiscent of General George Patton's push in December of 1944, where his tanks outran his supply lines in an effort to pursue and decimate them enemy.

Schwarzkopf's blitz left broken-down vehicles like so many dying and dead carcasses littering the landscape. It was near impossible for detention operations personnel to keep up with the main body of combat support troops, or to establish facilities, in such a fluid combat zone. And once the Iraqis began to surrender, there needed to be a place to put them, and fast. There could be no Bataan Death March, like the Japanese perpetrated on U.S. and Allied troops at the beginning of the Pacific Theater War of WWII. We had to accommodate the prisoners who, by Geneva Convention, had the right to be treated with dignity and respect, and were entitled to nearly the highest level of treatment by their captors. The Iraqi troops wore uniforms and carried their weapons openly, requirements to earn the high status of prisoner of war (POW).

The 800th MP Brigade did what it had to do to accommodate the hordes of pathetic Iraqi soldiers. The brigade desperately begged engineer units to help construct hasty holding areas by plowing berms in the sand to forge corrals, but more often than not, simple triple-concertina (barbed) wire pens were erected and had to make do. Sally ports (enclosed gateways separating holding areas and open areas in a prison camp) were thrown together by hand by Reservists, some of whom were carpenters, contractors, and builders back in their civilian jobs in New York, New Jersey, Connecticut, and Pennsylvania, where the majority of brigade personnel came from. Guard shacks and towers were similarly tossed together with wood, hammer, and nail. If they were available, tents were erected for detainees along with hurriedly posted shelters and lean-tos to help protect the defeated masses from the unforgiving sun.

Meals-Ready-To-Eat, or MREs, were given to the prisoners, but many of them balked when they learned several meals contained pork. Water was scarce and plumbing was nonexistent. A mass exodus from the holding areas needed to take place in order to prevent a human tragedy. These prisoners needed to be well cared for, or their relief over not having been executed upon surrendering would soon turn to riotous thoughts, and then potentially deadly behavior.

Enemy Prisoner of War brigades have lots of different units. Some are large, like the Internment/Resettlement (I/R) battalions, with hundreds of soldiers, and some are small, like the tiny twelve-person processing teams or resettlement detachments. The whole concept here was that EPW camps were not supposed to house prisoners for long periods of time, and according to the rules, after hostilities cease, prisoners are supposed to be handed over to either the "host" or third-party country, or repatriated back to their own country. The International Committee of the Red Cross was the third party go-between in all of this. Prisoners would be taken to border areas in order to meet up with the ICRC and representatives of either the host country or third country or country of the prisoner, and either an exchange or release would take place. There were lots of prisoners to process for release.

This was accomplished in a professional and respectful way that would make anyone proud to be an American. I had the esteemed privilege of coming into this band of MP brothers in January of 2000, just before the big EPW conference at the Merchant Marine Academy in Kings Point, Long Island, New York. Enemy Prisoner of War units from across the country, all Reserve units, came to discuss doctrine and prepare for the next machination of EPW operations, whenever that would be.

I was a newly minted captain, but since I hadn't had an official promotion ceremony, my commander, LTC Hendricks, insisted I wear my previous rank of First Lieutenant (1LT). Promotions came slowly in the Reserves. Most of us spend maximum time in rank before getting promoted, especially in combat support units. Officers in combat units, such as the infantry, artillery and armor, are said to get quicker promotions, and probably mostly for good reason—they are expected to be the tip of the spear in battle. And so I spent the requisite three years as a second lieutenant, and the requisite five years as a first lieutenant. For this reason Reserve officers tended to be older than their like-ranked colleagues in the Regular Army.

The conference included a special "BLD" session for the six units designated as Brigade Liaison Detachments. These were units born of a belief that if the next war were in a desert environment, which after the Gulf War is all we really trained for, there would need to be additional command and control elements on the ground in the EPW compounds, to help the Brigade support the EPW clusters. An EPW cluster would consist of three battalion-sized EPW camp operations, grouped together for efficiency and survivability. They were supposed to be part of a larger logistical establishment, protected by infantry or military police, or some of their organic elements, along with other combat support units like transportation and maintenance. It was like a little town in the middle of nowhere, but between the backs of our frontline troops and the fronts of our administrative support, or combat service support units, such as medical, finance, and supply.

The BLD's job, while co-located with the EPW camp battalion with the most senior commander (usually a lieutenant colonel), was to provide the brigade commander—who in the Gulf War would be maybe up to five hundred miles or so away from the EPW camp cluster—eyes and ears on EPW operations. More specifically, the BLD would be there to work external support for supply, medical, transportation, engineering, and legal issues. The BLD was designed to give the staff sections of the cluster battalion's direct assistance, but also ensure that the brigade commander's intent was being executed in the EPW camp cluster.

So, to a senior EPW battalion commander, was this BLD extra help, or was it a spy group for the "Old Man" (brigade commander)? At the conference we literally rewrote the job descriptions of each branch officer represented in the BLD. Branch area experts, including myself in the Medical Service area, discussed objectives of the mission vis-à-vis our branch specialties. The several commanders in the room, who each seemed to need to make a comment on each change proposed, tempered all this, of course. It was very slow going when the leading positions of Senior EPW Officer and EPW Officer were discussed. These were the leader positions within the BLD.

The Senior EPW officer was the de facto commander, even though the line and position were not a traditional commander's position, being the senior officer, a lieutenant colonel, he was perceived to be the commander of the unit, and so carried that title and authority, even though it was not official or written anywhere. Every unit in the Army has a commander, and these BLDs would be no exception. There was only one problem. There were other lieutenant colonels in the audience who were EPW battalion commanders, and commanders in reality as well as in position, who seemed to resent their equally ranked colleagues in these little piss-ant, twelve-person, blip-on-the-screen units. There was also a full-bird colonel in the audience who, little by little, tried to swing his rank around like a blunt instrument.

"LTCs should not have C2 (command and control) in an EPW camp," the bird-colonel said. "The camps have to be run by the camp commander, period." It is treacherous ground one walks on when contradicting a superior officer, even in an environment where the free flow of ideas is encouraged. It is done with the utmost respect and decorum, else the offending junior officer be dismissed and ordered into submission, either by word or striking glance. Lieutenants and captains were silent. The challenger had to be another field-grade officer; if anyone, a major or lieutenant colonel needed to say something. Finally, one did.

"Sir," an LTC started, in a restrained and reverent tone, "with all due respect," the phrase that disarmed even the most terse superior for a least a sentence or two, "the doctrine is in place so that even though the EPW battalion commander and the BLD commander are the same rank, the BLD commander represents the brigade commander's intent, and therefore the battalion commander should yield to the BLD commander with regard to operational and strategic operations."

The bird-colonel frowned, "The senior battalion commander is in charge of the cluster, and is in charge of force protection, and therefore calls the shots."

"Sir," the LTC countered, with a little more authority in his voice than before, "the senior battalion commander is in charge of the tactical situation, and most likely internal issues, but if the BLD commander represents the brigade commander's intent, then the BLD commander should have final say on overall mission issues."

The bird-colonel rose, and with force in his voice said, "Not if the EPW battalion commander has date-of-rank on the BLD commander." Date-of-rank, or date someone was officially promoted to the next rank (a.k.a. seniority) determined pecking order amongst like-ranked soldiers. In high level groups, if position didn't dictate pecking order, rank did. And if rank didn't, then date-of-rank did. It could get down to one officer being promoted a day ahead of another, or even down to the hour of the pinning-on ceremony if both were promoted on the same day, although officially, the day of promotion is all that could be considered. Unofficially, tie-breakers could also consist of how one earned their commission: ROTC (Reserve Officers' Training Corps), OCS (Officer Candidate School), service academy (West Point) or direct commission. One more way, field commission, was rare and only happened in extreme circumstances on the battlefield. In any case, the bird-colonel's comment was seen by most as a little ridiculous, and he lost some credibility with it. The LTC had a point, and it was one that gained the most influence amongst the majority of officers, and so was written into the job description and mission statement of the BLD commander and of the unit.

The decision-making model in the military is consensus: decidedly undemocratic, as it tended to mean whatever the senior-ranking commander wanted is what happened. All the really good knockdown, drag-out fights over courses of action would take place between staff officers, and usually behind closed doors. Once the courses of action were presented to the commander, and there had better be at least two or three choices laid out, and the commander decided on one, that was it. No more discussion, no more in-fighting, no more bellyaching about what was best. The commander's decision stood because the commander outranked everyone else, and was ultimately personally responsible for the outcome as a result of his decision. Good Navy captains go down with their ship, and good Army commanders go down with their plans—never giving excuses for falling short, never seeking scapegoats for defeat, never second-guessing their staff. Bad commanders squirm and moan and groan and point; bad commanders don't last long in wartime.

The conference ended with clear definitions of duty for the members of BLDs, and that was what those in my unit who went to the conference were looking for (a current list of the position duty descriptions along with a purpose statement about BLDs can be found in Appendix B). There were heroes in our midst there at the conference, and though I didn't know it yet, many of the officers there had survived the Gulf War enemy prisoner of war challenges, and had come together before to write the initial doctrine for these liaison detachments. These men were invested and needed the plan to succeed. There were a few though, who weren't as sure about the plan, and thought that instead of the BLD the Army should just increase the number of staff officers in an EPW battalion. That would make the battalion staff too top-heavy. Too many officers in one place at one time is usually not a good thing. U.S. Army officers—good ones, at least—don't always play nice in the sandbox together. They are headstrong, nearly always right, and taught to go forward, not backward or sideways, and are trained to seize the initiative. It is nearly impossible to get an Operations officer (S-3) and a Security officer (S-2) to agree on anything. In fact, they are trained to disagree. When war-gaming possible courses of action, these two staff officers, the two most important next to the commander himself, play devil's advocate against each other; the operations officer in control of the U.S. courses of action, and the security officer in control of the enemy courses of action. The operations officer studies the mission, the resources available, the commander's intent, the weaknesses and most likely approach of the enemy; while the security officer studies the bad guys—what they eat, where they sleep, how they think, and comes up with spectacular counters to anything the operations officer can conjure up. It's like playing three-dimensional chess, with bishops flying over pawns to take queens, and knights traveling in crescent-shaped paths to corner unsuspecting rooks. United States Army officers are taught to think out of the box. They are taught to create on the battlefield and to anticipate the unexpected. They are trained to be flexible, efficient, confident, and lethal. Captured German generals in World War II were said to quip, "It is difficult to defeat an enemy who doesn't even read their own manuals." We read them, but see them more as guidelines than as rote plans to be followed blindly to the death.

This brings to mind one of the most offensive myths about U.S. Army officers by civilians: that we are rigid, inflexible, as well as disciplined and unfeeling to a fault. Nothing could be farther from the truth. U.S. Army officers are some of the finest human beings on the earth as a group, and are just as diverse as the population itself, if not more so. U.S. Army officers are trained as counselors and human resource managers. We are trained to manage finances, supplies, equipment, and time. We are compassionate and confident. We are loyal and reverent. We are the best there is at what we do—mainly because we have to be, or people die.

OCS

I entered the Empire State Military Academy (ESMA), the Officer Candidate School for the New York State Army National Guard, in Peekskill, New York, after about three years in the National Guard of California and then New York. Administratively promoted from Private First Class, or E-3, to Staff Sergeant, or E-6, for pay purposes during the course, and wearing the rank of Officer Candidate (OC), I went through the same academic course work active duty Officer Candidates did at the Active Duty Officer Candidate School at Fort Benning, Georgia, only at ESMA I and my fellow Candidates schooled intermittently, as Guardsmen, for 14 months, while our Active Duty counterparts did the residential course start-to-finish in about 12–14 weeks. As Guardsmen, we did two solid weeks at the beginning (Phase I) in the spring, 12 months of weekend drills (Phase II), and then two more solid weeks after that (Phase III). The most difficult part of the course was getting motivated to take the mental, emotional, and physical abuse one weekend per month in Phase II. Were it not for the mutual support of other candidates especially that of O.C. Reynaldo Hylton, who refused to leave me behind, even when I begged him to do so sometimes on Friday afternoons before driving up with him on the weekends, I would never have become an Officer in the United States Army. Teamwork, leadership, and loyalty were in very high supply in that Office Candidate class. I would often comment that those whom I thought would make the best officers, fell by the wayside, month after month, because they could not "take" the pressure and head games perpetrated by our Tactical Officers (TAC Officers), and simply refused to come back up to the mountain academy just several miles south of the U.S. Military Academy at West Point. Abuse? Yes, we were made to feel like useless maggots, much worse than any treatment I received at the hands of U.S. Army Active Duty Drill Sergeants in my enlisted basic training at Ft. Bliss, Texas. Our TAC Officers were newly minted second lieutenants, eager to unleash the frustrations of the hazing they had received during their time as Officer Candidate's just months prior to our induction. This was insulting on several levels, one being due to the fact that in OCS all the candidates come from the cream of the enlisted and NCO ranks. We're not novices; we understand and appreciate what it means to be a soldier, but therein lays the problem. They don't want us to be soldiers; they want us to be officers. The other frustrating issue was the perception of the lack of respect shown to us as human beings and mature individuals in our own right, as teachers (my profession at the time), police officers, business men and women, parents, and college students to name just several occupations and responsibilities we faced between once-a-month weekend drills. It was hard to function in civilian society, me a public school teacher, coach and dean of students in a Manhattan, New York City public high school, and then be expected to take orders and abuse from those who I felt were no better than I, and in some ways, professionally inferior. This was different than the training I received as a private in Basic Training, because the professionalism, perfection, and excellence our Drill Sergeants maintained was in sharp contrast to the loose, offensive and seemingly random nature of our junior TAC Officers. Actually getting to classes in OCS was a welcome relief from the even childish behavior displayed by our TAC Officers. Many of our instructors were NCOs and officers, who treated us all with respect and even deference. And although I have never discovered the reasons for the behavior of our TAC Officers, it was agreed on by myself, OC Hylton and others, that we were constantly being tested to see if we had the temperament and determination to become a member of one of the most exclusive professional groups on the face of the planet, a United States Army Officer. Words cannot describe the pride, joy, and humility I felt upon graduating from the Academy and pinning on that shining gold bar. While I was in Officer Candidate School I was elected the Honor Committee President, whose job it was to organize the committee that would be called on to investigate any allegations of misconduct by an OC, and then recommend an outcome by our commander. We did this twice during the 14 months of the class, and recommended reinstatement on one case and expulsion in another.

Officer candidates take an oath upon induction that "We will not lie, cheat, or steal, nor tolerate those who do," whether during drill weekends or not.

Any legal trouble or conviction would end our candidacy. The slightest infraction could find an OC in front of a release board, who upon finding an OC unfit, would tell them to gather their belongings and then leave the academy immediately, kind of like a tribal council on my favorite TV show, "Survivor." And admitting guilt of an infraction, although admirable, was not a way out of the consequences. There were no second chances. So, like baseball and church, many attend and few understand, and fewer still, fully appreciate and function at the very highest level. I learned many lessons in tolerance, self-control, teamwork, loyalty, and flexibility while an Officer Candidate, but there were two lessons that helped shape who I am as a person, husband, father, Christian, colleague and employee since. The first lesson was learned during my military ethics course, the instructor for which was a "mustang," or former NCO who was field promoted to the officer ranks while serving in Vietnam. Any officer who had been an NCO for very long had award ribbons on his chest that gave away his prior service, mainly the NCO good conduct medal. This Lieutenant Colonel (LTC), who sported embroidered rank and other insignia on his BDU uniforms (when most insignia, by regulation had to be in the form of sewn-on patches), told us the story behind his field commission. He was on patrol with his infantry unit in the Mekong Delta area of South Vietnam. His unit became engaged with a superior enemy force, and it soon became apparent that unless they were resupplied and/or reinforced they might be overrun by the enemy. Members of the then NCOs unit were dropping like flies and running out of ammo. Finally, helicopters came and braved withering fire by the enemy in order to retrieve the able members of the instructor's unit. However, once back to the safety of a U.S. military base, the LTC discovered that some members of his unit were left behind, and the helicopter pilots had been ordered not to return because of the enemy's strength. The LTC told us he used a .45 caliber pistol to convince one helicopter pilot he was indeed going to return to the delta and then retrieve, dead or alive, his missing unit mates. He said he was called into his commanding officer's quarters after successfully bringing back his left-behind comrades, some dead, some alive, and thought he was going to be court-martialed. He was wrong. He received gold bars, a silver start with "V" for valor device, a Purple Heart, and the admiration and respect of everyone in his unit. He told us that at the time he was not thinking of his own safety, or that of the helicopter pilot, but of his oath and the Army credo to never leave a buddy behind. The point was also that Army officers are expected to think on the battlefield, where soldiers are taught to react. Not that officers don't react and soldiers don't think, but those aren't their main functions. During World War II, German Army officers criticized their American counterparts by saying we never read our own manuals. We read the alright, we just got creative on the battlefield, and were trained to do so, under the mantra of always putting completion of the mission first. That is why it is offensive to hear some say we should "bring home the troops from Iraq and Afghanistan." Hell, we still have all volunteer troops in countries we defeated in WWII,

namely Germany, Japan and Italy, and having troops in a now democratic Iraq and burgeoning democracy in Afghanistan have proved
our worth as liberators and friends to those and every free nation on
earth. Come home? The mission is not complete. Loyal soldiers don't
quit the mission; they accomplish it, no matter what. The LTC
reminded us of that. The question came up to the LTC after he finished his story, would he have pulled the trigger if the pilot, whom he
described as "a friend," refused to return for the other members of his
unit? The LTC said the weapon was not loaded, and that his friend
would probably have gone on the rescue mission without the threat,
but that he did it to expedite the rescue. The second OCS experience
I'll never forget came during Phase III, in the mountain woods above
the Hudson River, during a break in field training. A TAC Officer
approached me and said he wanted me to sit down with a fellow OC I
had rated lowest in the class. We rated each other from time-to-time,
and those who were consistently rated at the bottom of the class were
boarded out. Just like that. If your peers don't think you'd make a
good officer, you don't become and officer. This was a gut check.
Who, during the normal course of their day, sits down with the person
they hate the most at their job, and tells them point blank why they
hate them? Well, that's exactly what I was being asked, or told, to do.
It shouldn't have come as a surprise that the person I rated the lowest
among the remaining OCs had also rated me the lowest. You don't
always get along with everyone.

But in this case, we were being asked to reconcile our differences,
or, who knows, maybe we could be boarded out if others felt the same
way as we did about each other? The OC had infuriated me on many
occasions. A former senior NCO, this OC had acted every bit the sergeant during the course. On a rotating basis, the TAC Officers
assigned us to different leadership roles within the group of OCs. This
OC, no matter his role, or lack thereof, was constantly interjecting,
correcting, and advising, as if he were a TAC Officer himself or NCO
in charge of the OC class. I was sure I wasn't the only one who felt
the way I did about him, but I didn't know how many might have
rated him lowest in the class. It didn't matter now, as the TAC Officer
had given us both copies of our written evaluations, and then told us
to read to the other what we had written. What I learned was that it
was infinitely harder to criticize someone to their face than it was
when you thought you were telling it anonymously. The lesson was
that if you have a problem with someone, let them know or let it go.
Talking, or writing about someone behind their back without giving

them an opportunity to explain or fix the problem was not honorable, professional, or fair. From time-to-time, at my civilian job, I am faced with unprofessional and cowardly behavior by others who think that by talking to me about the deficiencies of others will win them favor with me, or degrade my opinion about the target of their wrath. Nothing could be further from the truth. I know that if someone is willing to trash someone else to me, then they are willing to trash me to someone else. I don't respect the behavior, and I don't respect the person behaving that way. Too few people behave in a truly professional and loyal manner. I was asked recently by someone whether, as an athletic director (part of my current professional duties) I valued the most in a coach, talent or loyalty. Without hesitation, I said that I valued loyalty the most.

§ § § § §

EPW operations plans were the same, especially before we got to try them out; a bunch of potentially useless words, blind to deadly realities in actual combat. The Gulf War was proof of that. EPW doctrine simply couldn't have predicted the scenario of spread-out units with no communication and extremely limited support. And now we were trying to fix that with these little BLD units. God would have to help us at some point, before the world would judge us too harshly, even while we were always head and shoulders above any other country in the world when it came to treatment of EPWs, civilian internees, and detained persons.

To add to all the debate, the field manual for EPW operations was being rewritten, but the preliminary word was it was being revised with a Korean peninsula scenario in mind, not a desert scenario. This upset the senior officers of the 800th MP Brigade tremendously. They had been through the last doctrinal blunder, however unintentional. And now, they thought, the next dumb-ass policies were being drawn up because some idiot in the Pentagon thinks the next hot war was going to happen at the 38th parallel. God help us, indeed.

I was a Field Medical Assistant, a captain in the Medical Service Corps whose job it was, among other things, in this unit—the 455th Military Police Detachment (Brigade Liaison Detachment (BLD))— to ensure the medical and environmental health and safety of prisoners (called "detainees") who are associated with the group who sent nineteen terrorists to destroy the World Trade Center's Twin Towers and the Pentagon on 9/11.

On Saturday, 5 January 2002, Brigadier General Paul Hill, then brigade commander of the 800th Military Police Brigade, gave the BLD a personal briefing regarding the probability of the 455th deploying in support of Operation Enduring Freedom the OCONUS (outside continental U.S.) version of our War on Terrorism. Although I wanted to believe this wasn't true, I knew no general would waste his time briefing people on nothing. So, it began to occur to me that something was really up.

General Hill explained that the 77th Reserve Support Command had tasked him with coming up with a plan to facilitate the incarceration of al Qaeda and Taliban prisoners, or "illegal combatants," taken prisoner by U.S. troops in Afghanistan. I felt paralyzed as the weight of what he was saying began to bear down on me. My wife, I thought, would be hysterical. My kids would suffer untold frustration and emotional pain. I couldn't go. I just couldn't go. "How long would the deployment be?" I asked LTC Hendricks. "At least a year," he said. I'd read news about some Military Police units being activated for up to two years for operation Noble Eagle, the CONUS (continental U.S.) version of the War on Terror. But, I had never really thought this would happen. I knew it could happen…but how long would I keep trying to kid myself?

We were told that we were "in the plan," and that the Department of the Army could reject the plan, modify it, speed it up, or slow it down depending on the needs of the mission. We had to wait now. We could know in a day, or a few weeks, but we would know sooner than later if the plan were to be accepted.

I began my military career much like the hapless and hopeless stars of the movie *Stripes* did, back in 1981. While watching TV, feeling sorry for myself, having graduated from college, earning a bachelor's degree from the University of Alabama, and master's degree from Teachers College at Columbia University, becoming a K-12 substitute teacher in my hometown school district in Southern California, college loans coming due, I witnessed a commercial promising a "second income," "marketable skills," and "loan repayment," all for only two days a month and two weeks each summer. What a deal! I was going to "be all that [I] could be." *Join the National Guard!*

Becoming a medic was the only thing that really appealed to me, other than flying helicopters and being a spy. Since I had become a health and physical education teacher and coach, and had already obtained a master's degree, I felt that gaining knowledge and expertise in dealing with emergency medical treatment would be a great advantage to me in dealing with injuries on-the-job. Besides, the recruiter told me, flying and spying were probably out of the question: "Very selective."

After taking entry tests and getting a physical, eventually I signed a contract of enlistment in the fall of 1985. I got the medic thing, called a 91 Alpha 10 ("91" being the medical enlisted series number for that military occupational specialty (MOS) of medical specialist/combat medic; "Alpha" being the military phonetic equivalent of the letter "A," in this case it designating the enlisted qualifier below the rank of E-5, or sergeant, and "10," which identified the course as being ten weeks long), got the loan repayment, a bonus, and a unit thirty-five miles from home, in Santa Ana, CA, close to my other part-time job in Anaheim (my most favorite job ever), as a Davy Crockett canoe ride "host" at Disneyland.

I was given the rank of PFC (Private First Class, or E-3) upon enlistment, as I did not qualify for a direct commission. I wasn't scheduled to go to basic training for several months, but was given uniforms, boots and equipment by my new unit: Headquarters, Headquarters Company (HHC) of the 1st Battalion of the 160th Mechanized Infantry Regiment, of the 40th Mechanized Infantry Division. I was assigned to the Headquarters Company in Santa Ana, even though my local recruiter promised me that I could perform my weekend drills at my local armory, Charlie Company, just a few miles from my house. I later found out that medics always drill with the Headquarters Company of a unit—and yes, my recruiter knew that. I guess it was revenge for when I walked out on him after he insisted I sign up for second and third choices of mechanic and foot soldier, respectively, just in case I couldn't get the medic job I wanted. I walked out, didn't call back, and didn't go back until he called and told me I could have medic for all three choices. My older brother had warned me about this trickery after he enlisted in the Air Force several years earlier.

My unit was a very good, seasoned group of guys who welcomed me and made me feel at home right away. My platoon sergeant, Mal, wore the Combat Medic Badge, earned for performing his duties under fire in Vietnam. My unit still had the Vietnam era "steel pot" helmets instead of the new Kevlar helmets, which were lighter, tougher and offered better coverage than the steel pot, but had no liner. In the old helmet, there was a liner, or shell, made of fiberglass, containing the leather headband and suspension. Once separated, the metal outer shell could be used for many things; a wash basin (the most popular), digging device, stepstool, you name it. The new Kevlars were not as versatile as the suspension webbing was integrated. Mal made sure I was included in everything—medical training, briefings, and outdoor drills. I liked my job right away and volunteered to go on advance party to set up the aid station on Friday nights, before the main body of soldiers arrived for training on Saturday mornings. This is when we would go to Camp Roberts, a quite beautiful place northwest of Los Angeles. The rolling golden hills and scattered trees were windswept by the nearby Pacific Ocean breezes. It was cool-to-cold there in the winter months. Those who went on advance party would eat in a restaurant on Friday night using government vouchers, then, at the end of the weekend, we'd get to leave for home as soon as everybody else got back to the armory on Sunday afternoons. Everybody else would have to unpack and put things away and we could skedaddle. And best of all, we would receive an extra half-day's pay for the Friday night work.

Mal made sure I was always with a trained medic, but also made sure I was given opportunities to fire the infantry weapons when we would cover ranges for the grunts (infantry soldiers). Before I even went to basic training I fired the M203 grenade launcher, M60 machine gun, and learned to setup and use military equipment such as a cot (not as easy as it appears at first glance), litter stands (a litter is the military term for a stretcher), hard-line communications between vehicles, and familiarization with the M114 and M113 armored personnel carriers, the transportation for the mechanized ("mech") infantry.

I even went with the 1–160th (1st Battalion, 160th Infantry) to Fort Irwin (a.k.a. the National Training Center or NTC) in the Mojave Desert, to participate in war games. The 24-hour operations at NTC were exciting, exhilarating, and exhausting. It seemed we trained for a week straight, but it was only a two day exercise with little "down time," and a lot of moving. The armored personnel carriers (APCs, or "tracks" as we called them), were so loud that riding in the back seemed like riding in a tin can being rolled along a gravel road. The cold desert nights forced us to use our too-hot Army sleeping bags. To breathe we'd have to stick our noses out of the mummy bag opening. The warmth from our breath caused condensation to form on the tips of our noses, which made them even colder than just being exposed. This juxtaposed the sweltering days in the tracks, which could heat up quickly in the punishing sun. We slept in or on the tracks, but never underneath or beside them as other maneuvering tracks and desert scorpions would make this a potentially deadly practice. Whether it actually happened or not, the stories flew fast and furious about the last time the unit was in the desert and some idiot put a cot between two trees and got run over by a track during night OPS (operations). In a mechanized environment it was just too dangerous to sleep on the ground.

Claustrophobia began to set in one long night when we must've gotten lost on the way back from an exercise. It was dark, dusty, loud and cramped as too many of us were squished into the back of a M113. I stood at one point and tried to trade places with the Track Commander (TC), whose head sticks out of the top of the track. If you're not first in line while traveling *en masse* in tracks in the desert you eat dirt, dust, and sand *big time* as a trade-off for getting some "fresh air." So, as the TC made way for me, I ate a bit of dust, dirt, and grime and slid back into my sardine's quarters. My feet needed to be free, my head needed silence. I couldn't sleep because of the discomfort and noise, but couldn't keep my eyes open for lack of sleep. I developed a tendency toward near panic. Not being able to get out of a tiny space from having sometimes sadistic older brothers who would put me in a clothes hamper as a young child and not let me out, and from being sardined into the back of my father's MGB 2+2 with my older brother and little sister when I was a kid. Luckily, I had never "lost it," neither in the hamper, the car back when, or now, in the track. I was somehow able to put myself in a safe, calm place in my imagination, in spite of being tremendously uncomfortable and feeling trapped. Praying helped, too.

One day, Mal seriously offered to sign me up for physician's assistant school. The unit had a need for one in a few years because the current one was now in medical school. I would really be in the medical profession and become a direct commissioned officer when I got out. I asked Mal what the commitment would be and he said, "Two years."

"Two years of weekend drills?" I asked.

"No," Mal said, "two years, full-time, and all expenses paid, including room and board." I couldn't accept. I had just spent six years of my life and gone into at least $20,000 worth of personal debt to become a teacher, coach, and curriculum specialist. How could I toss that all aside and start over? It intrigued me, and from time-to-time I do still think about how my life would be different had I gone down that road, but I declined.

While getting a physical exam for a promotion at Disneyland, a doctor diagnosed me with bilateral inguinal hernia. I was not feeling any discomfort, but Disney refused to allow me to go back to work. Disney paid for a second opinion from a local doctor in Anaheim. He found the same thing and recommended surgery. My basic training date was approaching in a few months, and I didn't want to jeopardize my new part-time career, or my loan re-payment. I told Mal at the next drill. He immediately sent me over to Long Beach Naval Hospital on a "line-of-duty" slip. Mal thought that all the heavy lifting I was doing all by myself to set up the aid station on advance party had been the cause of my condition.

I saw a physician's assistant at the hospital, who also confirmed the condition, and agreed that doing the heavy lifting was probably the cause. I had the surgery at Long Beach Naval Hospital not long after that, and the Army paid for everything. I recovered quickly, using a cane at first to get around with, but soon I was walking, and then running, getting ready for basic training.

I swore in at the Los Angeles Military Entrance Processing Station, the depot for the region. Soon after that I was on a plane, headed *not* for Fort Leonard Wood, Missouri, as my original orders stated, but to Fort Bliss, Texas, or "Fort Blister" as we called it because of the blistering heat. Not a blade of grass within a day's ride, and home of the Air Defense Artillery School and the Sergeant Majors Academy. The heat wasn't that bad after a few weeks, as I reported in the fall. It was more like Southern California, where I grew up, with desert mountains, rocks, gravel, and sand. I don't even remember seeing trees.

My drill sergeants were impressive human beings. The Army takes the top 5 percent of NCOs and assigns them to drill sergeant school. Of those, many do not finish the school. The ones who do are squared away, sharp, and on the ball. They got up before we did and went to bed after we did. They looked, acted, and trained us perfectly. I don't remember one flaw in any of them. Some seemed meaner than others, but they were by and large very consistent with us and by the end of the eight weeks of basic training, we knew in our hearts that they cared about us deeply, and wanted us to be successful and happy in our military and personal endeavors.

The drill sergeants pulled no punches. Day one was harassment and intimidation. In-your-face confrontations were the norm at the slightest indication of resistance, hesitation, or "tough-guy" attitudes. The drill sergeants would break you down right there on the spot. One of the first orders of business was a show down inspection of all personal and military clothing, equipment, and supplies. You dumped everything out of your duffel bags, and, one by one, held up items called out and put them back into your duffel. God help you if you picked up the wrong thing or tried to put things into your bag before being told to do so. The method reminded me of my fourth grade teacher, Mr. Nesbitt, who was a super type "A" personality: very friendly and nurturing, but you had better listen carefully and do exactly as he said or there was a price to pay (like, no recess, or clean the blackboard after school). He improved my listening skills significantly. And the listening drills he had us do in the fourth grade were coming in handy now, as I avoided any special attention from the drill sergeants.

My goal throughout basic training was not to be noticed, to be the "stealth private." My plan was to do what I was told when I was told to do it and to the best of my abilities. This tended to work. I could do this. I am a very good follower. Problem was, going into basic training at age 24 and with a master's degree kind of made me a target, both from the younger guys and from the Drill sergeants. The drill sergeants wanted me to use my skills to help teach other soldiers how to do things after I picked up on the skills. This generally worked out well and seemed to gain me favor with the drill sergeants as well as with my basic trainee brethren. I did not feel resentment from any other recruit, even though I thought I might.

I did get "smoked" once however, as an individual. We were constantly getting "smoked" (or made to do physical training at the drop of a hat, and until muscle failure) as a platoon because of the mistakes of one or two individuals. These individuals would rarely get "smoked" alone, especially in the beginning, because the Drill Sergeants were attempting to teach us to work together, and that we were only as strong as the weakest guy. We caught on to this, not in the least because our eventual and best platoon guide (fellow recruit selected by the Drill Sergeants) was a former Marine and re-enlisted Army to take advantage of the G.I. bill and other benefits. He was older than I was, too, but he was majorly squared away, which helped us all stay away from getting "smoked." As time went on, there was less and less group "smoking." The drill sergeants were beginning to pull out "ate up" (lousy) soldiers and "smoke" them individually: They told us this would eventually happen when they were satisfied that we understood and demonstrated that we were working together as a unit, and doing whatever it took to keep each other in line. We took the togetherness thing very seriously, with the guidance of our former Marine Platoon Guide. We even had a "blanket party" or two for guys who were not doing the teamwork thing. Blanket parties were simply putting a bar of soap in a sock and once lights were out and everyone was in bed sneaking up on a recruit who was messing up all the time, a couple of guys holding him down and the rest of us filing by and whacking him on the stomach with the soap-filled sock. The severity of the blow depended as much on individual feelings for the recruit as well as how much trouble he had caused for the group. This was never meant to injure, but to get the guy's attention. The victims never told on the group, no one was injured, and the practice worked. I don't remember ever having two blanket parties on one guy.

There were a few recruits who insisted on bringing contraband into the barracks. God knows where they got the stuff from, some of it. There would be the occasional show down inspection, or the drill sergeants would mosey through our lockers and personal belongings while we weren't there. They wouldn't break in, but if you left your foot locker or wall locker unlocked, they would trash it by throwing all your stuff all over the room, and would hang on to any contraband to embarrass you with it later. Some of these guys would smuggle food from the dining facility, like little boxes of cereal, fruit, etc. I understand why they did it, too. We were rarely given even five minutes to eat chow. We'd march over to the Dining Facility drop our gear in formation, line up heel to toe (literally, your toes had to be touching the heels of the guy in front of you, and the guy in back had to do the same), at the position of parade rest, a modified position of attention which required you to place one hand over the other in the small of your back, feet slightly spread and at a forty-five degree angle, and face forward, not looking at anything but the back of the next guy's head; no talking, no moving. When the line moved, you'd have to come to the position of attention, heels together, feet at forty-five degree angles, arms to the side, and then you would have to "march" forward one step, return to the position of parade rest, wait, position of attention, one step, parade rest, wait, and so on. All the while, the Drill Sergeants would be harassing you: "What are you looking at, Private!?" "Eyes forward, Private!" "Are you in love with me, Private?" "No, Drill Sergeant!" "Then why are you looking at me, boy?" "Heel-to-toe, Private!" "Get in, shove-it-in-your-hole and get out!" No sooner would you sit down with your food then you were told it was time to leave. And if you ever had to be asked twice, you were in for a personal smoking, which more often than not would result in your losing what little breakfast you were able to ingest, but not digest. At first, you would load up your plate. Everybody always said Army food was not the best, but you could eat all you could. Well, "all you could" turned out to be "not much," at least in the beginning. So what we did was get only as much food as we thought we could shove into our mouths in the time they gave us. If we finished, we were never harassed about getting more food, but you had to be fast. I began to eat a bowl of cereal, yogurt and an apple or banana for breakfast. I would have bites of all three in my mouth at one time, just shoving it in. Eventually this eased up, too. And when we returned form the White Sands training area in nearby New Mexico, after our second of three phases of training, we no longer had to stand in chow line heel-to-toe, and we got time to eat. We were finally allowed to drink soda and have desserts. Prior to going to the desert, no recruit was allowed these things.

I eventually got my one individual smoking. And it was from the "The Smoke Master" himself—The tallest, meanest, Panamanian-American you ever wanted to meet. He was actually the drill sergeant of a neighboring platoon, and he was famous for smoking anybody who even looked like he was going to mess up. Often we would get back from the day's training and his platoon would be doing push-ups while we were being dismissed. He had the loudest voice of any drill sergeant, and seemed to enjoy the group smokings as well as the individual smokings. He spoke with a slow, distinct southern/Spanish accent, and with impeccable diction, and he would laugh and smile, and sometimes sing songs, often in Spanish, while he was putting smokees through their paces. He was relentless, too. He would rarely put a number limit on the smoking calisthenics he'd have somebody do. Most of the other drill sergeants would give a smokee or group a number of repetitions to do, like 10, or 20 push-ups or donkey kicks at a time. The Smoke-Master would say: "*Drop,* Private!" Most of the time he wouldn't even tell a person why, but before he was done with you, you knew why, and were swearing to God you wouldn't repeat the offending behavior. The protocol for recovering from the smoking would be to ask permission, and this was usually done after the requisite number of repetitions was completed. Since The Smoke Master didn't usually give you a number of repetitions to do, he would catch you in a rhetorical nightmare:

Smoke Master (SM): "Drop, Private!"

Private (P): Drops.

SM: "*Push!*"

P: (Begins to count push-ups out loud) "One, Drill Sergeant, two, Drill Sergeant," and so on. (After about ten to twenty push-ups private asks permission to get up.)

P: "Drill Sergeant, Private Jones requests permission to recover!"

SM: "Who told you to stop?! Push, private, *push!*"

The process would continue for as long as The Smoke Master wanted it to. It was scary.

My downfall came just a week or so from graduation from basic training. We were training for the practical skills test in our company training area. One of my Drill Sergeants asked me to go see The Smoke Master and ask him a question about something. The trauma of the experience has since erased from memory the trivial nature of the mission. I dutifully got out my notepad and pen, and marched quickly over to where the neighboring platoon was training and addressed The Smoke Master: "Drill Sergeant, Drill Sergeant Lee would like to know if..." He stared at me, looking me up and down. I immediately began to panic inside, thinking, "*Why is he doing that?*" and "*What did I do?*" I was paralyzed. It didn't take but a moment later for the words to come out of his mouth: "*Drop Private!*" I made the mistake of attempting to speak; he caught me before any words came out. "What, Private? Were you trying to speak to me? Were you trying to make an excuse for your sorry ass? I hope not." I began to push, after throwing my leather work gloves on the ground to protect my hands from the heat and rough pavement of the parade grounds. It hit me almost immediately as I began to push. I had left the top left breast pocket of my uniform unbuttoned after I hastily removed my notepad prior to coming over to him. The Smoke Master noticed it immediately when I approached him. He was giving me time to correct the mistake before he dropped me. I'd seen him show mercy to recruits after the desert phase, and had actually not smoked guys after they corrected themselves. So I immediately began to work the angle. I didn't push all that fast, but not too slowly, either. I said, "Permission to speak, Drill Sergeant?"

"What, Private?" The Smoke Master replied.

"I know what I did wrong, Drill Sergeant."

"What, private?" he said. "I failed to button my top left pocket after I got out my tablet to take notes, Drill Sergeant." Silence. He was obviously enjoying himself. Silence meant more push-ups. I continued and it wasn't until I truly began to struggle and reached muscle failure that he allowed me, after I asked for proper permission, to recover. I asked my question, which I must've written down, and then returned to the safety of my own platoon.

After basic training, I returned briefly to California, but was miserably lovesick. I was no fun to be around, complained a lot about things, and was generally depressed. It wasn't a good time to get a teaching job in my home district. I didn't go back to work for Disney, which hurt, but I was thinking all along that I would return to New York, where I had met my future wife the year before while at Teachers College.

I met her in August of 1985, I had just gotten off my motorcycle from a summer camp counseling job in New England, walked in to my graduate housing apartment building, adjacent to Teachers College, and there she was. Five foot six, short blond hair, pale green eyes, sexy smile. Sandra worked part-time behind the front desk while studying at TC. I got my room keys from her and later, after cleaning up, asked for directions to Yankee Stadium to watch the Yanks play my favorite home-town team, the California Angels. "What's your name?" I said, "so I don't have to call you 'Hey, You' anymore?" Later that week we went out to dinner in Chinatown, and then had dessert and coffee in Little Italy. She then walked me into the ground all the way back to Midtown Manhattan before I gave up and demanded we take the subway back to 120th and Amsterdam. She walked my legs off! After nearly twenty-five years, five children, and three deployments, I have never looked back, except with fondness and love.

Theodore Gareth Granger was born at 9:38 p.m., Wednesday, 23 January 2002. His mother was spectacular. No meds (pain medication), no doctors, no quit in her. Labor started the day before, after 5:00 p.m. She and I were up most of the night, trying to get through the contractions, which came in at six, eight, and ten minutes apart or longer. Sandra finally fell asleep a bit past midnight. I got dressed, put her bag in the minivan, got the baby seats situated and started heating water for coffee. I returned after 1:00 a.m. to find her still sleeping. I had a snack, turned off the now boiling water and watched a bit of news on TV. I went back up at 1:15 a.m. and she was awake, but not in active labor.

I went to sleep, and was awakened by Sandra after 5:00 a.m. She was having more intense contractions, five to six minutes apart. I called my new commander's home, LTC Alvin W. Grosse, who took over from LTC Hendricks due to an undisclosed health problem which left him undeployable, which broke his heart; I left my home number and a message. I then called the unit Executive Officer (XO), Major Pauline B. Peterson, and got her out of bed to tell her I wouldn't be coming in. I called the Reserve Center after 8:00 a.m. and got permission from LTC Grosse to have a four-day pass for the event. I had to meet the unit at our Mobilization Station, at Fort Dix, New Jersey, before midnight on Saturday, 26 January. No problem.

Sandra and I went to the hospital and found Neerah, one of the University Hospital midwives. Sandy was hooked up to monitors for a while, but her contractions were no closer than eight minutes apart. We went to the cafeteria to have breakfast, and then went back to Labor and Delivery. Still, no closer than nine or ten minutes. Deloris James, another midwife from the practice, was on duty, and she said active labor could take place anywhere from four hours to two weeks.

We were stunned and disappointed. We told her I was on a four-day pass and asked for suggestions on what, if anything we could do naturally to get this baby to come, and soon. Deloris said she could "augment" the labor with Pitocin, but if Sandra would drink a lot and eat something, that might get things going. So we went home, which thrilled Harrison, our second-born son, who was three at the time. Sandra ate chicken soup and drank a couple glasses of water, then lay down with Harrison to take a nap and actually slept for over two hours. She woke up with intense labor pains and about five to six minutes between contractions. Grandma and Grandpa (Sandra's folks) came over to take care of Harrison and get Benjamin, our first-born son, who was six at the time, off the school bus.

Unfortunately, there were no labor and delivery rooms available when we were admitted, the worst part of the whole experience. They put us in a critical care cubicle about the size of a shoebox. We were there for over an hour and a half, until a room was finally available. Sandra had thrown up in the cubicle, and was getting closer to active labor.

"Labor" is a kind description for what could easily be termed "torture." But Sandra did not complain; she simply wanted it to be over. Finally in Labor and Delivery, Sandra took a shower, and prepared for the task ahead. We tried to make her as comfortable as possible, and after a while, Deloris broke Sandra's bag of water. She then said Sandra could begin pushing when she felt ready.

It took thirty to forty minutes before good progress was made. Sandra had to learn how to push all over again. She did a phenomenal job. Deloris was masterful at coaching Sandra to "birth" her baby. I held her left leg during the pushing, and fed her ice chips and wiped her brow with a wet washcloth between contractions, which could not have been more than a minute apart.

Instead of getting three ten-second pushes out per contraction, like I thought I remembered from Lamaze classes from Sandra's pregnancy with Harrison, Sandra chose four shorter pushes. She worked hard and never quit. She wanted to at one point, near the emergence of Theodore's head, but went right back to work at the next contraction.

The most beautiful, wondrous, exceptional experience of my life was when my children were brought into the world by the most courageous, selfless, and beautiful woman I know. She was not torn or in pain afterwards, like she was with Benjamin, and somewhat with Harrison. And although Theodore was "grunting" a bit with excess fluid in his lungs, which eventually subsided, he breast-fed immediately and was a pro from the start.

He and his mother were so healthy, the hospital was willing to let them go home early, were it not for Theodore's bad reaction to anesthetic prior to a planned circumcision, we could have all been home after only one night's stay. Sandra and Theodore stayed the requisite two nights and came home on 25 January.

Sandra's recovery nurse was Laura Ecke, wife of the 800th Military Police Brigade's Executive Officer, Colonel Alan Ecke. This was an amazing coincidence and a blessing. Sandra had someone to talk to who understood what we were going through. Colonel Ecke had recently returned from a deployment to Kuwait, so the tie of military spouses was formed. The day nurse cried when Sandra went home, knowing she and Theodore and his brothers would be without me. It began to sink in with me, as well.

Harrison assisted on the trip home by "pushing" his mommy's wheelchair to our minivan. The candy striper assisting us did the real pushing, but coached Harrison along. He was the proudest of all and wanted to hold Theodore immediately upon arrival. The precious cargo seemed to acknowledge his older brother, and regarded him several times when he spoke, and before crying his sweet, cat-like cry of "Naaa, naaa."

I broke down and silently sobbed for a few moments, kissing his sleeping little head as I said goodbye. I'd shed tears many times the day I left and the previous days, but only in Sandra's presence or alone. Now, it was hard to hide my emotions from the older boys, so I just held my kiss on the perfect little forehead I'd seen brought into the world not 48 hours before.

I felt like a criminal leaving. A man should never leave his family for any reason. But duty, honor, country call. If not me, who? If not now, when? Do I leave my country to defend itself against crazy individuals who would indiscriminately kill civilians and military people, and possibly my own children, or do I anti up, pitch in, and do my share?

Getting Ready

"Those who want to reap the benefits of this great nation must bear the fatigue of supporting it."

—Thomas Paine

26 January 2002, 9:29 p.m., Fort Dix, New Jersey. I'm here now, sitting in a three-bunk room, wishing I'd wake up in my house, with three boys and my wife. I want it to happen. I need for it to happen. I'm crying inside at my separation. I don't want to feel too sorry for myself: I saw on CNN this morning, a story about seventy-eight babies being born to sailors on an aircraft carrier of five thousand that just rotated back to the States. At least I was there for Theodore's birth. I'll never forget it, and will always be in awe of my wife's strength and determination and the miracle of my children.

When Sandra picked up the phone tonight, Sunday, 27 January 2002, 7:01 p.m., I heard Theodore's cry. It was a hungry cry, confirmed by my wife, who intimated that Theodore had two states, sleeping and "nooking" (breast-feeding). The other two boys were being boys in the background. We closed the conversation with, "How do you leave a newborn baby?"

I am doing all I can to protect myself from this. LT Bay (our logistics officer) lives close by, so he's been staying the night at home with his wife, who is four months pregnant. MAJ Peterson (our XO, and an MP officer) saw her significant other last night. CPT Wolfe (our JAG officer) is seeing his new bride tonight. They all claim it is very hard to say goodbye each time. Bay even said he wishes he were in Guantanamo already.

I wish I were home, warm in the love and hugs of my wife and boys, doing my job as husband and father. If I took it for granted

41

before, I pray I do not ever again. It sounds like it's time for the obligatory "promises" stage—you know, shock, disbelief, anger, deal-
making, acceptance; the stages of death. *I promise to be whatever it
takes to get me home honorably.* Sandra still asks me if there is any
way I can get out of this. I told her that there were no honorable ways,
but, honorable to whom? To her, the boys, or to my government? Are
they mutually exclusive?

To whom do we owe "the last full measure" of our lives? It's an
age-old quandary—full of good, correct, and righteous answers—
none of which would comfort a little boy or a grieving wife, and none
of which would relieve an ounce of pain, nor fill a barren heart.

*Dear God, please let me live through this, to see Theodore crawl,
then walk, and then play with his brothers. Please let me see Benjamin marry and fulfill his boyhood dreams. Lord, please let me see
Harrison's talents develop and bring him happiness and success.
Please, God, let me live to be with Sandra in our old age, reliving our
past and playing in our future. I ask this in Jesus' name, Amen.*

We were in NBC (Nuclear, Biological and Chemical) training early
this morning through 2:00 p.m., and then we were given private briefings on terrorism and the "Rules of Engagement." I had to make up
for the time I was away. I have CQ (Charge of Quarters) duty from
2:00 a.m. to 6:00 a.m., so I'll only get a few hours sleep. LTC Grosse
has a DVD player and some movies, so I guess I'll watch *Vertical
Limit.* I don't think I've seen it before. I'll try to sleep some more
after the flick. Up at 6:00 a.m. ("on duty"), then delivery of the night
report to "A" Company, the Active Duty folks who are doing our Soldier Readiness Processing. I get to go to the head of the line tomorrow
morning in hopes of getting me through and caught up with the rest of
the troops, who'll be getting their tuberculosis screening test and then
going to first aid training.

Tuesday is our CIF (Central Issuing Facility) day for picking up
our chemical protection suits. I've been told we're also getting two
sets of hot weather BDUs (Battle Dress Uniforms) and two pair of
black jungle boots. I need to pick up a few things myself, such as shoe
polish, handkerchief, one new uniform, rank sewn on my Kevlar
cover, etc.

We're very busy, but there is also lots of down time; good ol' Army
"hurry-up and wait." I wish we were at Gitmo already—if indeed
that's where we're going. Sometimes I wonder. There is nowhere to
go, really. Can't go into town with the Hummers (HMMWV—Highly
Mobile Multi-Wheeled Vehicle), and the fifteen-passenger van

assigned to the unit has to stay on post as well. In spite of this, the LTC says we'll celebrate on Thursday night if we get validated (cleared for deployment). We've got the weapons qualification ranges on Wednesday, so we'll see about that.

I love you, Sandra. You are truly a strong woman, and beautiful in your strength. You are tenacious, brave, and true. And I love you more than life itself. I'm sorry I'm not writing to you directly. I suppose I should. How about tonight while I'm on CQ duty! Yeah, that's it— with messages to the boys. Count me in. Until then, good night, my love!

I SRP'd today, Monday, 28 January 2002. We did Soldier Readiness Processing at home station (Uniondale) in October of 2001. A garrison support unit came in and pretty much did everything this one did, except for pre-processing briefings, medical, and dental. Today, I was whisked into the processing a little early (7:15 a.m.) and was out by noon. That's lightning speed in Army terms. I did have to sit through over an hour and a half of briefings, but managed to get my I.D. card done beforehand. I went right to medical processing first; told by my compatriots, who days earlier had processed while I was home with Sandra and Theodore, that medical was the longest station to go through; I wanted to get it out of the way.

They had my records and I had brought copies of my recent physical just in case. No problem, they had everything. I went to inoculations first. I needed five, including yellow fever, flu, and tetanus. I also needed one other and a PPD, which is a "wheel" shot given just under the skin on the forearm so that it makes a small blister—I remember giving those in medic training and how steady you needed to be in order to make the blister between layers of skin. A reaction within forty-eight to seventy-two hours may indicate TB (tuberculosis). I also needed an HIV blood draw, and an SFC named Gentle did the best job I have ever felt; it was painless and efficient.

A female specialist did all my shots except for the PPD. After about three of the five invasions into my body with small hard cold steel implements, I was beginning to feel a bit woozy. I had let them know that I had had trouble in the past with nausea and fainting when given shots. One or two were not a problem, but any more than that and I was at risk.

When I was in junior high I had bronchitis, and even had adaptive physical education because of breathing problems associated with the condition. My mother took me to the doctor once for allergy tests during this time. The plan was for the doctor to place over fifty different types of chemicals one may be allergic to under the skin on the shoulder, just like a PPD. I think I made it through just about twenty-three or so before I blacked out. I was sitting down and slid right out of the chair and onto the floor. I called the experience a "bad trip." I dreamt a painful dream while I was blacked out. All I remember of it now is the pain and a lot of buzzing and colors. I came to and the test was over. Apparently, I had a mild reaction to all twenty-three chemicals put into me, but none serious.

At one point the female specialist bounced a needle off of my left deltoid. She said she was sorry, but then reinserted the needle. *Ouch!* That one hurt, going in *and* going out. I felt nauseated, and told them so. There were four medics working in the area. I rested a minute or two, was given water, and recovered quickly. She gave me one more shot and then I had the PPD, which she asked the senior medic to do. *Thank you!*

At each station they were familiar with my situation. "Oh, yeah, you're the one who had the baby." It was kind of nice because I got to tell a lot of people how proud I was of my wife and Theodore. At the chaplain's station I was made into a spectacle because of my admitting I left my wife and two-day-old son to come here, and I got an opportunity to express my feelings to a chaplain. I was numb, but nearly broke down at the mail station, where I was encouraged to write a letter home. *The torture has begun.*

29 January 2002. I'm listening to President Bush give his State of the Union address, and getting bad vibes from his very strong saber-rattling at Iran, Iraq and North Korea. *God help us.* He spoke about increased funding for defense, airport and border security, anthrax vaccines, police and firefighters, etc.

We are at war. The President's three goals are to defeat terrorism, keep the homeland safe, and revive the economy. These are bold words, and important actions. But are they impossible goals? We'll see.

The newest rumor has us leaving Fort Dix on 6 February 2002. We finish our training tomorrow on the ranges. We'll do day-, NBC-, and night-fire for qualification. Validation could take place on Thursday or Friday. If this is all true, we're hoping we can get a few days back at home before we go. I told Sandra about these possibilities, but cautioned her that these were predicated on us being released if the new rumors are true.

Wednesday, 30 January 2002. Qualification day. Early trip to the zero range ("zero" means to adjust the sights on the weapon to suit the individual), I zeroed on the first try. You must group five of six consecutive shots within a four-centimeter circle (about the size of a quarter) in the "center of mass" portion of a stationary paper target placed 50 meters down range. Next, it was on to the NBC (Nuclear, Chemical and Biological) range, where we had to don our protective masks then put at least eleven out of twenty rounds into a large green stationary silhouette. Max Wolfe asked me if I wanted to enter into a contest with him to see which one of us could hit the clips holding the paper target to our green plastic silhouette target. I balked at first because I didn't want to "bolo" (get less then the minimum requirement) by missing the target trying to hit these stupid clips, so Max said he would limit the contest to five rounds each. I agreed, but after shooting twice at one of my clips (and missing), I decided to just go for "center of mass." Max, of course hit one of his clips. I took a picture of him smiling with his prize—proud marksman. It was especially significant because Max was the unit lawyer, a JAG (judge advocate general corps) officer of legal pedigree: his father is a respected retired judge in Brooklyn, N.Y.

Later, when qualification came, I fired in the first firing order. I qualified, but shouldn't have. I experienced two consecutive jams. I performed SPORTS (upon experiencing a jam, one needs to Slap the magazine, Pull the charging handle, Observe the chamber, Release the charging handle, Tap the forward assist, and Squeeze the trigger to remedy the jam) to the "T," but had to physically clear my weapon on the first jam to remove a stuck round. On the second, SPORTS did the trick.

I qualified after missing at least six targets on the first group. I had six extra bullets to put into my second magazine, which gave me twenty-six rounds total. I shot two rounds at several targets that I missed on the first shot. I squeaked by with a twenty-three hit score, the minimum score needed for qualification. Never before had I come this close to bolo-ing. I'd never shot "expert" before, but had always shot "sharpshooter" which is the second highest scoring category. It didn't matter because we all ended up waiting for Specialist Betty Java to "Q," or qualify. She finally did it and we all moved on to the night fire range, where we were given instructions on the qualification methods and requirements.

Night fire was actually "dusk" fire for the first twenty rounds, so hitting the target, which seemed only ten yards away, was "like eating a piece of cake," a favorite Army saying that is usually shortened to, "piece of cake," when the easy accomplishment of something is anticipated. We moved to the twenty-five-meter range and it was dark. The red flickers of the enemy gun flashes (computer controlled LED lights in the targets down-range) were quick and faint. I had to fire over the rear sight, like they taught us in BRM (Basic Rifle Marksmanship) training, instead of sighting through the rear sight like in daytime. I "Qd" on the first round. Max hit twenty-nine of thirty targets. *Super Shot Wolfie!*

31 January 2002. We found out we would get to go home for Super Bowl weekend! We are all giddy and can't wait to go.

1 February 2002. I got a lift from 1LT Bay to a New Jersey PATH train station and from there took a train into Manhattan and then on to Port Jefferson, where Sandra picked me up. I would reverse my steps to return to Fort Dix a few days later. Sandra was soft and warm and loving. The boys were like jumping beans. We laughed and played and had a great time, and I was completely exhausted by the early evening, falling asleep in the recliner with Harrison in my lap.

3 February 2002. Super Bowl Sunday. Due to the attacks of September 11, and the NFL schedule being moved back one week, Super Bowl XXXVI was moved from the original date of 27 January to 3 February. One week between the semifinals and the big event was much better than the previous two weeks between the two games. Not enough time for too much hype; this was good, but I was dispassionate, and lonesome, as my boys had all three gone to bed with their mother near half-time. It didn't matter much to me that the underdog Patriots beat the favored Rams by a last second field goal. I sulked and felt sorry for myself, which was becoming a more and more familiar habit. It makes me sick that I complain and bitch and moan so much now. It's pathetic.

I called Dr. Wine, my civilian boss, who told me the school board wanted to "pay me for a year." I couldn't believe it. Most people who had the "best" situations were getting their salaries matched. I was going to get both. And he said he would keep my medical benefits coming as well. I told him I could not feel more supported. I am truly humbled by the generosity of the school board.

The Ruby sisters, star basketball players on the high school varsity girls' basketball team, were featured in a spread in *Newsday* today. The byline said Gregg Sarra wrote it. I should write him a note of thanks. He actually did a good job and had a good angle: They regularly beat up on the local boys at street ball. Too bad Gregg doesn't realize, or maybe he does, that boys don't play basketball in the town where I am the athletic director and school district resident. They play lacrosse. We're six-time (in a row) and current defending Suffolk County, New York Champions in lacrosse. Ask anybody, they'll tell you!

Theodore is growing; opening his eyes more and I think he knows me, and can be comforted by me. I worry though if he will remember me when I return from my deployment. I am almost certain he won't. I love him; God, how I love my boys. For some reason, I am most saddened and haunted by leaving Harrison, though. The middle child needs his daddy. Not that the other two don't, but Harrison is old enough to feel the loss, but too young to be able to deal with it. Or is he? Human beings are the most adaptable creatures on the earth. Maybe this will just teach him the lesson sooner. But is it too soon?

Benjamin is strong, stronger than we give him credit for. He still needs his daddy, if for no other reason than to temper the fierce love of his mother, manifested sometimes in direct confrontation. Benjamin needs close contact, needs to know he's being watched and loved.

Words can't describe the hurt empty feeling of saying goodbye. The little boy pouts of Harrison go straight to the heart. Benjamin is a joy, with his innocent smile. Sandra tries to smile, but really can't as she holds back the tears. I rage at the terrorists for taking me from my home and family. My rage is fed by the two dark empty spaces that once were the Twin Towers—a stark and constant reminder of 9/11 for all those who ever saw them and now cannot. I feel the "quiet and unyielding anger" described by President Bush in his speech to the nation that day. On September 20, in his speech to Congress, the President said, "I will not yield; I will not rest; I will not relent in waging this struggle," the struggle to fight and win a global war on terror. He said, "Every nation, in every region, now has a decision to make. Either you are with us, or you are with the terrorists. From this day forward, any nation that continues to harbor or support terrorism will be regarded by the United States as a hostile regime," and that "we will pursue nations that provide aid or safe haven to terrorism," and that "we will meet violence with patient justice." Patient justice, indeed. I hope Gitmo lasts forever, or until the last terrorist on earth is prosecuted.

4 February 2002. Days run into weeks quickly here at Fort Dix, it seems. We now have a friendly betting pool going regarding when we think our bird will fly us to Guantanamo. I have Saturday, 9 February 2002, "wheels up" by 11:00 a.m. At five dollars a pop, it's just something to pass the time. The highlight of any day is going to the post

library to get online to do email. I got six emails from Sandra today, and got to see first photos of Theodore. I actually took the best photograph of the bunch; one of Teddy sleeping in his car seat after I put him in it at the curb of the hospital. He's not even two days old. The sun is hitting the side of his face: The innocence, the tranquility, the beauty. The other one I really like is of Sandra, Harrison, and Theodore at the hospital the day after he was born. Mommy and Harrison are lying behind a prone Theodore, with Harrison obviously excited, happy, and enjoying his new baby brother. Best of all, Sandra is smiling, enjoying Harrison's enthusiasm.

We're eating more "off campus" these days. All three meals "out" as it were: The bake shop for a bagel, the PX for sandwiches, and the German/American restaurant just off post for dinner—just a typical day. All pretty good compared to what we've been getting at the post dining facility. It's a little expensive, eating out so much, but lifesaving none-the-less.

We got the word today. On Friday, 8 February 2002, at 5:45 a.m., we will be picked up outside the barracks to be taken to a Boeing 757 at McGuire Air Force Base (across the street) for a flight to Cuba—wheels up at 9:00 a.m. We received the hard copy orders at about 4:00 p.m. I lost the pool by a day and two hours.

I can picture it, the naval station at Guantanamo. I've seen pictures on the Internet. I've studied the military topographical 1:25,000 meter scale map, and I've seen a few pictures in books, magazines, newspapers, and on CNN. It looks a little like where I grew up in Southern California; arid, with few trees, and with tall brown-tan grass, scrub, cactus, dirt, and sand. Oh, and it looks hot. But we'll see. It's still winter, right?

We ate at McGuire Air Force Base dining facility (DIFAC, pronounced "DEE-fack") tonight, all of us but Max (his new bride is in town), 1LT Lee Bay (went home to his wife in Jersey), and the LTC, his wife is in town as well. 1LT Bay's wife is pregnant with their first child and may deliver during our deployment (I'm not sure what's worse, leaving your two-day-old child, or missing the birth all together). The McGuire DIFAC was a million times better than the Army dining facility; polite, cheerful crew, tasty, healthy foods and lots of variety—and inexpensive, too. They even have mentally challenged civilians busing tables. We're going there for breakfast tomorrow.

First Sergeant Michelangelo from the Headquarters (HQ) in Uniondale stopped by with CamelBaks for all of us. That's a plastic bladder and padded insulator that you carry on your back and drink through a flexible plastic tube with a bite valve you position near your mouth; the shoulder strap has a clip for the tube which easily bends up to the mouth. They're really cool, and an issue item (so we don't pay for it!). We have some packing and cleaning to do tomorrow, then, poof! We go.

Thursday, 7 February 2002. The packing is done. The cleaning will happen at 4:00 a.m. We swept out the room, and will mop it and our bathroom tomorrow. We loaded a twenty-foot shipping container with our duffels. Max had to help me get my last duffel closed. I guess I did travel too heavily after all. We stand tall for the trip to McGuire at 0545 hours tomorrow, as planned. We're taking our weapons on the commercial charter, but have to put our bolts in our pockets. We also had to put our pocket knives in our duffels—no carry-on Leatherman tools, knives, etc. M-16s and 9-millimeter handguns are OK, though. Ludicrous, considering we're the "good guys," eh? What, they don't feel safe with us on board?

I can hear the jet engines in the night. I can't believe it's true. I suppose I won't believe it until I'm actually there. I think a lot about just getting settled. I want to do my job and all, but I also want to get settled in—a place to unpack, a place to call "home" for a while. I know that will all come soon enough, but not soon enough for me. Next entry from thirty thousand feet?

Camp X-Ray

"These are the times that try men's souls."

—Thomas Paine

8 February 2002. 1055 hours. Make that 35,000 feet. Probably off the east Florida coast, flying North American Airlines. Meal was fine. Lots of soda and water to drink. Coffee by my side. M-16 under my seat, barrel facing toward the outside of the aircraft.

We are on our way. Recent news (CNN in the waiting room of the air terminal at McGuire Air Force Base) says that the Taliban will be treated under the auspices of the Geneva Conventions, and Al Qaeda will not. Max says that's kosher. He's reading an MP course manual; he's going for the Military Police branch area of concentration. Even though he can't branch transfer because he's an attorney, he wants to be MP-qualified, which is admirable—and also useful to me as a resource.

I hate the Taliban and Al Qaeda for separating me from my wife, family, job, and friends. This sucks. We've all been reduced to adolescent humor by the last week at Fort Dix, which saw us doing absolutely nothing of value. Up at 4:00 a.m. this morning to clean and move out. We sat on a bus for about a half hour, and then processed through the air terminal.

They gave us boarding passes we did not need. They made us put the bolts of our M-16s in plastic bags and put them in our pockets. Those with 9 mms had to remove the barrels. Then for the pre-flight safety briefing, they told us we needed a knife for the life rafts. Oh, we had to pack the knives and leathermen, remember? Then for the meal we got these really hard, sharp plastic knives to cut our food with. I should have saved mine for the raft.

The pilot said we were 30 minutes ahead of schedule, "I don't know if that's good or bad," he said. Guess. Estimated time of arrival is 12:21 p.m. No hats on the tarmac. It's 85 degrees Fahrenheit in Guantanamo; I can't wait. Maybe if we can get midair refueling we could. There we go again with the adolescent behavior. It's tough not to fall into. It's a constant tendency in times of sheer boredom or stress. Especially for men, I think.

There is a deeply serious side to what we're doing. And it is slowly seeping into everyone's demeanor. It's beginning to show on the faces. It's nearly show time. One of the flight attendants said she thought we might be a spectacle when we arrive, insomuch as we would be the first commercial airline to land at Gitmo since they first started shipping prisoners there. Whoopee.

Lord help us. Lord be with us. Lord forgive us of our sins and give us peace, the knowledge and strength to carry out our missions to the very best of our abilities. Lord, keep us safe and out of harm's way. Lord, help us treat our prisoners with due respect and courtesy, and let our prisoners be enlightened by your grace and good will through us. I thank you oh, Lord, in Jesus' most precious name I pray and thank you, oh Lord. Amen.

8 February 2002, 1210 hours. Arrival at U.S. Naval Station Guantanamo Bay, Cuba (a.k.a. GTMO, or Gitmo, pronounced "GIT-mo"; sometimes said as a pun for "get more" as in, "git mo' at Gitmo"). Warm sun, cooling breeze, pictures taken on the tarmac. Waiting in the hangar for our gear, dogs sniffing duffel bags. Our hosts are meeting us inside, taking us for a ride to the landing on the leeward side of the bay, waiting for the ferry. General Lehnert (Marine one star general in charge of the incarceration mission of JTF 160), Congressman Larson, press, getting off a boat. Boat ride to the windward side, orientation briefing (two minutes), in process (five minutes), meal card (a half-minute), and medical screening (two minutes). Then it's off to Windward Loop and our "hooch," or Army domicile. A hooch could be a pup tent, a cave, a general purpose tent, bachelor officer quarters, or—as it was in this case—a condo.

WL 11-C (Windward Loop, hooch "Eleven Charlie"): Two bedrooms, one-and-a-half baths, living room, eat-in kitchen. Good, new furniture, heavy, solid oak head and footboard, pressed wood laminate dressers and wall lockers. Beds with no hardware, spring frame on the floor. Because I snore, I'm alone on the bottom floor of the two-story condo. Four wall lockers make a wall between the kitchen wall and my bed space, making a narrow hallway. I also use the closet shelf in the hallway for my shower items. Shopping at the NX (Navy Exchange, a.k.a., NEX, pronounced like the word "next," without the "t" on the end), dinner on Marine Hill (dining facility, chow hall, or in Navy-speak, the "galley"), not as bad as the Fort Dix eatery, not as good as the McGuire facility. The Marine Hill Galley (called "Quick Hall") has a large cafeteria feel to it, with a touch of diner. The dessert carousel is glass-encased and well lighted. Help yourself. There are booths around the perimeter with good views of Guantanamo Bay from nearly every seat.

I can only make collect phone calls today. Speaking with Sandra, wishing I was far away from this place, not believing I'm here, wishing I were there, with her now, holding, kissing, hugging, loving. Children far away, I feel them hurting, wondering, hoping their daddy would come back home. I'm with you, boys, always with you. Look at the moon, I say. Look at it each night at 7:00, and I'll be with you there...eating cheese and crackers like a *Wallace and Gromit* picnic!

9 February 2002. A day that will live in infamy. There are thirty-eight new arrivals. I am allowed to observe the in-processing of the new "detainees" (not "prisoners"). Radical thoughts flood my mind and psyche as they are individually taken off the buses. Hatred and empathy collide in an emotional train wreck.

I am reminded that when Donald Rumsfeld was here in late January, he said that although the Al-Qaeda detainees were not entitled to the protections of the Geneva conventions, he expected us to treat them within the spirit of the conventions.

The detainees are humbled to the core, most of them, as they are taken to the shower, clothes cut off of them, to wash themselves and to be observed by ninety-one Bravos (medics) and MPs. A towel is placed around their waist and they are escorted to the medical screening tent. Three NCIS (Naval Criminal Investigative Service) agents are present. One takes two swab cultures from the inside of each detainee's mouth, opened by the detainee on the command of an interpreter. Fear, contrition, anger, and ambivalence are all apparent on the faces of individual detainees.

Next is the rectal exam for concealed weapons. Detainees are quickly bent over a table, and 1LT Don Tiva, 115th MP Company, physician's assistant (PA) and former Special Forces soldier, is businesslike and professional. E-5 Sergeant Mathias (also a civilian Registered Nurse) jots down notes as 1LT Tiva calls off observed injuries, body markings, and deformities to her. Later, Navy corpsmen and nurses will make rounds to follow up on those in need. Navy nurses stand by in case of emergencies in the processing tent, and Petty Officer First Class Juanita, of the Naval Hospital, stands outside the tent in case of emergencies in the shower area. Sergeant Mathias is assisted by Army Medic Specialist Hastings, from the active duty 988th MP Company.

Detainees are then made to kneel down on a tarp covering the pea gravel floor of the processing tent, which covers the entire inside-the-wire area of Camp X-Ray. Before the towel is removed, gray gym shorts and a new, clean orange pair of pants are put over the feet of the detainee, rolled up over the ankles, and then the detainee is instructed to rise. As he does so, the shorts and pants are pulled up and the towel is discarded. An orange scrub shirt is then put on the detainee and they are fitted with a leather traveling belt with metal loops through which the shackle chains are looped. Observing the process and lurking around inside the tent is a representative of the International Committee of the Red Cross (ICRC).

I chat with 1LT Tiva, the medics, the Petty Officer First Class, and the FBI folks, but not with the Red Cross representative. He's about six foot four inches tall, maybe mid-to-late forties, longish graying black hair, a paunch in his blue-shirt-covered belly. I don't hear him speak, but I am extremely curious about what he is thinking and doing. Is he simply looking for the obvious? Does he really suspect the detainees will be mistreated in his presence?

I've heard from LTC Grosse that the ICRC has had "issues" with treatment and procedures, but that they have been worked out. Apparent rough handling at certain points in the transportation process were initially complained about, but were resolved when it was pointed out that there was a psychological necessity to establishing dominance and control. Instructions were given once to the detainees, usually in English. If they were not complied with, none-too-gentle physical force was applied.

Master Sergeant Jefferson, our Vietnam combat veteran and acting First Sergeant, told me he observed this on the tarmac this afternoon when he witnessed the loading of the detainees onto buses at the airport. He said a huge MP would bark in the ear of a detainee at the foot of the bus steps, *"Step up!"* If the detainee did not step up in a second or so, the MP would grab the chain between the shackles on the detainee's legs and the detainee would be thrown onto the bus, head first.

At Camp X-Ray, the commands were, from bus to holding area, "Get up!" "Walk!" "Head Down!" in the medical screening tent, the volume lowered a notch, but the commands were still given, "Open Your Mouth," "Eyes Up," "Bend Over," "Don't Look Around."

I saw four interpreters on this day, one Marine and one Army in forest BDUs (Battle Dress Uniform, standard battle dress of all services, with brown, black, green, and tan amoebas all over, a.k.a., "tree suit") and two Air Force interpreters in DCUs. The Marine and Army interpreters looked as though they were of Middle Eastern descent. One young corporal with sleeves up, crisply pressed, couldn't be more than twenty or twenty-one. He was firm, businesslike, and professional. He was very direct and verbally forceful with the detainees. He would first inquire as to the dialect of the detainee, and establish if they could speak English. According to Captain Roberts, S-1 (Personnel Officer) of the 115th, about 95 percent of the detainees said they did not speak English. The MPs told me almost all of the detainees knew some English. So far twenty-six nationalities are represented, including: French, Spanish, British, Australian, Danish, Belgian, Russian, German, Bosnian, Tajikstani, Pakistani, Emirati (UAE, or United Arab Emirates, is a sovereign country on the Persian Gulf coast between Saudi Arabia to the north and west, and Oman to the south), Saudi Arabian, Kuwaiti, Iraqi, Yemeni, Bahraini, Syrian, Qatari, Algerian, Libyan, Chadian, and Moroccan. Detainees have identified themselves as Al Qaeda or Taliban, but not many.

The young Army interpreter, according to CPT Roberts, has only been in the U.S. for three years. A Saudi national who came to the U.S. to become a soldier, he never crossed the line of decorum during his interpreting, but was right there, walking it, being intense but not threatening; close, but not touching. The other Arab interpreter, a U.S. Marine E-8, was almost docile. Unless he was speaking to a detainee he held his head and eyes down for much of the time I was in the medical in-processing tent. He would address the detainees from the side and slightly behind them, speaking closely to the ear. His face would contort slightly in concentration when the detainees spoke. It was hard to understand them because they had surgical masks on to help prevent the spread of any airborne diseases they may have been carrying.

The Air Force interpreters wore DCUs (desert camouflage uniforms). Both were nonchalant, but businesslike. They operated mostly in the identification tent, where detainees were fingerprinted, photographed, and issued a new ID bracelet. They were forceful, like the young Marine, and seemed to be taking in everything that a detainee did; they were one tone below a bark at times, maintaining a psychological advantage. It was important to get through the in-processing phase quickly and without incident. The mission was most vulnerable at this point, but the security measures were carefully planned and executed to prevent any type of disturbance that might endanger the mission.

At first, all the detainees looked about the same to me: medium brown skin color, dark hair (shaved), no facial hair, ectomorphic or mesomorphic, but no one too muscular. I was aware of my inability to discriminate, and worked hard to notice subtle differences in build, facial features, skin tone, muscle mass and tone, so soon I began to see them more as individuals. Large and small noses, eyebrows thick or thin, round vs. oval head and face shapes, small to large ears, and skin color variations from pale to dark brown.

A sixteen-year-old Chadian boy, tall (maybe six-foot-two-inches) and very thin (maybe one hundred forty pounds), collapsed in the shower. Petty Officer First Class Juanita treated him with two IVs of Ringer's solution using 22-gauge needles. The Chadian boy was placed on a litter and put in the shade. There was a jam in the laminator in the ID processing tent, so the whole operation waited about a half-hour before it was up and running again. The Chadian was eventually brought into the medical processing tent. He shivered, as did many of them although it was warm; the shower, shade and breeze combined to have a chilling effect.

He looked particularly scared and disoriented, and very thin, but not emaciated. He looked healthy physically, but behaved more like a sickly eighty-year-old. I could not help but feel compassion for this man/boy. But the feeling was met by a stronger feeling of deceit. As a dean of students in two New York City public high schools years ago, I was often duped early in my career by sweet-looking, fast talking streetwise criminals in children's bodies. But with the help of my older brother Gary, a former Elite Guard E-6 in the Air Force, and current security executive at an Oregon university, and with training and guidance from Mr. Milton Wadler, long time security officer in the NYC public schools and trusted friend, I began to become a student of human behavior.

In graduate school at Teachers College-Columbia University, I took a course from Professor M. M. McKenzie called "Psycho-Social Aspects of Human Movement." Professor McKenzie described his experiences and experiments as a pioneer sports psychologist. He hypothesized on many aspects of human behavior and was a proponent of deciphering one's honest responses based upon involuntary eye movements. For example, "Down Left" (DL) meant the subject could be experiencing an emotional response to the question; a potential lie is indicated here if the subject is being asked a question that requires a cognitive rather than an affective recall. So, if you were to ask a subject his name, place of birth, date of birth, these are all questions that should elicit straightforward, cognitive responses. They're questions that should take very little if any thought. Pauses, stutters, quick DL eye movements, might indicate fabrication.

Not to over simplify Dr. McKenzie's hypothesis, and with respect to his ongoing study, this tidbit and others, in practice, proved quite valuable. And combined with advice from my brother, who taught me how to "set up" and interrogate subjects, were invaluable. The "set up" was simply chatting up the suspect; small talk to get them relaxed and comfortable. Ask them how they are doing, how they feel, what they had for breakfast, etc. These questions and conversational topics would be used at the same time I would be studying the suspect's behavior, especially eye movements and facial expressions, which would almost always begin as tense, worried, and fidgety. I need to say that the "set-up," more often than not, also led to a guidance referral. The simple answers to these seemingly innocuous questions would tell a sad tale of neglect, poor nutrition, and health, which all can lead to poor performance in school and, therefore, possibly misbehavior. Often, the kids would say they had nothing for breakfast, or "a candy bar and a soda," or similarly poor nutritional items. Big on the list were bagels with butter or cream cheese. These kids got little or no quality protein in their diet, and therefore their energy levels would tail off around 10:00 a.m. or so. They were quick to get caffeine fixes through colas, or even coffee. So they would pick-up again around lunchtime, then crash again in the afternoon, which is when you'd see the junk food binges furnished at the corner store: Twinkies, chips, soda, candy bars, etc.; on to another energy rush, then another crash. It's something I had to battle constantly as a teacher and coach; getting kids to take control and responsibility for their energy levels is a huge challenge, especially if they're hooked on certain sugary or fatty foods. Yes, they get addicted to the candy bar and soda for breakfast. Then it's uphill from there. Poor nutrition leads to a domino trail of effects that follow people the rest of their lives. And it adds to stress in these kids, which none of them need.

After a few minutes of innocuous small talk, the suspect would become more relaxed; eye and facial movements would become more natural. When this occurred, and I was sure I had a good model of honesty to go by. I would use three rapid-fire questions, but even-toned and with a non-threatening delivery, similar to the three mentioned previously: "What's your full name? Where do you live? What's your phone number?" Occasionally I would get the cognitive eye movement of "Up Left," on these questions if a suspect had to think about the answer, but what came next would prove to be the clincher in nearly every case.

The question following the "set up" would always be the one I really wanted answers to, such as: "Did you steal so-and-so's Walkman?" The response of an honest person who is wrongfully accused is usually calm and quickly delivered. The response of a dishonest person, who is a thief, is usually that of anger. The body contracts in fear, the face contorts, pupils narrow. Future questions are now used to confirm the hypothesis of the thief: "Where were you at such-and-such time? Do you know so-and-so? Did you know that so-and-so had a Walkman? Do you have a Walkman in your book bag?" And so on, and so forth. We would inevitably search the suspect's bag or locker, depending on what our intelligence suggested. This would generally freak out guilty parties. They'd frequently argue and fight verbally about their right to privacy. The "*In loco parentis*" condition of educators to students while they are in school allows educators to question, search, and discipline students without ever having to get parental permission to do so. We are literally "in place of the parent."

The eyes of a liar are seared into my brain. The tall Chadian was to me a liar, a "get over," a shirker, a "goldbrick." I could be wrong, but former Navy SEAL and current E-6 91W (Staff Sergeant, Senior Medic) William David told me our tall friend was "faking it." "He's just tired," he said. And, I added to myself, wanting a bit of attention and conversation. He was very talkative. Wanted to know where he was. We could not tell him. He wanted to go to the bathroom. We could not let him just yet. He didn't want the body cavity search. We had to conduct it. I considered him dangerous because I believed he was dishonest.

Monday, 11 February 2002. I accompanied LTC Grosse to the Leeward Airport for the arrival of 34 more guests. While waiting for the ferry on the Windward landing I had a longer conversation with Staff Sergeant David. He had received forty Red Cross brassards for the medical personnel working with Joint Task Force 160. I praised him and ordered him to distribute the armbands to every Army medical person, in accordance with Department of the Army Pamphlet 40–19, which describes the rationale for the wear of the armband. I have been wearing the armband since I arrived so as to easily identify myself as of the Army Medical Department. The DA PAM (Department of the Army Pamphlet) gives authorization to wear the marker only to those directly involved with the treatment of patients or the administration/supervision of treatment, which covered me, the Field Medical Assistant of the BLD and JDOG (Joint Detainee Operations Group).

I believe that it is important to wear the Red Cross for several reasons. First, it is a safety issue if someone is injured and there is a medical person in the area, but no one knows who they are. So it easily identifies medical personnel. Second, it can't hurt on the public relations side of the house. There is positive PR in displaying for the consuming public and all those who care about the health and welfare of the detainees to have all medical personnel easily identified visually—it says we care, and that's important. Third, the "we care" environment is very important to the perception of the detainees themselves. They are constantly surrounded by Americans. They are reminded constantly, and for good reason, who is in charge, that they are under our control. But they are also constantly observing and experiencing American culture—through our conversations, interactions, food, sundry supplies, and fair treatment.

LTC Wellborn, the 115th MP Battalion Commander, has said to LTC Grosse that the prisoners are happy with the level of medical care and attention they are receiving. SGT Mathias, a 115th 91B (medic) who is also a civilian nurse, told me that the detainees will attempt to get attention by claiming they have a medical condition that requires attention. Lieutenant Commander (LCDR) King, the Navy officer in charge of the Camp X-Ray Medical Facility, told me that two days ago she received a complaint from five detainees who were adjacent to each other in a unit. They all complained of abdominal pain, nausea, etc. But when they were triaged, they were fine. She said that every complaint is taken seriously, even though she suspects many of the complaints are bogus. Each complaint is triaged and a decision is made as to whether or not the detainee can be treated in the unit, in the Camp X-Ray Medical Facility (a one-story plywood hooch with an entrance hallway and four rooms, three for examination, one for administration and for storing a few supplies) or at the Fleet Hospital (constructed using DEPMEDS, Deployable Medical Systems—with an X-ray, lab, and surgery ISO (International Standard of Operation) containers that are connected to temper tents, which are metal-framed and lined sectional tents, with vestibules that connect the tents and ISOs. The whole system is fully powered and air conditioned by 150-kilowatt generators). The final piece of the medical pie is the Navy Hospital Guantanamo Bay, which is just a few miles from Camp X-Ray. The hospital is fully staffed and supported, and the food is some of the best at Gitmo.

The detainees cannot help but know we are interested in their physical well-being, "Wild Bill" being the exception. I heard about Wild Bill on my first day at Gitmo from 1LT Tiva, who, when asked about the condition of the detainees said there was one, Wild Bill, who decided he didn't want to behave. His real name is Abdul Razaq, born in 1976, in Afghanistan. He has attempted to eat his blanket. He has eaten his own feces, and has drunk his shampoo. He has taken bites out of his flip-flop sandals ("Yes," 1LT Tiva said when I asked in disbelief whether or not he was kidding, "bit, chewed, and swallowed."). He would ball up his stool and throw it at the MPs, and he would masturbate in front of female MPs. He urinated in his canteen, put pebbles in it, hung things from his penis, and tried to wash his unit floor with the contents of his waste bucket. He was diagnosed as schizophrenic in Kandahar before being transported. He was annoying to his flight guards, made bludgeons with his clothing and stones. Dangerous? Yes. Sick? Very.

A grand debate ensued over what to do with Wild Bill. Should he be isolated, should he be subdued, should he be medicated? "Yes" was the answer to all the above. They separated him and Commander King said that if his behavior remained unacceptable he would be taken to a Camp X-Ray medical tent, restrained on a hospital bed and medicated. She said a psychiatrist was on call. It is important that the other detainees see that we are trying to take care of him, so, the Red Cross armbands are a good idea; visibility, PR, psychological advantage over our enemy.

Staff Sergeant David told me he was in Mogadishu, Somalia, in October of 1993, during the "Black Hawk Down," battle of the "Black Sea," the local name for the certain part of the city where the battle began. He was a sniper on a perch one kilometer from the center of the city. I asked him if he had killed anyone and he said he couldn't tell me. A few seconds later he held up seven fingers. I mentioned how frustrating it must have been not to have been able or well equipped enough to have gone in during the battle. He agreed and said that that was the worst part of it. He said the only weapons he and his SEAL Team compatriots had were sniper rifles and 9mm pistols. He married after getting out of the Navy, then joined the Army and told his wife he was going to be a medic, thinking he wouldn't be deployed as a medic. He said she left him just before he reported for medic Advanced Individual Training (AIT).

We waited at the Leeward landing for an hour before heading up to the landing strip; there would be no cover for us there. We waited another hour at the landing. We were told the plane would be "late." We were originally told the detainees would land at 12:30 p.m., but they didn't touch down until 1:20 p.m.

Once down, the plane taxied right in front of us. As soon as the plane came to a stop, a crew of Air Force aircraft maintenance people went to work: several on a recharger, one on a forklift, two doing other maintenance and one assisting the airman on the forklift arrange off-loading ramps. After about ten minutes, one of the airmen near the plane made a large waving signal with his arms, and the Marine escort approached and circled the plane. Eight Marines on foot with locked and loaded M16s and wearing Kevlar helmets and body armor (flak/bulletproof vests) and four Humvees, two with M60 machine guns on top, two with Mark 19 grenade machine guns. Soon the airman signaled with both arms, closed together in front of and above his head and then opening them similar to how the rear of the aircraft would open. Then the two buses and QRF (Quick Reaction Force—a squad of Marines in riot gear carrying M16 rifles) in a five-ton truck deployed near the tail of the aircraft, a C141 from Andrews Air Force Base.

Soon, the detainees were escorted onto a modified school bus. Painted a dull, dark gray, the buses were stripped of nearly all their seats. There were only seats in the very back of the bus and just behind the driver's seat. There were a few steel bars overhead for MPs to hang on to. The detainees were made to sit on the floor of the bus and face rearward, or "aft" as the Navy and Marines say.

We left as the second bus began to fill with detainees, as we didn't have transportation down the hill to the Leeward landing, and needed to beat the convoy to the ferry or we'd be left behind. After the ride across the bay, we drove in vehicles waiting for us on the other side behind the convoy to Camp X-Ray. We didn't stay long this time, but long enough for one of the detainees to faint from the heat and possible dehydration. The medics and corpsman worked quickly to get the detainee to the shade and attempt to start an IV. They were unsuccessful getting fluids to flow on the first two attempts, but went to a larger-gauge needle and eventually pushed fluid into the detainee's veins. A corpsman helped the flow by squeezing the air in the bag down on the fluid inside. General Lehnert stopped by to check on the casualty and cautioned us about pushing to fluids too fast, why, I don't know, there was no danger in doing so as far as I knew. The detainee almost immediately began to look better.

Standing beside me was the ICRC pediatrician, who noticed along with me that during the treatment of the casualty, his escort guards disappeared. It was a strange feeling, to be standing over an alleged terrorist or Taliban soldier, someone who, given an opportunity might very well kill me without a second thought. He was shackled at the feet, but not the wrists. He moaned almost imperceptibly, and moved his head slowly from side to side. He also moved his arms slightly, probably from the coolness in his veins.

After about sixty seconds or so of the detainee not being guarded, two MPs ran over and nearly overreacted to their negligence. The larger of the two guards pushed the detainee's shoulders down onto the litter. The smaller stepped on the chain between the detainee's legs. After about five minutes, the two MPs switched positions after the smaller one asked to be relieved. When the larger MP stepped on the chain between the shackles his foot was so large that it actually touched both shackles and drove them into the orange socks, flesh, and bone of the detainee's shins. I exchanged glances with the ICRC doctor and knelt down to adjust the shackles. The smaller MP and I spoke to the larger MP to get him to adjust his foot. The problem was that the width of the litter was so narrow that the detainee could not move his legs any further apart and still keep them on the litter. But after I adjusted the angle of the shackles and pulled some slack on the chains, the shackles no longer dug into the detainee's leg.

Several detainees would have cuts and or abrasions from the shackles, either on their wrists or ankles. 1LT Tiva and the in-processing treatment team medics and corpsmen were very good at dressing and treating any of these injuries the detainees had. The bad guys were indeed receiving excellent medical care, despite the consensus feeling amongst everyone I had spoken to about our feelings of hatred and distaste for them. This was a professional group, a dedicated and skilled assemblage of caring, honest, and forthright individuals. I was proud to be in their company, but definitely shared their feelings of anger toward the detainees. After the IV bag emptied, the casualty/detainee was helped to his feet and processed. He seemed able and willing to do so.

To be fair, we did not know the circumstances under which they had become detained persons. We could speculate, but only a very few were willing to fess up to their political affiliation, at least to us.

Interrogations were being conducted daily which yielded valuable information, not just information that would help prevent further terrorist attacks, but information that would reveal a detainee's affiliation, reasons for being affiliated with whomever, and information about who they were and where they came from.

14 February 2002, Valentine's Day—and my eighth wedding anniversary.

Friday, 15 February 2002. I accompanied the LTC to the plane again today. This time lunch was served beforehand and we ate ten minutes before leaving for the Windward ferry landing. SPC Java, our unit clerk, and SPC Silverman, our S-2 and intelligence processor, joined us. Down at the landing I hooked up with SSG David to discuss one of the litter patients on the incoming flight. The detainee was said to have a fracture of the left femur, untreated and un-sedated—or even given pain medication. Apparently, the wound was not a recent one and had healed somewhat, improperly of course.

Also on the trip was Navy Lt. Wesley Christiansen, an eye, ear, nose and throat physician from the fleet hospital. He would receive the detainee fitness report from the Air Force flight surgeon. He was assigned to the Fleet Hospital a month ago and has had no patients. Again, the overwhelming need is for orthopedics. So, Navy Lt. Christiansen feels his services are not necessarily needed in this scenario.

The plane arriving today would be a C17 Globemaster. It would be carrying twelve new guests, one litter patient, and one detainee who was reclassified from litter to ambulatory at the last minute. The latter patient is supposedly suffering from shrapnel wounds in the buttocks. All other detainees are reported to be in good condition. I share this information with Major Renfro, the Marine Joint Task Force (JTF) Public Relations coordinator and with the ICRC pediatrician.

About fifteen minutes before the arrival of the plane, Air Force Colonel Donald Alexander, commander of the Air Forces on Gitmo, sat down in front of me at the tarmac (there are about a dozen railroad ties set perpendicular to and about twenty yards from the tarmac, used for setting pallets of cargo, they are inviting resting places while we wait). The Colonel asks me about the condition of the detainees, so I give him the information I have. We chat about the aircraft being used to transport the detainees and the planning and execution that go into the movements.

It can be quite complex, as he explains that today's' flight is a thirty-hour, nonstop flight from Kandahar, that will have refueled in the air three times before reaching Gitmo. He said the plane "took rounds" (was shot at) upon liftoff from the airport at Kandahar. He said the quick reaction force at the airport there responded but found no enemy. It is reported today in a SIT REP (situation report) that there is a force of about twelve thousand bad guys in and around Kandahar. The invading Northern Alliance apparently took bribes and let them go with their weapons in October.

Colonel Alexander explained that the "aerial ballet" of refueling a single plane three times en route to a destination is tricky. The main planning headquarters must reserve airspace and pre-position fueling planes and back-up fueling planes along the route. Coordination must take place between several different CINCs (Commanders-In-Charge), such as Central Command in Afghanistan, and Southern Command here in Gitmo. He said the problems with the aircraft rarely happen in the air, but are more likely to happen when starting the engines, which explains the need for back-up aircraft.

I was curious as to why the planes were apparently not escorted by U.S. combat aircraft, considering their payload and value. I prefaced my question with the obligatory, "I know you probably can't tell me this, but...," and he paused before answering. Combat aircraft were "on the ground," he said, and could respond in time to any threat from the air. "They're here, but they're not here. If you know what I mean," he said with a squint. I didn't, but didn't tell him. He seemed to like to talk, was tall, thin and wise-looking, and very friendly and personable. He said the main threat here was from the ground.

I'd heard the story from Chief Petty Officer Sutton, who gave me a ride to the Pink Palace (former dental clinic on McCalla Hill, painted Caribbean pink, and the command post for the BLD and the 115th MP BN) yesterday. Sutton works for the Preventive Medicine Department, NAV HSOP GTMO. A month ago a uniformed Cuban soldier, carrying an AK-47, surrendered for political asylum near the child-care center. How he got there was anybody's guess. But Sutton was visibly upset even by recalling the apparently fresh memory. He went on about how the Cuban soldier could have killed or taken hostage the children in the center. The Chief lives here on the Island (what we called Gitmo from time-to-time) with his wife and kids. He said they addressed the issue with the facility commander, who he said assured them security measures would be improved. I'm not sure how that would happen. Hell, one of the first things they had us do when we got here was give up our weapons. We turned them in right after in-processing. Do I feel safe and protected? Somewhat, but stories like this don't help.

The plane arrived ten minutes late. The maintenance crew did their thing. The plane was not nearly as noisy as the C141s that had run this mission before. This plane was twice the size in the fuselage, and the engines must have been twice the size as well—but comfortably noisy. SSG David went right onto the plane after Marine security forces deployed and the rear hatch was opened. The flight surgeon came out to meet me and LCDR Christiansen. He confirmed the injuries, told us he gave a detainee medication for headache, but nothing to either the detainee with the leg wound or the shrapnel wound.

SSG David soon emerged from the plane, sought us out and asked to see the detainee manifest. SSG David said the wounds were at least a month old on the leg patient; he hadn't looked at the shrapnel patient. For some reason the litter patient was not off-loaded first, I guessed it was because SSG David needed to do an assessment of the detainee first, and the MPs decided to off-load the healthy ones in the meantime.

SSG David said the detainee's vital signs were good and so were the distal pulses. He said the detainee had lost his toenails on the injured legs' toes. The SSG would ride back to Camp X-Ray with the casualty. On the ferry ride back, I again shared what I knew with Major Renfro and the ICRC doctor.

Once at Camp X-Ray, the litter patient was moved to the low shower area, next to the regular showers; this bathing area, also concrete, had a concrete lip around a ten-square-foot graded slab with a drain. There were several spigots for washing, and a two-foot lip half way around the shower near the spigots, which were between this and another low shower adjacent to it.

Several people were working on the patient, whose orange detainee clothing had been cut away. The detainee's genitals were exposed, but someone quickly covered his lower body with a towel. He was lifted again several times, to be bathed, which was accomplished by Sergeant Mathias, the civilian nurse and Army medic, and by others when they needed to examine his wounds.

Indeed, there were several scars between the left knee and hip of the detainee. He told the interpreter, who relayed the information to me, the ICRC doctor, and General Lehnert (who was always around during in-processing), that the wounds were incurred "two months ago," and that he had been seen at at least two medical facilities in Afghanistan that said they could not help him. Apparently, and according to Commander King, Camp X-Ray medical facility commander, the detainee would need surgery and the facilities available in Afghanistan could not handle such a case. We were obligated to provide at least the same level of care offered to our own soldiers to this and all detainees.

The wounded detainee had a half-dollar-sized round scar just above and to the outside of his left knee. A few inches above that scar, another scar—about eight inches long and somewhat cigar-shaped—extended vertically along the leg toward the hip. The scar was dark pink and after several minutes of examination and after they rolled him slightly over for his body cavity search, both wounds began to ooze bright red blood. The wounded detainee was carried through the rest of in-processing, with a medic holding his IV bag. The escort guards had handcuffed the detainee to his litter.

18 February 2002. At our ten-hundred hour briefing, our JAG officer, Captain Wolfe, told us about this Friday's holy day for the detainees. They will be fed before sundown, fast, and then will be fed again after sundown. Then, on Saturday, they will receive a special "feast" meal consisting of lamb stew, traditional pastries, as well as baklava and dates. *Mmmmmmm, tasty!* I wonder if I were to be captured by the Taliban or Al Qaeda they would give me a roast beef dinner with all the trimmings on Christmas Eve?

CPT Wolfe also told us that the detainees are "becoming more disobedient and are testing the guards." He also said "the guards are finding weapons on some of the detainees. Such as a six inch welding arc, and a two-inch piece of metal, sharpened into a point." He told us that "the detainees are attempting to get the guards to engage in conversation with them." One detainee even asked a guard to read the Koran to him.

There are only two forms of allowable punishment for detainees: confinement and reduction in privileges. There currently is no area for confinement, and the only privilege that has been taken away so far for the most disobedient and those who have constructed weapons is the elimination of their daily fifteen-minute walk outside their unit.

I met briefly with Navy Lieutenant Commander Guillaum yesterday. He is Navy Captain Phillips' assistant at JTF headquarters (a.k.a. "Puzzle Palace"), down the road from the "Pink Palace" (JDOG Headquarters). He is a Medical Service Officer like myself, and welcomed my input and observations. I told him about the experience I had with LTC Grosse the day before, when I took the LTC to the Joint Aid Station on Windward Loop, unit 1C. I took the LTC in and the corpsman was interviewing another soldier. The corpsman was half dressed in an untucked T-shirt, belt flapping, and blouse hanging on his desk chair. The floor hadn't been swept recently as dirt and dust bunnies were apparent. A beer bottle rested on the seat of an outdoor picnic table bench, visible through the sliding glass door to the rear of the condo.

One Army medic, in T-shirt and running shorts, whom I'd met and seen work at Camp X-Ray, was on the desktop computer in the dining room, playing a computer game. The E-6 in charge was in T-shirt and shorts. He leaned in, said hello, and asked if the colonel had been helped yet. We told him "no," but he didn't help us. When the first patient was done, and left the aid station, the colonel was seen by the corpsman. A few minutes later, another soldier came in and was immediately seen by the E-6.

At one point, an African-American soldier came in complaining of an ingrown hair. The E-6 went into the kitchen, which is adjacent to the living room where the aid station was set up, and asked a gaggle of three medics and corpsmen, "who wants to do the ingrown hair?" There were varying excuses made by the medics and corpsmen. When we left, the soldier with the ingrown hair had still not been treated.

The laundry room, which was visible from the aid station treatment room (living room), was a pigsty. Dirty clothes, uniforms, and running shoes littered the floor and shelves. The trash can in the kitchen, a large thirty gallon can, was overflowing. Dirty dishes were in the sink, and there was a cot and sleeping bag set up outside in the tall grass of the back yard. The medicine and supply cabinet was disheveled. Items were not necessarily grouped. The appearance was messy and disorganized.

I mentioned these things to LCDR Guillaum, who said I should mention it at Tuesday's medical staff meeting at the JTF. I will. If they need a quality control officer, I'm it. Captain Phillips asked me to review the standard operating procedures, so I got them from LCDR Guillaum, who gave me two documents. The first, "Chapter 6, Commanding Officer/Mission Policies, Standard Operating Procedure, 500 Bed Fleet Hospital," the SOP for the DEPMEDS (Deployable Medical Systems) Fleet Hospital on Radio Range, was down by the beach, which I also visited today. The second document is a "Department of the Army, United States Disciplinary Barracks, Fort Leavenworth, Kansas, Standard Operating Procedure, Crisis Intervention Services for Inmates."

I will read them soon. But now I am in the middle of rewriting 1LT Tiva's and SSG David's SOP for in-processing detainees, which was given to me by SSG David. It's a very good start, but is not entirely being followed, and needs adjustments.

Mission First

"If we do not hang together, we shall surely hang separately."

—Thomas Paine

18 February 2002. I spoke with SSG David and 1LT Tiva individually today about the in-processing SOP. We all agreed on minor changes. My challenge now is to get it written, approved, and in the hands of the medical staff of the JTF tomorrow. I set high standards for myself—perhaps unnecessarily, but then again, I like to surprise people.

On the ride home from work today *(God, I hate that I have to call this place "home" for now)*, LTC Grosse intimated to me that there was a particularly uncooperative detainee at the camp today. COL Johnson, the current JDOG commander, asked the guard in charge of the detainee what the matter was. The guard said the detainee simply would not do what he was told. COL Johnson is a slight but fit man in his late forties; sometimes he has an easy smile, but he is more inclined to wear a poker face. COL Johnson allegedly went to the detainee's unit and asked him what the problem was. The detainee allegedly said that this was all just a game. COL Johnson supposedly replied, "Yeah? And it's a game you'll lose," and walked away. Later he had the detainee moved to an end unit—the furthest southeast cell—catches the sun most of the day—with little or no shade. Take that and no walking privileges, and Akbar will bake.

I saw the movie *The Majestic* tonight, alone. MSG Jefferson and SPC Paul (our unit vehicle driver and MP) showed up and sat behind me. I think MSG Jefferson wanted me to feel guilty for not calling them (they live in a hooch a few doors up the road from me)—but did he call me? Sometimes we just want to be alone and have a good cry.

I feel like such a bastard for not being with my wife and kids. I look at their pictures every day. I have the ones I took when I was home for Theodore's birth, one of Theodore sleeping in the chest carrier with his smiling mother looking at him, and a close-up of Theodore just sleeping. There was one of Harrison holding up a small purple wooden toy train named "Lady." his rosy cheeks puffing out ever so gently and softly. Will he still have those cheeks when I see him again? *Oh, God, please don't take that away from me, my sweet, sweet little boy. Harrison, I'm so sorry I'm not there for you. I love you so.* And there was one picture of Harrison and Benjamin, their cute faces belying the confusion about where and why their daddy has to go. For what? For whom?

Nearly every week Marines die in plane or helicopter crashes. What's going on? Isn't anybody paying attention to us here and in Kandahar, Kabul, Uzbekistan, and the Philippines? We're dying. Our families are suffering. Let's get it done.

The Majestic is a Jim Carrey movie set in a post-World War II, Anytown, U.S.A. Carrey plays a man with amnesia who gives a town a hero after so many have died serving their country. He turns out to be someone else, but comes through for the townsfolk and himself in the end. People have given their lives for this country so many times before. For so much more, it seems. But really, when you think about it, this is a just cause. This is about enduring freedom and noble eagles. This is about us, the United States. This is about everything our forefathers, however flawed and imperfect, wanted for their children and grandchildren; the freedom to do and be what and whomever they chose.

The bastards who are now thinking they are in control, not being obedient, even in the clutches of their most hated enemy will have an exacting price to pay. It may not come tomorrow, it may not come soon, but it will come. And when it does, they will not be prepared for it. They will cower and shrink away. They will shiver in the cold of isolation. They will break under the pressure of two hundred and seventy million-plus voices; of the U.S., of all nations on earth, of all languages and cultures and religions and creeds: Hear us and heed us. We are coming to find you, and when we do, you should be most docile, or we will end your life and with it your quest for evil. With each drop of an American's blood you spill, thousands of your drops of blood will stain the battlefield, which we will gladly take to you. You, our enemy, have no idea what we are capable of, nor should you wish to know. Because knowing is pain, suffering, and death. You will lose most soundly. And once you've lost, your name will mean nothing.

CPT Granger with newborn Theodore, January 25, 2002.

Harrison (L) and Benjamin, 3 and 6 years old respectively, January 25, 2002.

LTC "Grosse" in his office, late afternoon. He was rarely in the office, preferring instead to visit the camp and spend time talking with the troops, and overseeing operations.

Fleet Hospital 20 staff. Navy CAPT "Romanov" kneeling bottom left. An unassuming and brilliant leader.

CPT Granger (L) with Marine General Lehnert, Commander of Joint Task Force 160 during stand-up of Camp X-Ray, early 2002. Max Wolfe took this picture while telling a joke about the General "bailing out" on us—this was the General's going away bash.

Camp X-Ray (center left). Final press conference held outside the camp before detainees were moved to Camp Delta.

Inside Camp Delta cell block. Pastel green paint was used to aid in keeping detainees calm. Open ceilings with air handlers aided circulation and helped keep the cell blocks cool.

Accommodations inside Camp Delta.

Roadside black Cuban rock iguana. The unofficial symbol and protected species of Gitmo.

Joint Detainee Operations Group (JDOG) Headquarters, Pink Palace (center), McCalla Hill, Guantanamo Bay Naval Station, Cuba.

Tending the Garden

"If you want to tell people the truth, make them laugh,
otherwise they'll kill you."

—Oscar Wilde

19 February 2002. There are sixteen detainees in the Navy Fleet Hospital, its sole purpose was the detainee health care mission. The direction given there is that the detainees will receive the exact same medical care that a U.S. Soldier, Sailor, Airman, Marine, or Coast Guardsman would receive, period. Of course, the way in which this high-quality care will be delivered will be much different. The detainees are shackled to their litters, both at the ankles and wrists. There is an armed MP on the ward at all times, as well as a uniformed Army Intelligence soldier most of the time—there to pick up what is called "passive" intelligence from the detainees. As soon as any of the sixteen in-patients are capable of returning to Camp X-Ray they will be moved and receive treatment at the Camp X-Ray Medical Treatment Facility (CXR MTF).

20 February 2002. A detainee at Fleet Hospital, #369, resisted a corpsman during treatment and then refused to eat. They are testing the waters to see how we react, who reacts, and with what degree of force. The MPs in the Fleet Hospital say they don't want more than two detainees up and about on the ward at any one time, which is nearly impossible to achieve because so many of the detainees require physical therapy. Then there's using the bathroom, X-rays, and various other reasons a detainee must get out of bed. The SOP is one MP for every two detainees, but it's too crowded, so we suffice with seven guards for now in addition to the armed floater. All other MPs do not carry weapons on the ward for fear of possibly having it taken away by a detainee. The one MP who carries the loaded weapon, a 9mm, is not allowed to come into contact with detainees for any reason; his sole mission in life is to shoot to kill if a detainee gets into a position

of possibly killing the MP or anyone else. Reasonable force is the rule of thumb, but we must be ready for the worst-case scenario, and they need to see we have that option should the need arise.

Detainee #459 refused treatment and medication. He complains the ward is too noisy and that he cannot sleep, which makes for a cranky and potentially dangerous detainee.

21 February 2002. As the liaison Medical Service Officer with the Navy Fleet Hospital, I carry important information back to JDOG HQ and share it in the form of a daily report or SIT REP (situation report). Today, Navy Captain Peter Romanov, Fleet Hospital Commander, wants me to tell my boss that they can take no more patients at the Fleet Hospital—not because of capacity constraints, but because of the lack of additional MPs. They need to keep the 2-to-1 detainees-to-MPs ratio. Yesterday's count of sixteen detainees and seven guards did not sit well with him. Two detainees were discharged, so today there are fourteen, and with seven guards and a rover, that's where CAPT Romanov is drawing the line.

There is also a detainee who may need medical evacuation off Guantanamo due to a potential neurosurgery emergency. We're not sure how that will play with the Department of Defense. So far they have been willing to authorize any specialty physician and any specialty equipment that the mission requires in order to keep detainees on the Island. What would it take to get one off and into the States for treatment? We may get to know soon. The potential emergency might not be avoidable. We have one neurosurgeon, and if something goes wrong we are in the soup.

CAPT Romanov has invited the Fleet Hospital guards to a barbecue at the Fleet Hospital AO (Area of Operation) at East Caravella Street (where the Fleet Hospital personnel have their condos), this Sunday. It's a very generous gesture. All Army personnel sleep in tents on Freedom Hill, which overlooks Camp X-Ray—all except for anyone in the command group, which is about two dozen or so of us.

Two psych patients are now on a round-the-clock, one-to-one watch. This is going to kill the Corpsmen, morale-wise. There should be a psych tech working with an interpreter and these detainees, or even a psychologist. Personnel numbers are tight, and specialties are spread very thin. There are two tuberculosis cases isolated in the Fleet Hospital now, and more alcohol referrals. Some of these guys were alcoholics, and are now dry instead of high, and they are going through withdrawal.

We should have phone service in the hooch soon. Sprint is the local carrier. That would be cool to be able to call home from the condo.

22 February 2002. The neurosurgery went well, so we dodged a bullet. There's a thoracic surgery scheduled for tomorrow, and a tracheotomy was done today on Detainee #205. A corpsman found a scorpion on him in the ward this morning; critters get into everything. Local grass cutting has sent the wildlife scurrying; a mouse was also caught in the Fleet Hospital today. Food in the Fleet Hospital has got to be policed better.

PSY OPS invited themselves to Camp X-Ray on the 19th and played the national anthem at dawn, and played Neil Diamond's "Coming to America." General Lehnert kicked their asses off the compound and told them not to come back. No more national anthem at X-Ray, and no PSY OP B.S. The PSY OP boys have a hooch down the street from us on Windward Loop. One of them bought a beach dune buggy jalopy from a local, and their driveway looks juxtaposed: half California coast hangout, and half military ice cream truck on steroids, with their new jalopy and banned PSY OP Humvee with huge speakers on the roof. These guys should just go home (he, he).

23 February 2002. I've been very busy lately, and haven't had time to write home much. I've done post cards and/or coloring books to Sandy and the kids, and I just answered one of my mother's letters. I have had pretty good luck with e-mail off of the Colonel's computer but there's no telling how long I can use it in a given sitting, so my writing is rather abbreviated. Even now, finding time to write lately has been a challenge. Gotta go!

24 February 2002. Colonel Johnson sat the 455th down at a meeting two days ago, and told us that we were officially his staff, the JDOG staff, and that he was going to use us as such. I gave him an updated biographical summary and a letter of introduction yesterday morning. Later, I approached him for a sit-down he asked to have with each of us regarding our functional area expectations, and he said that would happen in the next few days or next week. Fair enough. It feels good to belong to somebody. Our first two weeks were spent trying to fit in somewhere. It wasn't too difficult for me, because medical missions are pretty obvious. The people are conspicuous and the tasks are straightforward: take care of the hurt and sick folk. Now that the detainee flow has stopped, there are lots of challenges ahead—challenges of professionalism. How do folks stay gainfully employed who don't know what they're doing? Thank God I know, or this would be more torturous than it already is.

I helped with the good-guy in-processing tonight. The 342nd MP Company flew in at nineteen-thirty hours, and was in-processed down the hill from the Pink Palace at about twenty thirty hours; SFC Silwain of the 115th MP BN gave the "creepy critter" and "common sense" brief, and I gave the in-theater medical brief using the materials Dr. Blount gave me a few days ago. 1LT Tiva and I revised the materials so that they make sense to Army folk. I think we did a good job, and I hope it's helpful to the new troopies.

Also on the flight were three flight surgeons and four senior NCOs, all Air Force-type. They have been "sequestered" (for lack of a better term) here from McGuire Air Force Base (how ironic). These folks have been doing the detainee in-flight medical care. Some of their *compadres* have been sent "home" to their derivative units; these seven were told to come to Gitmo and wait until the detainee flow starts again.

I got their names, ranks, MOSs, hooch numbers, and phone numbers and invited them to my hooch for snacks and drinks this afternoon. I spent the morning trying to find someone to tell me what to do with them. I suspected Captain Phillips would know, but it is Sunday, usually a day of rest for permanent party Navy commanders here. I went to the zero eight-thirty meeting at Fleet Hospital and CDR Williamson told me Phillips was the guy, but I went hunting for an answer anyway. Good thing. I ran into Navy CPT Israel at the Navy Hospital, and he told me to attend tomorrow's ten thirty meeting at the JTF Headquarters (a.k.a. "Pleasure Palace" or "Puzzle Palace," take your pick). He also said they would all most likely be turned over to Dr. Blount for assignment.

I enjoy my daily morning trips down to the Fleet Hospital. It is several miles from the Pink Palace and has a beautiful sloping straight road that comes over the last hill to the water. You can see the Navy Fleet hospital in the distance, which meets the horizon in all its desert hills glory. The road from the crest of the hill to the hospital is just under a mile long, gently sloping down. I have seen two large iguana (four-to-five-footers) crossing or attempting to cross on my drives. Each attempt to get photographs however has been unsuccessful. They are quite wary of me. Not like the much smaller iguana I photographed a few days ago while briefly exploring a divers' concrete walkway and staircase that goes right down to the water.

Specialist Nosh Silverman, our intelligence guy, does work at the Fleet Hospital and I drive him back to the Pink Palace after my morning meetings and a brief look-see inside. On our way back one morning we took a fifteen-minute look at the divers' area—for "fully equipped experienced divers only," according to the sign. It was a great, picturesque view of crashing waves on a rocky cliff. We walked down the low steps of the staircase and took a few photos. On our way up, as soon as we stepped off the last step, we saw a small iguana, perhaps twelve to fourteen inches long. It didn't seem too startled, so we took a few quick snaps. I got into a low crawl position (I had fantasized about this opportunity the first time a big iguana got away from me. I imagined that if I had gotten into a low crawl and slowly approached rather than walked in, the animal wouldn't run away. I was right!). The little fella didn't move. So I got what I considered to be very close, perhaps as close as two feet or so. He complied at first, and then ran a little bit and got out of range. I got up, moved around a bush to head him off, and once again, he posed. I got down, got a few more snaps, and he decided to move on. Having grown up in the desert mountains of Southern California, the flora and fauna of Gitmo entranced me—it was like a surreal flashback—and "hunting" iguanas with a camera reminded me of the countless hours my brothers, friends, and I would spend catching lizards and snakes on Rattlesnake Mountain, a finger of the Sierra Nevada's just across the street from where I grew up, in a place called Rubidoux. I took the photos with a new camera I bought at the NX. The film was cheap. Four rolls of film for about the same price as a disposable camera. But I haven't seen any of the pictures—the NX photo lab equipment is on the fritz, so I'll have to wait to see what's become of the iguana photos. I hope they're good enough to send to the boys.

I spoke to them last night when I called from the Pink Palace while waiting for the three-four-deuce MPs to get in. Harrison was sweet and said he loved me and wanted me to come home right away, and that he hoped I didn't get lost. I was excited to talk with him, maybe too much so, and he got off the phone right away. I do my best to allay his fears, but I'm not sure how well I'm doing at that.

Benjamin sounded great. But he needed to tell me that he had elbowed his brother to the ground and was sent to time-out. He said Harrison had made him mad. He also said that he was mad because I wasn't home (*dagger to the heart!*). This is absolutely the biggest emotional test I have faced in my life, rivaling seeing and hearing my parents fight as a child. Rivaling having to take a loaded .22 caliber revolver from my first stepfather, who in a drunken stupor after my mother told him they were through, drew the weapon on her. Rivaling my mother being stalked by her eventual third husband during the second husband crisis. This is worse. In those crises, except for the first, the arguing part, I had some control, and exercised some initiative to relieve the situation. Yelling parents has to be the most hurtful thing a child bears, except perhaps losing a parent, it strikes at the heart of a child because it messes with their sense of stability and security, whether or not they consciously understand it.

Poor Harrison, he views me as "lost." In his three-year-old mind and heart, that means I am gone...his version of dead. Does he even believe it's me who calls? Will he remember me when I get back? People tell me he won't remember this when he's older. How can that be true? "Losing" your daddy has got to be a conscious, emotionally significant event. It has to be remembered somewhere in the psyche. *This is the ultimate price I pay.* Death would be cruel, but having to suffer the pain my small son is experiencing is tantamount to torture, or, better yet, terrorism. I blame the Al Qaeda and Taliban for this. There has to be someone, something to blame here. It's just the way things work, but it's just scary, and not Richard Scarry.

25 February 2002. Every day I go down to the Fleet Hospital (FH) and attend the morning staff meeting, I also speak to the guard NCO-ICs (Noncommissioned Officers In Charge), SFC Giap and SFC Snodgrass. I talk to them about how their guards are doing, the guard procedures, how the detainees are doing, etc. They have some color-ful nicknames for the detainees. There's "General," "Stumpy," "Ivan," "Turtle Boy," and "Smiley." General is named for his per-ceived intelligence and language skills. He speaks several different languages well, including English. Stumpy is an amputee. Ivan is a detainee from Russia, who speaks Russian. Turtle Boy ("Half-Dead Bob" to the Air Force medical folks that brought him here) spends 99.9 percent of his time in the fetal position, head under blanket. Smi-ley smiles when spoken to or looked at.

The guards have been in a questionable morale mode for some time due to long hours and no days off since they hit the ground, cer-tainly the last group here to still be on seven days a week, but there is a pinhole at the end of the tunnel. The 342nd MP Company, who just flew in two days ago, has been getting oriented to the Fleet Hospital, and SFC Giap told me today that they are still scheduled to start help-ing out on 28 February. He said the three-four-deuce will take mid-night shifts and help out with swing shifts, and the 115th will take day shifts and help out with swing shifts. He was scheduled to meet with his counterpart with the 342nd today.

Navy Petty Officer Third Class Ladd is my hero. I see her nearly every morning in the detainee ICU (Intensive Care Unit) ward doing physical therapy with detainees who are not shackled. She seems to hold together fairly well. You can't tell that it affects her, but I know it does. While about five soldiers and I were being briefed regarding a press event, she asked the PAO (Public Affairs Officer) if she could discuss emotional issues with the reporters. The PAO asked if it was related to her interaction with the detainees. She said it was, and that she felt conflicted. We all do. The PAO told her that it would be alright.

I saw the dressing changes of a couple of detainees yesterday. One had stainless steel rods attached to just below the wrist and just above the elbow. Between the rods was about an eight-to-ten inch by two-to-four-inch piece of flesh missing from his left forearm. It looked as though a large animal had taken a chunk out of his arm with one vicious bite; battle wounds took on myriad forms. The physician supervising the dressing change gave a thumbs-up to the detainee, with just a hint of a smile and said, "Looks good." It did "look good," from a medical standpoint. It looked clean. There was bright red flesh exposed, some fatty tissue here and there, but there was no oozing pus or other indications of dead, decaying or otherwise infected tissue.

26 February 2002. While at the Fleet Hospital today I observed three detainees interacting quite jovially: General, Ivan, and Stumpy. Ivan glanced at me several times and appeared to be shielding me from his expression. I believe he was smiling but I couldn't quite tell; it could have just been a knowing glance. General was talking to Stumpy mostly, and Stumpy would reply with animation, nodding and moving excitedly. General and Stumpy would laugh occasionally, and share their laughter with Ivan. This went on for several minutes. *Interesting,* I thought. *They seem comfortable and well.* They obviously feel safe, and although they were communicating in Farsi or some Arabic language, they were speaking freely, and loud enough to talk over Ivan, who was between the two of them and listening intently to their conversation.

At the 1500 hours JTF Medical Staff meeting, Dr. King ran down the current list of known infectious diseases: three cases of malaria; one confirmed case of TB and one suspected case, with both patients in the DACU; two hepatitis cases, with testing being done to determine the type; and several cases of unidentified legions that are being investigated. There are also five psychiatric cases currently being treated at CXR. Yesterday, a detainee "punched" a guard. When I relayed this information to COL Johnson he pooh-poohed it and said, "It was a push with the leg." So much for accurate reporting. But the "punch" was communicated in the context of mounting aggressive behavior on the part of the detainees. The detainee was being returned to his unit after having seen medical personnel at the CXR Medical Facility, and the incident was reported at the medical staff meeting by LCDR King, the supervising doctor at the CXRMF.

Weigh-ins are done for the whole detainee population every 15th of the month, re-weighs are done on the first of the month as necessary. There are ten detainees who are currently on the first-of-the-month schedule. Detainee sick call is way down. The CXRMF is currently seeing only fourteen to eighteen detainees per day for sick call. Previous numbers were in the high 30s. The last thing put out is that the OPSEC (Operations Security) people have started going through trash to see if any classified or other potentially compromising information is being improperly discarded. I wouldn't be surprised if they go through our mail or listen in on our phone conversations as well.

LTC Grosse and I are having COL Johnson and CPT Yuel over for breakfast tomorrow. I fancy myself a closet chef, so I'm cooking omelets: two eggs lightly salted and peppered with a splash of milk, whisked with a fork, immediately mixed with green, red, and yellow peppers, and then onion when it hits the preheated buttered pan. Diced and seeded plumb tomatoes added after about ninety seconds, then about a quarter cup of shredded mild cheddar and Monterey jack cheese. Cooked lightly, and then a sprinkle of the cheese on top and popped into a warmed oven on a warmed plate to wait for all four omelets to be made; served with whole wheat toast with a choice of strawberry jam, peanut butter or butter (or a combination thereof to the taste of the guest). Oh, and a sprig of parsley on the omelet as served. I am toying with the idea of frying frozen hash browns, which is a risk. I've never done it before, but there is a first time for everything. Pancakes are out this Saturday, as it is the date of the 0700 5k and 10k fun runs. You get a T-shirt if you run. I'm in for the 5k (3.1 miles). I gotta have the T-shirt!

CPT Yuel just walked in and put up a new (official?) OPSEC prevention sign: Lower right half of the 8 1/2" x 11" portrait-oriented sign is a picture of a WWII G.I., helmet chin strap un-snapped, smiling broadly, holding up with his right hand a canteen cup of what we assume is coffee (or pick your beverage), with the following caption in the upper third of the sign: "How about a nice cup of shut the f**k up." *Cute.*

There was recently an indiscrete incident here. A second lieutenant was caught in a compromising situation (disrobed from the waist down) with a female nurse. He is allegedly married. Current problem in the investigation, find a copy of the marriage certificate. Yes, married men fooling around while in the military are in violation of the UCMJ (Uniform Code of Military Justice). It's called infidelity.

27 February 2002. The detainees at CXR are getting "uppity." I heard a report today that a couple of the blocks are not eating in protest of "abusive treatment"—being incarcerated, being interrupted

during prayer, a general lack of respect for their religious beliefs, which is a bit silly considering we give them Korans, allow them to pray whenever they like, and even spray painted in Arabic the direction of mecca on the guard towers so they know which way to face when praying. They are also refusing to shower or take medication. A detainee was placed next to "Wild Bill," and was "begging" to be moved. While at the Fleet Hospital today, the three *caballeros* (Ivan, General and Stumpy) were more subdued. No laughing, talking, or carrying on. Ivan got his physical therapy today. He's moving better than last week. I think he should be moved back to CXR, just my opinion, but he seems healthy enough to go.

Breakfast with the colonel and Yuel went fine. The new toaster either burns the bread or doesn't toast at all. But the omelets were very good, just like I planned. I did the frozen hash browns and that turned out well, also. I told the colonel at one point that I thought the new cases of hepatitis among the detainees (two so far) was something that scared me. They could be infecting themselves on purpose for several reasons. One, they could be trying to get medical attention for a variety of reasons, including to establish sympathetic relationships with medical personnel, change of scenery, get to the Fleet Hospital to attempt an uprising. Or, two, they could be trying to infect the guards. I told the colonel that the detainees could be spreading their feces on things they know the guards touch, and even though the guards wear protective gloves, if the guards touch their eyes or mouth or other transmutable surface with an infected glove they could become infected. Seventy percent or more of all non-battle injuries/illnesses are gastrointestinal. It is an angle. Colonel Johnson didn't seem impressed, but then again, he never seems impressed. But he did compliment me several times on the breakfast, and he cleaned his plate.

Fear. Hatred. Loathing. These are the things I felt as I watched him, this time with two large MPs right behind him, and Navy Petty Officer Third Class Ladd right behind and between them, then the NCOIC behind her. Ivan didn't look around. He held his head at a downward cant. I could tell he was listening to what was being said around him. There was light chatter about his improvement. Several guards who were not involved in guarding him at the time were chuckling as he went by. Ivan's gait was stilted, as though he couldn't control all the muscles in his leg. His gait was herky-jerky, but better than before. He looked healthy and alert. He looked like if he wanted to, he could attack anyone around him on a whim. He didn't. He just stared at the floor a few paces in front, but looking alert nonetheless.

I had a daydream today about us being issued our M-16s. I've wanted mine, with ammo, intermittently since we got here. I didn't like putting it in the armory. I understand why we did it, the "threat condition" or THREAT CON doesn't indicate that we would need them. Just the same, I'd rather have my M-16. Call it what you will— false sense of security, psychological crutch, irrational? I don't really care. Issue me the damn weapon and I will take good care of it. I will sleep with it, clean it, love it, and use it if I have to. Guess I'm not feeling too safe here lately, eh? I daydream that the bad guys are coming over the hills and I have my M16 and I plug away at 'em—nice idea—but I don't have my sixteen. Why not? Threat level. Ah, every day is a Monday, and life here is a vicious circle.

28 February 2002. JDOG needs the fire and bomb threat plan from the Fleet Hospital today. Certain cell blocks of detainees at CXR are not eating, showering, or taking medication. Is/Should the "Starvation Info Handout" available in all needed languages? If they know that not eating can cause permanent damage to their organs, would it make a difference? Word is the detainees are protesting against general conditions by not eating or cooperating. Second case of detainee aggression was reported against a guard at CXR; detainee struck a guard. The detainee with the ex-fix refused treatment. 59 detainees are refusing medication, including malaria prophylaxis, so the series must start over. A guard was accused of disrespecting a detainee by removing a cover from the detainee's head, which is not allowed. Lack of information about their future has detainees upset.

1 March 2002. The JTF 160 "Fun Run" is tomorrow morning. I'll be doing the 5k (3.1 mile) run. There's also a 10k—too rich for my blood.

On NPR (National Public Radio) this morning I heard a report that nearly 200 Afghan rebels detained here at GTMO were on a hunger strike because one of them had their turban removed during prayer. Turbans are not allowed because they can be used to hide weapons. General Lehnert decided to allow turbans, but said they could be searched at any time.

There are currently two detainees being treated for dehydration at the Camp X-Ray Medical Facility (CXRMF). Both received four liters of fluid, one is now eating and drinking, the other is still refusing to eat or drink.

I am involved with the Hunger Strike SOP revisions, just communication issues. It will be revised to include procedures used at Fort Leavenworth, Kansas, the site of the U.S. Military Prison, which interns only U.S. prisoners. The talk is about at what point we intervene. The current SOP addresses only a hunger strike, not a thirst strike (specifically saying it is so rare it would not be addressed). The bottom line is we will force-feed them, and we will force fluids. We will not let them die. They may have valuable information, and we are compassionate human beings sworn to provide the same care to the detainees as is offered to U.S. personnel, or better.

Several guards at the Fleet Hospital were bragging about their conversations with some detainees. They said if you were caught trying to purchase an AK-47 in Kabul there was a penalty of a ten-year prison term. AK-47s go for $600 American dollars, they said. Russian made grenades can be had for $200.

Turns out the detainee they call Ivan is not necessarily Russian, although he speaks Russian. The guards say he is from one of the "Stans" in the Afghanistan region. I read up on them in a recent issue of National Geographic. I bought the February Issue at Fort Dix nearly a month ago. Last week, the Naval Exchange here just got the January issue, which I had already purchased at Fort Dix in mid January. The Navy Exchange is woefully under-stocked. They seem to get perishable food stuffs regularly, from God knows where or how, but other items like padded mailing envelopes, books, magazines, computer accessories, etc., are much more far and few between. The Jamaican managers always say, "h'it should be on the next barge, mon." The barge was how almost everything got to Gitmo, and if Gitmo was out of something, from McDonald's fries to TLC, it was said to be "on the barge." The film shop is still not operational. The technician from the States has been here for two full days and I am not encouraged. I still have one roll in, and one roll to give, and nearly halfway done on a third. I still don't know if my new camera is any good.

The guards seem to have some hostile tendencies toward the medical staff at the Fleet Hospital. Each "side" is accusing the other of being too friendly with the detainees. The guards feel the medical staff is too nice. The medical staff feels the guards are too buddy-buddy with the detainees. Neither side seems to trust the other to do their job. I wonder if it would be the same if the medical personnel were Army. I tend to think not. Army folk wouldn't put up with the contempt and flippant behavior even I have witnessed. As a liaison all I can do is listen and communicate. I told COL Johnson about my observations. He listened intently and with concern on his face and asked me to pass the info on to CPT Eisen, the 115th MP BN S-3 (Operations Officer). I did. I also ran into Navy Captain Phillips, the JTF Surgeon, and told him. He thanked me kindly and said I was performing a very valuable function. I appreciated that and told him so. After I spoke with him I couldn't help but feel a little disloyal. But I wasn't being disloyal toward the troops and Navy personnel I observe at the Fleet Hospital. My loyalty has to lie with my country, my commanders, and my conscience.

SFC Bragg is very upset about having to take Muslim sensitivity training. Since the hunger strike began with the detainees, the Navy Lieutenant Muslim Chaplain has suggested, and gotten his way—insofar as his opinion—that all U.S. military personnel should receive the training, especially the guards. How about some freaking sensitivity training for the freaking terrorists? How about a little rehabilitation—*A Clockwork Orange* style? Maybe we should get together a visual tribute to their brutality and savagery; show them pictures of the Twin Towers being destroyed, people jumping out of windows a hundred stories up to avoid being burned alive, the Pentagon being hit, people running and helping each other, the wreckage of the plane that went down in Pennsylvania due to a revolt on the plane by passengers? How about we teach our captives a little about American resolve and American character?

These guys couldn't possibly have it better anywhere else on this planet. They have plotted and trained to kill and probably have killed in the name of religion or greed or bloodlust, you name it. The international nature of the captives speaks to the appeal for some lowlifes to pursue clandestine opportunities to fight and kill and maim, and yet they are treated like unfortunate children being held against their will for no good reason. Give me a break! These murderous miscreants would slit the first American throat they could, and enjoy every minute of it. I have no doubt about it.

I went out to Camp X-Ray today. I really should get out there more during this hunger strike. The physician on duty, LCDR Ravenbush, told me she was concerned about protocol regarding dehydration casualties. She was nervous about how many detainees were not drinking. I went to Command Post (CP) 1 with Army Captain Lopez, who is a civilian nurse, credentialed by Navy Hospital Guantanamo Bay (NH GTMO) to work in the CXR Medical Facility; a Navy nurse with some Arabic language skills came, too. We discussed the situation with the Battalion Commander, LTC Wellborn. CPT Lopez suggested we use juice to entice the detainees to drink in order to assess who was really drinking and who was not. I decided to go around to each cell block and ask the NCOIC's if they were tracking fluid intake. Several said they weren't aware that they had to do that, several others said they suspected certain detainees were not drinking, one detainee even told the NCOIC that he wasn't drinking because he didn't feel well. I passed that word along quickly.

All in all, two in "A" block were not eating and suspected of not drinking as well. "B" block had thirty-three not eating and two also suspected of not drinking. "C" block had eight not eating and one suspected of not drinking. "D" and "E" blocks said all their detainees were eating and drinking, and "F" block, which I missed on my tour, radioed in to CP 1 after I returned, and reported twenty-nine not eating and zero known to not be drinking.

The plan to have interpreters go with medical personnel to ask each detainee if they are drinking went forward, and I briefed the team before they went out to do this. "Don't mention eating," was their instruction from CPT Lopez. The point here was drinking. I'll find out tomorrow if the plan was successful and whether or not they got a hold of juice.

Before going to CP 1 the first time, I went to the CXRMF to assess the situation. They were just getting fluids into a detainee who had apparently passed out. The man's eyes were fluttering and his body was limp as he lay on an exam table inside the facility. There were two med techs working on him, the ICRC pediatrician, and Dr. Ravenbush. CPT Lopez introduced me to her and we chatted about protocol. I told her that Navy Captains Phillips and Romanov were concerned about the lack of a workable SOP. CPT Lopez mentioned the "do not resuscitate" question, and Dr. Ravenbush wanted to know what she should do if she got more than ten dehydration cases at once. She needed to know how many were not drinking, now. Just before CPT Lopez and I left for CP 1, the detainee being treated inside came to consciousness; they were running the IV wide open, at almost a stream. The detainee wanted to talk. The Navy nurse who eventually went with CPT Lopez and I went in to talk to the detainee. She came back to us in a minute and said the detainee told her that after they were done putting the fluids in him; he wanted to go back to his cell and see *Allah* (his God). He wanted to die.

LTC Wellborn told us that the hardest hit by being locked up in eight-foot-by-eight-foot cells were the Yemenis. He said they were a nomadic, free roaming people, and that they were going stir crazy. *Good*, I thought to myself. *I'm getting fed up, too.* LTC Wellborn said the majority of the captives were getting restless and wanted out. He said the Europeans among them were handling the confinement the best.

Yesterday, when the media were all over CXR, General Lehnert spoke directly to the detainees on the loudspeaker. The speech was translated. He told them he didn't know what was going to become of them. He really didn't know. None of us do. He told them he did know that in a month or two they would be moving to more permanent quarters, now being constructed on another part of the island, and that that should give them some indication of their fate.

When I got back to the Pink Palace, a bit after 1600 hours, COL Johnson came into his office, where I was doing e-mail and asked me to call CP 1 to get a current status on the detainees in the CXRMF. I told him that when I was there, there were the two dehydrated detainees out in the holding tents next to CXRMF, the one is from the previous night, and one now eating and drinking, and the other not eating or drinking but getting fluids pushed. There was one more in the MF for a dental procedure. When I called back, the Medical Officer In Charge (MOIC) said they only had the two dehydrated detainees outside in a tent left and that both could go back to their cells within the half hour.

That was the plan. Fluff 'em up and get 'em back in their cells. There would be no trip to the comfortable, cool Fleet Hospital for these chaps. And of the seventy-two or so still not eating, if nearly all of them are drinking, we look pretty good. So, you decide how accurate the NPR report was.

2 March 2002. The run went OK. We got up at zero four-thirty to run a 5k at zero six five-five. What's wrong with this picture? I got a XXL t-shirt; they were out of XLs by the time I finished, so Sandy gets a night-shirt. I wonder what she'll think of it. On the back, a green geographic picture of Cuba, with a red star marking the location of Gitmo, and surrounded by the six official seals of the Joint Task Force, Department of Defense included. "JTF" was screened above the island, and "160" below. On the front, a disk over the left breast, about three inches across. In small, almost tiny print, "Joint Task Force 160" curved around the inside top of the disk, and "Guantanamo Bay, Cuba" along the inside bottom. Inside the circle, another island of Cuba, mini medallions of the service seals on the bottom, with about a two-inch tall Mr. Banana Rat in orange detainee clothes and hat. This image is phenomenally politically incorrect. I wonder if CNN will pick up on it.

I had the rest of the day off. I went home, took a shower, slept, and made myself a multi-pepper, onion, cheese, and tomato omelet with hash browns and whole wheat toast, and a glass of orange juice on the rocks. *Mmmmmmmm, delicious!* I napped again, went to the NX, saw that the film shop was still being worked on, came home, started laundry, snacked, laid down, and just got up to write this. I'll go into the office after the laundry is done, try to get on line, go to Mickey D's for dinner, then go see the 7:00 p.m. movie, *Joe Somebody*—I have no idea what to expect.

3 March 2002. I can't wait to call Sandy and the boys tonight. One call a week is not enough for me. I think I'm going to start calling on Wednesday mornings as well. Sandra says that Harrison is getting a little more violent with Theodore and Benjamin. I know he's hurting inside. He's old enough to really miss his daddy and young enough to not understand why his daddy is away. I really want to see him and hold him and reassure him.

FBI Director Robert Mueller visited Gitmo today and was hosted much of the time by LTC Grosse. The LTC shook hands with the director shortly after he got off the plane and the director asked if there were any Marines in the group. The LTC stepped forward, and although was obviously in Army uniform, told Mueller that he had served in Vietnam as a Marine. With that, the Director slapped the LTC on the back and told him he would be his escort. Director Mueller was mostly interested in the hunger strike detainees according to the LTC, and he was briefed on our plan.

The plan is in place now for breaking the hunger/thirst strike, at least for those who want to eat but are getting peer pressure from the detainee leaders. The guards have been told to move certain individuals who are not eating, in blocks "B" and "F" especially, to the other blocks where there is no hunger or thirst strike. They eat and drink when they get there. Another approach that will be used is offering hot tea to those who are cooperative. *Rewarding expected behavior.* A child psychologist might say that is dangerous territory in that the reward may become expected. They say, "do not reward expected behavior." But we are desperate (too strong a word?) to end this strike and get the media down. They feed on things like hunger strikes (pun intended). We'll see.

A guard at Fleet Hospital (FH) had the idea that if you take out the really militant detainees and put them in "A" block, the smallest and most well-established block, and isolate them, then their influence would be diminished. But the unknown always creeps back into the psyche. We don't know the power or threats wielded on the hunger strikers by the detainee leaders. They may have said to the minions that if they refuse to strike, when they are released, they and their families would be murdered. Who knows?

Again, concerns about the four hundred and fifty new laborers from India we are getting to help build the new confinement facility at Radio Range, to be called Camp Delta. There is severe unrest in

India right now between Hindus and Muslims. It is getting worse, as hundreds have been killed over the past four days. Will our laborers be Hindu, Sikh, or Muslim? And even if they identify themselves as one or the other, how do we know they are being truthful, and are not just looking for an excuse to get close to their Muslim brethren behind the wire? Have we let our guard down about such things because we're afraid what to say around the Muslim chaplain?

Even more security measures have been employed around the Fleet Hospital. Road obstacles, more concertina wire, concrete bollards, telephone posts laid horizontally here and there, talk of crew-served weapons inside the medical facility.

I discussed this with Navy Captain Romanov, the FH commander. He is concerned as well about the threat level and what it means to the security of his post. I mentioned to him and to COL Johnson in my daily report that there are potentially serious implications to not iden-tifying the FH and medical personnel with the Red Cross. Legally, if the FH or its medical personnel are not identified within the require-ments of the Geneva Conventions, and an attack happens, whether by sniper or by a larger force, the enemy combatants can say that they did not know they killed or wounded medical persons or that they knew they were destroying a medical facility. If however, the facili-ties and personnel are marked, there would be no excuse, and legal ramifications would be great; the case would be cut and dried.

Question: Would potential infiltrators want to rescue or kill the detainees? Would putting red crosses everywhere tip off where the most vulnerable detainees are? Would it help or hinder the enemy? Do we consider this or simply follow the rule of law? I say, if anyone will listen, we follow the rule of law. Ours is not to consider the law as a tactical advantage or not in my opinion, in fact, tactically speak-ing, the Red Cross is not required on medical personnel—it's the commander's call. But are we in a tactical combat situation? It would depend on the threat level. Are we at THREAT CON "Bravo?" And if we are, what are the requirements? The Navy and the Marines don't want anything to do with the Red Cross. They're always in fluid, tac-tical scenarios with bullets flying. So, why do we have armed guards and armed patrols around Fleet Hospital if there's no threat? And if there is a threat, why aren't we all armed and identified by Geneva Convention standards? Commander's call.

In FH today, I witnessed some bandage changes. SFC Giap is teaching English to detainees, things like "IV." He pointed to the IV device of a detainee this morning and asked, "What is this?" He had to ask two more times and the detainee finally nodded, saying, "Eye VEE, eye VEE." SFC Giap smiled at him, nodding and said, "Number one." He paused for a beat and then asked the detainee, "Who's number one? Who's number one?" The detainee dutifully said, "Giap number one. Giap number one," and smiled.

I checked *Newsday* online today, and my school district was defeated by Copiague in the County Championship girls' basketball game last night before a thousand fans at the State University of New York at Stony Brook. We were ahead at halftime by six points, but they came back on us, using the "box and one" against Nickie Ruby. Their superstar was pretty much shut down by Ally Ruby, and she was held to a season-low sixteen points. But we lost 55 to 48 in the end. Too bad, but we're still in the State Tournament.

Rules of War

"Put none but Americans on guard tonight."

—Gen. George Washington

4 March 2002. I was asked by Major North to attend the Chief-of-Staff's 0730 meeting at JTF Headquarters. I didn't resist, but I suspected it was her meeting to attend. I was proven correct when after the meeting the Chief of Staff, Marine Colonel Mears, told me he wanted our S-3 (Operations Officer) "here every morning," and that it was an operations meeting and not one for medical staff.

Army Colonel Hamberg, an Air Defense Artillery (ADA) officer, presented General Lehnert and about ten other officers, some Navy, some Marine, some Air Force, a PowerPoint presentation on the Air Defense of Guantanamo Bay Naval Station.

It is interesting how after six months of operations here, they are just now getting around to this. There is a cylindrical space above Guantanamo Bay that is U.S. airspace, but all around us is either Cuban or international air space. It poses a serious problem if a hijacked airliner is crossing the northern route over Cuba. Once inside U.S. airspace a plane could cause serious damage. Believe me, after 9/11, almost everybody is looking at aircraft differently these days.

The suggestions for force protection from the air include, "toning down," or painting all the buildings the same color, so as not to give away certain targets that may be easily identifiable by their color, such as the Bachelor Officer's Quarters (BOQ), which is a white multistory hotel-looking building, with very distinctive aqua trim, which can be seen distinctively from quite a distance, including from the oversight towers in Cuba proper, which surround the base.

Fratricide was mentioned as a possibility. I've thought about this myself. Why wouldn't the bad guys want to kill those who are in custody to prevent them from talking? Sounds kind of far-fetched or from a movie, but wasn't the idea of a passenger jet being flown into the World Trade Center rather far-fetched as well?

Then there is the question about the Red Cross. In Department of the Army Pamphlet (DA PAM) 27–1, *Treaties Governing Land Warfare,* Chapter VI, *The Distinctive Emblem,* Article 41, states: "Under the direction of the competent military authority, the emblem of the Red Cross on a white ground shall be displayed on the flags, armlets, and on all equipment employed by the Medical Service." That's pretty clear. If one wants to enjoy the "protection" of the Law of War, one must play by the rules. In war, as they say, rules are meant to be broken, especially if you wish to take the advantage. What possible advantage could there be to intentionally striking a medical facility: The "horror" effect, to shock, to terrorize, to get better news coverage?

I think it is better to identify medical facilities. If you do not clearly mark, in accordance with the law of war and various other international agreements including the Geneva Conventions, and the enemy strikes, hits or destroys a medical facility or medical personnel, what explanation could you give to your commander or to the grieving families of those injured or killed as to why you didn't follow the rule of law, especially if the perpetrators say they did not know they were medical facilities or personnel? Conversely, what could you tell these same folks if those marked facilities were singled out *because* they were marked with the Red Cross?

6 March 2002. Nine American soldiers have been killed in the past few days. 2,000 American and Afghan forces have been in a fierce battle, named Operation Anaconda. One Special Forces troop was killed early in the battle, and eight more were killed two days ago. One fell out of a helicopter while it was taking off and was hit by an RPG (Rocket Propelled Grenade). Another helicopter came in with troops to rescue their fallen comrade and witnessed him being executed. They hit the ground and were chewed up by Al Qaeda forces. On TV this morning they interviewed the family of one of the slain soldiers, a twenty-one-year-old Ranger, who was one of the rescue forces; just a kid.

So, *they* execute *their* prisoners. We play by the rules, or at least we do when the world is looking. And if the world is looking closer, we go above and beyond by listening to the ICRC and the Navy Muslim

Chaplain. It is easy to hate the detainees when looking at them as the enemy. I know that no matter how "human" or friendly they seem, at the first opportunity they will kill or injure an American. They are dangerous, conniving criminals who have led dirty, nomadic, soldier-of-fortune lives. They are addicted to fighting and killing. It gives them a rush of adrenaline and endorphins, which alter the chemical composition of their cranial juices, and produces the most dangerous state of being a human can experience. The "fight or flight" instinct takes over and they savagely destroy anything or anyone they perceive as a threat.

Seven more detainees have been given fluids intravenously today; one forced, who took five liters of fluid, according to COL Johnson. The camaraderie at Fleet Hospital continues to improve, with guards, medical personnel, and detainees seemingly getting more and more use to each other. There is a routine now, what we call a "battle rhythm." One detainee has even asked to go and speak with another. What could make him ask such a thing and think we would allow it? After several weeks in the environment, the guards are happier because they've been reinforced and are getting days off. Things are good at the Fleet Hospital, so why not ask, I suppose?

9 March 2002. Hot sweet tea, snacks, large Korans, English and Arabic language books; these are the things being offered and given to those detainees who are cooperative. The JIIF (Joint Interrogation Intelligence Facility) guys give the detainees cigarettes and McDonald's food when they take them into the JIIF huts for interrogation. It is an interesting strategy, using rewards for expected behavior. Or is it a way of developing trust in order to elicit information?

There is an Army NCO who goes around with an interpreter whose job it is to collect information about how the detainees are doing and whether or not they have any complaints. My job is to filter out the medical complaints. Some detainees want to know what will become of them, or what their status is. Some claim they have a father or son they wish to be next to. Some want to be moved next to those who speak their language. The Algerians want haircuts (this was accommodated). Some ask for better food, more variety in the meat, or more food. One even said he was glad some of those around him were not eating because he was allowed to have some of their food, but normally there is not enough, he said.

Two nights ago the third leading man in the Al Qaeda network was paraded through Camp X-Ray for all detainees to see with COL Johnson and LTC Grosse. He was taken to the Navy brig, up by Navy Hospital Guantanamo Bay. He will stay there, and they will move another there soon.

The Fleet Hospital is up to fifteen detainees now. The physical therapist tech, HM Ladd, was featured in this weeks *Gazette,* the local newspaper which is also available online from the Gitmo website. Good story. It's a tough job, working with unshackled detainees. Helping them get stronger and healthier. I observed her and her counterpart today working with two detainees. They were tying rubber surgical tubing to the litter stands of the detainees they were working with and having them pull the tubing toward them to increase strength in the detainee's arms. One detainee was obviously not tested by the amount of tension on the tubing, and it was far too easy for him to pull it up, so Ladd doubled the tubing over. The detainee could barely pull it up, and Ladd said, "C'mon, you can do it," which he did, complaining and struggling. Then, she said, "Now do thirty," and walked to the other detainee.

There is definitely a mood change on the wards. Five detainees are in the North Ward, and ten in the South Ward (my titles). I walk through and observe from five to fifteen minutes every day. I see a lot of dressing changes and some treatment. I see a lot of physical therapy. As these guys heal, they have to work out. I wonder if they fake pain and immobility in order to stay longer at the Fleet Hospital, where it is cool and they get a lot of attention. I think I wouldn't want to get well very quickly, either, knowing what I would be going back to.

10 March 2002. Tomorrow marks six months since the attack on the U.S. by Al Qaeda forces, masquerading as citizens, who hijacked four commercial aircraft that eventually killed thousands of innocent Americans and several hundred foreign nationals in the World Trade Center's Twin Towers, the Pentagon, and in a plane that was suspected to have been diverted by passengers and crashed in an open field in rural Pennsylvania.

The feelings rush back, the raw emotions. On CNN this morning they had a widow, a grieving mother, and a New York City firefighter who lost colleagues. They are sad, bitter, and frustrated. I too, am sad, bitter, and frustrated. My mission is impossible, and I don't even have direct contact with the detainees. But it bugs the hell out of me that they are living it up in the Fleet Hospital. Yet, it is required that they receive quality medical care. And guards and medical personnel are human beings. They seem to be getting closer and closer to their charges. Smiling more, talking to them more. It is far different than what I saw a month ago.

What I saw a month ago was a nearly silent ward of some frightened some timid detainees, guards, and hospital workers. The guards were stern and unhappy, pulling mostly twelve-hour shifts with no days off. Hospital staff was a little intimidated by the guards, and probably scared or at least wary of the detainees. And the detainees I'm sure were frightened as well: a bunch of people walking around them with various medical instruments poking and prodding them, injecting them, and taking them here and there for tests and X-rays. I wonder if they thought they would become medical experiments.

They are all one now. Almost what you would see if American soldiers were being treated. The only difference would be the restraints on the detainees. The guards might be the occasional buddy who comes to see the wounded. It really is uncanny.

12 March 2002. Things are really heating up around here. People are speeding up planning and contingencies regarding receiving more detainees. At the same time, issues arise about current operations and the Joint War Fighting Task Force will be down here next week to pick our brains about what has gone on so far.

My computer is hooked up, so I can e-mail Sandy and the kids regularly and without feeling rushed when I use the colonel's machine. I also have hospital e-mail on line. Lots of good things are happening but there is also a lot of work to do. The zero eight-thirty meetings at Fleet Hospital have become really important, as a guard has been accused of harassing a detainee (#75) who seems to have more and more problems with guards. Well, according to hospital staff, he's been abused by the guards. There are a least three guards who have been requested by FH command to be reassigned out of the Fleet Hospital. The FH also has commended certain MPs for their professionalism, positive performance, and cooperation. It is necessary for both the "jailers" and the "caregivers" to compromise and work together.

The abuse was reported to be such things as slapping the detainees on the head to wake them, and removing their bed coverings in an urgent manner.

13 March 2002. The situation here is deteriorating rapidly. We would probably need some outside independent opinion of that, but it seems so to me. It seems that just as we are gaining experience and savvy about this detention medicine thing, personnel changes are made and we have to start all over again. Mistakes made in Vietnam, aside from even getting involved, include rotating troops. Experi-

enced, efficient soldiers were taken out after twelve or thirteen months, to be replaced by less experienced, less efficient greenhorns. In World War II, the Civil War, and other conflicts, soldiers stayed in the field until they were killed, wounded beyond quick rehabilitation, or until the conflict ended.

But there may be dangers to keeping certain people here in the FH. There are now manifestations of previously identified violent ideation on the part of guards. Soldiers are being transferred. Now detainees are being transferred to the brig. One detainee began to bang his head against the bars in the brig. There is more and more psychosis becoming evident in detainees. Behavior in all personnel is deteriorating, the detained and the free. It's scary. I'm scared. I must find a way to communicate this feeling effectively, maybe to the commander, maybe to the Navy Muslim chaplain, *maybe to nobody.*

If I were a prisoner of war, my "Code of Conduct" requires me to attempt to escape and resist. What do we think their code says? Be nice? I feel there will be incidents. I feel there may be a detainee or U.S. suicide. Five U.S. personnel have been sent home because of psychiatric problems. Then what? We already have probably a dozen or so detainees who are psychiatric cases. The number is growing. Do we think by continuing this game they will get better? Is there any "rehabilitation" going on? Is there any education going on? Should there be?

Is confinement in an eight-by-eight-foot cage punishment? Is it worth it to say these folks have probably hardened themselves by now to any attempt on our part to rehabilitate or release them into a nonviolent world? Or do we just hang on to them indefinitely until they all become infected with the culture of maximum confinement until they are all hopelessly committed to the destruction of civilization, or at least Western civilization? Isn't that the way we got them in the first place?

Oh. Lord, please forgive me for my sins, for they are many and varied. I am weak and need your love and strength to see me through this dilemma. I need to be whole when I return home, in your good graces, for my wife and family. My boys need me to be whole and sane. Thank you, oh, Lord for your faith in me, for your love and kindness. In Jesus' name I pray and thank you. Amen.

17 March 2002. Things are changing around here fast, on a lot of fronts. Home front: Just avoided major catastrophe. Sandra e-mailed me two days a go saying she had received a letter stating that our health insurance, dental insurance, and eye care had all been termi-

nated. I forwarded her e-mail to Dr. Wine, and he got right back to me saying he would take care of it. I believe him, and trust him. Do I have a choice? This is just one more reason for me not to be here.

BLD front: Two of our officers are severely pissing off the commander. They went into work today and were unable to confirm the total U.S. personnel in the JDOG (Joint Detainee Operations Group). They made a printout of CPT Yuel's power point presentation on JDOG strength, but it was weeks old and needed to be verified. They were unable to do so. LTC Grosse, at the hooch with me for a day off (he's suffering badly with arthritis), got a call from Marine COL Mears, the JTF-160 Chief of Staff, to come on down to the JTF HQ to verify the numbers for the general. LTC Grosse had just put a TV dinner in the microwave for lunch, was in T-shirt and shorts and in severe pain. He left lunch, got dressed and took a hummer down to JTF HQ. When he got back he said the General was "hot." He was upset that our officers couldn't get the info right. The Chief called them "stupid." When LTC Grosse met COL Johnson, who just came back from 10 days at Fort Hood with his brigade staff, said LTC Grosse could send them home as nonessential.

CXR front: CNN reported that two U.S. personnel had been removed from Camp X-Ray for psychological reasons. I called Commander Baily, the new SPRINT leader, and she said she didn't know anything about it, but had been called by the General who told her he may have said something to the press that may have been taken the wrong way. CDR Baily told me that she and her two assistants were interviewed on Thursday by the press, but that she had no knowledge of any soldiers who were psychological cases. She was a psychiatrist, not a psychologist. And the only person she knew of having any problems was a Marine who was being sent home because of personal problems at home. There's also a detainee in the Brig who has not eaten in four days, and a detainee who keeps banging his head on the concrete. LTC Grosse said LCDR King told him she'd keep treating him as long as he keeps banging his head.

I went shopping today. I bought Sandra a royal blue polo shirt with "U.S. Naval Base, Guantanamo Bay, Cuba," embroidered around an image of a lighthouse. I hope she likes it. I got the boys some patriotic stickers and a post card with a kitten sitting next to some American flags. I really love my boys and miss them terribly. *God, I hope this is over soon.*

Dennis Jones, an old friend of mine, e-mailed me two days ago. He gave me the Web address of his girlfriend Rose's site, "Visual Poetry."

She does professional videography. She had several sections, one with the heading "Biography," which was especially touching, with portrait photographs of extreme and subtle human emotions of joy, happiness, and love. I nearly cried. I thought this was a great idea for an anniversary or birthday gift. The "Weddings" section was great, too. A section titled "Life Is Art" was filled with beautiful images of the human form. I e-mailed Rose from her site, telling her what I thought of it, and she e-mailed me back thanking me and saying she was grateful for me serving my country. I had said a few nice things about Dennis in the e-mail and she thanked me for that as well and agreed.

I emailed Dennis back after having lots of problems sending an e-mail with attachments from the Web browser, but finally was successful e-mailing from my new medical e-mail address. I sent him pictures Lieutenant Commander Gene Montpellier took of the New York City flag and the U.S. flag that flew over the Pentagon on 11 September. They were both raised over Camp X-Ray and Freedom Heights, respectively, at 0800, 10 March to the playing of our National Anthem. I was there when Gene took these photos. I also sent him two more Gene took, one of the front of Camp X-Ray, and one of a large iguana that was posing in front of a Marine's Humvee.

18 March 2002. I have been asked by LTC Grosse to read reports from a quality control soldier who goes around to each cell with an interpreter and asks the detainees how things are going. They tell him and he moves on. I read the reports to glean medical and preventive med information from them. I give the information to Navy Captain Romanov, who is asked to act on it. The information is non-classified, so he doesn't need to worry about the source, or whether or not his attention to the information will compromise further information collection, even though he was concerned about that.

Captain Romanov is an exceptional officer. He is unassuming, exceedingly intelligent, I would even say brilliant, and in a non-threatening, professional, and even gentle way. He is almost subconsciously concerned with ego, but not his own. Uncannily sensitive, he can be direct in such a way as to communicate absolute clarity, but with just the right twist of humility and self-effacement that you can't help it but want to do what it is he wants immediately and to the best of your ability. He is ultimately concerned about the details. He thinks and plans three months out, and probably further if you asked him to admit to it. But even as focused as he is on the little things, he does not micromanage. He trusts and demands of his staff the very best, but is so easy about it they don't realize perhaps that they are being encouraged with a crop. It's like the seamless relationship of a rider and his horse. There is love and care in the relationship, and they function as one when they work, but it is clear who is in charge, and it is so abundantly clear that it never needs to be discussed. It just is.

When I first mentioned the information to him, it wasn't clear to me how all the information was reported. I thought perhaps some of it was picked up passively or indirectly. So, Captain Romanov began to hypothesize about what value there would be if they were to approach the medical complainers at a certain time or place, or whether or not to bring them in to be treated even if their condition did not warrant it, in order to glean more information from them. The situation was cleared up when I was told the medical information was not classified and was all solicited openly.

19 March 2002. There was very lively conversation among the detainees at Camp X-Ray this afternoon. I was looking around for preventive med concerns due to some of the detainee complaints about snakes and bugs. Indeed, there was tall grass and weeds, some of it adjacent to the cells, some of it on the perimeter of the cell blocks, and a lot of it adjacent to the inner and outer fences. Prev Med should have had that stuff gone a long time ago. One wonders what would cause the detainees to have such excited conversation. There is a lot I don't know, and perhaps that is for the best; after all, curiosity killed the cat, and released all the evils of the world from Pandora's Box.

The drinking water and hand-washing situation is not ideal, either. Drinking water is placed in a canteen, which does not have a lid or cap, and detainees are not allowed to cover it as a precaution against them keeping items in it. But the water is not regularly filled, and left uncovered has let bugs and even frogs in. LCDR King had the idea that if we could get clear plastic gallon-sized water jugs, we could keep the water full and not have to worry about concealment of contraband, and the detainees could keep a cap on the jug without having to worry about being accused of concealing anything. I liked the idea and told LCDR King that I will pass it along. I told CDR Guillaum about the Preventive Med concerns and he'll pass them along to Navy CAPT Phillips.

On my way out of Camp X-Ray, the detainees began chanting. Of course I did not know why, or what they were saying. Next time I run into an interpreter, I will ask him. But apparently, the excited chattering I heard when I came in was about something. One of the guards told me that "D" block had been chanting earlier in the day. That's a previously "good" block. But the strategy has been to move "trouble-makers." Well, if you move a troublemaker without rehabilitating him, guess what? He instigates even more. Hell, I knew that from working as a dean of students in New York City's public schools. That's how they handled it too, at least when I was there. Before I got there in the early eighties, they had what were called "500" schools. The rowdy, unsocialized screw-ups would get sent there, one school per borough. Let them ruin the education of each other, not those who want to learn. They discontinued 500 schools shortly after I arrived on the scene. It was probably too successful. Not enough excitement in the other schools, I guess. Then the strategy was to transfer them— *Great; new killing, stomping, stealing, and robbing grounds.* Kids lick their chops at opportunities to start anew. Unfortunately, for the kids who were introduced to their new tormentors, no one cared enough about them to protect them from these antisocial predators.

So, at CXR, if you're bad, you get new friends. This was easy enough to figure out. No secret was ever made of it. Besides, how do you keep secrets from nearly 300 folks who have nothing better to do than to study your every move, your *every* move. They get to organize a whole new group of people.

Hicks, the Australian, supposedly wrote a letter home that some-one told me about. Hicks said he loved his family, and didn't want them to believe the stories in the newspapers that he is worth 10 nor-mal fighting men. *Right, you just want to kill an American before you go on to your next horror show. Not on my watch, Bubba.* Upon arrival we were told of Mr. Hicks' famous first words upon hitting the tarmac at the Leeward airport: "I'm going to kill an American before I leave this place." Lovely fellow, that one.

20 March 2002. I took Navy Captain's Phillips and Hartman to the Joint and First Aid Stations. Coast Guard LT Porter and Chief Presley did a great job cleaning up the aid stations and answering questions of the JTF Surgeon. They're good guys and later I returned to thank them and get the name of their commanding officer. I called their CO later and told him what a great job they're doing; way above and beyond expectations.

Later, I went with Navy LT Daniels (Matt). Turns out he's a home-boy from suburban Riverside, California, my home town. He is from Fontana, California, just about eight miles or so from my boyhood home in Rubidoux, a suburb of Riverside. He went to the University of California at Riverside. We chatted a lot about the town, and how much the Gitmo landscape and weather reminded us of the desert hills we both are so familiar with. He asked me when the last time was that I was there. I honestly don't remember. It has been a long time. It was probably around 1986 or 1987. Matt and I went out to the Radio Range site, where Jamaican and Indian workers are building the new compound for the detainees and U.S. personnel.

The laborers from India were quite friendly, waving, smiling, and saying "hello." Bob, the safety officer for the contractor, showed Matt and me around. We also went to the Windward side airport, and at the east end of the runway, crews of foreign laborers were building the new incarceration "units" from steel containers, knocking down one wall and replacing it with steel mesh.

The new units are about five feet wide and eight feet deep, which is less moving space than the current units, which are approximately eight feet by eight feet. There is a stainless steel toilet bowl in the floor with a hole and two footpads, also stainless steel. There is a small blue stainless steel sink with one pressure-release faucet. This will be the lap of luxury for the vast majority of these detainees. I'm sure they won't appreciate it.

Leaning Forward

*"According to the Laws of Thermodynamics, only a fraction
of the energy of a system can be converted to work. Which
fraction are you?"*

—M. J. Granger

23 March 2002. It's not real. This all can't be real. I belong at home, with my wife and boys. Harrison is hurting. I know it. I feel it. He is confused and lonely without me. His mother is attached to his newborn brother, his older brother consumed with his older world and friends. Harrison is alone without me and it is hurting him. He lashes out at his little brother, the easiest prey. His mother he beseeches for love, but she can only hug him with one arm. He needs two. *God, let me at least go home for a week to help mend the wounds and heal the hurt. I need to go home for a week to help, to be with them, my life manifested in flesh and blood and spirit. God, give me strength to see and hear and be what I need to be to be whole and be a good husband and father, and, unfortunately so, a good soldier; there is no one to blame but myself. Living with the guilt is not living. It is existing, surviving, just getting by, the most useless kind of life there is. But I must make it through. I WILL make it through to the end and see my family again and it must be soon.*

I spent several hours today checking on the environmental and hygienic status of Camp X-Ray. I went through every cell block and walked past every cell. At one point, I told a detainee who was beseeching me to speak to him by repeatedly saying, "Sir, sir!" Finally, I told him "I'm sorry, I cannot talk to you." And he stopped. In retrospect, I probably should have spoken with him. I needed to know some important information only he would have been able to tell me about critters; something I was looking for. But, I didn't listen.

I waited until I spoke with SFC Stern, the author of the reports I read from which to glean medical and preventive medicine information in order to write my own reports to Colonel Johnson.

24 March 2002. Yesterday I went into the camp to give my own little survey of the environmental and hygienic conditions. I psyched myself up for it by agreeing with myself that I would not make eye contact with them. For the most part I kept my promise. It wasn't bad because the guards seemed happy to entertain me. One block even gave me an official escort. Two others had someone come with me, as a curiosity I think more than anything else. The troops were fresh, just came on duty, would be there for eight hours, and were in good spirits.

It was hot as be-Jesus. I had rolled my sleeves down and applied my SPF 45 sunscreen, and it proved wise as over two hours later I still got a bit pink on my cheeks, nose and neck. The sun baked the guards in the sally ports, the double-gated five-foot-by-five-foot or so cages that separate the prison alleyways from the cell blocks.

I took my time, going slow in order to get into a careful rhythm so as not to miss anything important. I looked for poor drainage (moss on concrete), vegetation, and critters. I found all three. I could have almost stopped after "A" block. It had standing water in some of the cells. "A" block is the oldest block, built several years ago for the Haitian immigrant days. It is smaller than the other blocks, and shows a few signs of decay; poor construction and lack of attention.

"A" block also had the most critter complaints. Detainees, once they got wind of what I was doing, were quick to tell me stories of scorpions on their necks, snakes coming into their cells, worms, frogs in their water, etc. I listened, but also trusted my own observations. I found the tiny inch-long worms, about a millimeter thick, in the wet stones next to the concrete foundation of an "A" block cell. Tiny white flying insects were also evident, about the size of the head of a pin, as well as an earwig. There was definitely something going on here. Not quite sure what. *Ah, my kingdom for an entomologist!*

I need to come back late at night or very early in the morning to look for other animals, such as spiders, scorpions, mice, and snakes. A black light would help, as scorpions show up quite well in the fluorescent beams. I found bees, ants, birds, and lizards, as well. All these animals I believe are attracted to water, and then to each other. I found no evidence of any food scraps. Not a crumb, which makes sense as most detainees complain about not having enough to eat. But one or two have actually complained about gaining weight! Water is the stuff of life, and it was fairly scarce; sourced only by one hose in each cell block, and the wash and shower areas. Most of the problems were where the sun did not hit the wet spots. The rows of cells in Block "A" are much closer to each other than in the other cell blocks, so the sun has trouble squeaking in, thus, the excessive moisture problems.

When I went through "F" block and the "Class Clown," a detainee pointed out to me by a guard as being boisterous, must've thought I was counting something, so began counting arbitrary numbers out loud in English, trying to mess up my count, as it were. A few other detainees joined him intermittently. I finished my work with a smile on my face. I never looked at him, nor did I acknowledge his silliness in any other fashion. But it was quite entertaining.

Today, "C" block had a mini "riot." The detainees threw their belongings out of their cells in protest of a detainee who is supposedly not well who decided he did not want to empty his own waste pail. Not all in "C" block did this, but many did. LTC Grosse said Colonel Johnson said, "They don't get their shit back until the 26th, that is, unless the General catches wind of it before then."

I have a feeling Colonel Johnson has something in store for these folks when he takes over as chief of staff. I am beginning to think that more and more LTC Grosse is the perfect JDOG commander. He's a Suffolk County deputy sheriff, who knows all the tricks of the trade. These are the guys who are not shy about having no compassion for the "carrot people." Yes, that's a slur upon the orange get-ups the detainees wear. Sorry. Not really. It's kind of an affectionate pet name for them. The nickname for Camp X-ray is "The Garden," because that's where we take care of The Carrots, some of whom are turning into pumpkins. LTC Grosse is an exceedingly nice individual. He is decent, polite, and respectful, but he also does not hide his belief that these detainees are exactly where they ought to be.

27 March 2002. "Kill the Carrots!" So reads Lee's dry erase board in our office, and covered with "Die!" all over it, courtesy of Max. Should the SPRINT Team (The U. S. Navy Special Psychiatric Rapid Intervention Team) see this? Or hear Max's cries of, "I want to kill myself!"? This is crazy stuff, but these are certainly crazy times. Lee has a wife and a little girl back home. Max has a new wife.

Navy Captain Romanov wants to talk with LTC Grosse regarding the use of the isolation cell constructed in the Camp X-Ray Medical Facility compound. Grosse wants it for whatever he wants it for, currently isolation for punishment. Romanov wants it for flexibility in putting a hunger-striking patient in there who they don't necessarily want to "reward" by putting him at Fleet Hospital, where it is air conditioned. Romanov also wants it available to the SPRINT folks in case they want to isolate and observe a psych patient. So, who will prevail? Grosse and Romanov are meeting tomorrow morning at fleet to talk about it over coffee. We'll see.

Sandra is doing an excellent job of keeping the kids aware of me. I send things and she has the boys e-mail me about what they think about it and such. I just filled another small package for the family: photographs, a Thomas the Tank Engine book for them to share, and the iguana crossing sign from the Army veterinarian. The vet gave them out as gifts to the JDOG staff before she leaves the Island next month to her new assignment in the Sinai. I remember asking her about the mission there and she had quite a bit to say about it. She said it was called the Multinational Force and Observers (MFO), an eleven-nation peacekeeping force located in the heart of the Sinai desert, just west of the Israeli-Egyptian international border. "The MFO is not a typical force," she said, "it is a unique organization, existing only in this one part of the world and for the sole purpose of monitoring compliance with the Treaty of Peace between Egypt and Israel. It has been in place, quietly going about the business of peace-watching, since 1982." Who knew? She said she's always wanted to go there. More power to her.

That reminds me. LCDR Montpellier and I witnessed an iguana getting killed. A small one was crossing the road in front of the Post Office. A white fifteen-passenger van was in front of the little thing, which was only about a foot and a half long. We were traveling the opposite direction, and stopped well behind it. The creature was crossing the street very slowly, but it was crossing.

Suddenly, and just as the little fella was safely on the other side of the road, and as the van began to move ever so cautiously, a much larger iguana, perhaps three and a half to four feet long, dashed out in pursuit of the first iguana. The larger lizard literally bumped into the side of the front left tire of the van and sort of bounced off of it. It looked as though it was going to retreat back to its side of the street, and the van was not going very fast at all, maybe five miles per hour. But instead, the large iguana turned 180 degrees toward the left rear tire, which bisected it and squeezed the life out of it. Blood spurted out of the animal's mouth and it lay there motionless, eyes open, dead.

Its body looked normal, as if it were sunning itself. But it was most assuredly dead. A pool of blood neatly formed to the front left of its mouth. The horrified but controlled driver of the MWR (Morale Welfare and Recreation) van slowly got out, knowing he had run over something, probably an iguana. He never saw it coming, as it raced from his rear left toward the vehicle. The only thing he could have done would have been to stop the vehicle after the animal hit his front tire. But with no sight of it and no tactile sense from the bump, the poor thing didn't have a chance. So, if you see one iguana crossing the road, there could be another one not far behind. The Army vet needed to be called, and the MPs had just arrived on the scene. The vet had told me once that she was obligated to retain all road-kill and other dead iguanas and send them to the San Diego Zoo, where they would by autopsied and their cause of death recorded. The black Cuban rock iguana's are a protected species and many are tagged with computer chips for tracking and studying. Their roving around the island like they do reminds me of stories and photos I'd read about cows wandering the streets of India.

The new Command Sergeant Major, a slight, sprite woman in her mid-to-late forties or early fifties (I give myself a lot of rope with which I could easily be hung here, but no one dares speak up about her age for fear of being wrong themselves), visited the JAS unannounced today. She evidently had some things to say to one of the corpsmen, but I have not interviewed that person yet. It seems she didn't like the messiness there. Join the club.

So, I went looking for her today so I could thank her for getting involved. I really could use her help, you know? She could help me track down Haskell and the other Coast Guard medic who are shadows around here. They claim they are only here to provide for their own people. What a scam; I wonder what they tell their commander? All medical assets on the Island belong to Navy CAPT Phillips, period.

28 March 2002. Max said that a detainee attempted to keep the M&M candy from his lunch meal to save for later (they are not allowed to save or stockpile food; they must eat it or return it at the end of meal time). The guards demanded the M&Ms, so, in an act of defiance, while the guards were entering his cell to confiscate the candy, the detainee quickly opened the bag and stuffed the entire contents in his mouth. Also, two detainees refused to eat the afternoon meal because they were not given the meal with rice and beans. I too have felt this way when on occasion I do not get the MRE of my choosing. MREs are Meals Ready to Eat; they are the military combat meal with about 1,200 calories each, if all items are consumed, and

there are twelve varieties, including a vegetarian meal, which we serve to the detainees. I completely understand their feelings on this subject. Perhaps we should allow a detainee MRE exchange so that they have an opportunity to trade up? *He, he, he.*

30 March 2002. March madness has a new face here in Guantanamo. General Lehnert went out with a whimper, spending one of his last full days of command at the camp handing out candy to and chatting with detainees, sort of like a St. Nick or Easter Bunny in cammies. He had stuffed his pockets full of candy and would even sit in the wastewater damp gravel outside certain cells and have little chats with the terrorists about their families and their fate. LCDR Montpellier accompanied the general as he spent two and a half hours going to each detainee and handing out the treats.

Was this last act an attempt to soften the terrorists to him? Was it to relieve himself of fear of reprisal, when and if one or more of these killers are released? Was it self-preservation? Was it disloyal and selfish? Or was it simply an act of empathy? Who had he discussed this plan with? And if he did discuss it with an inner circle, his XO (executive officer), COL Mears, or his wife, what possible rationale could he have given other than the ones I mention above? Who the hell is he, representing us, and the United States, to show compassion and kindness towards our avowed enemies? What gall, what presumptive asininity! How dare he take for granted my faith and loyalty in him to be a staunch and unemotional leader of this just confinement!

Our medical and guard personnel struggle every day at the fleet hospital, at Camp X-Ray, at the JIIF, in the Pink and Puzzle Palaces, the motor pool, in the galleys (Navy-speak for "kitchen"), and for what? For him to go and fireside chat and give candy to murderers? Incredulous!

Commander Dickenson, the new JLSG (Joint Logistics Group) commander, said last night at Rick's (the officer's lounge), that he may disagree with the general's behavior, but would not disparage him. His job was too difficult, too high-profile for it to be a traditional warden type position. I am paraphrasing, but the gist was: *cut the Old Man some slack.* I was mildly sympathetic to that view at the time; I am less so now. I said that perhaps the general was privy to important information that we underlings were not in a position to have a "need to know." That's one of the standards for one to receive classified information; a need to know meant you had the authority or position to actually do something with the information. Perhaps the general had a need to know some information that led him to do what he did.

Perhaps he was told to do it. We are quick to assume that just because somebody wears a star on their collar that it means they can do whatever they want to do. We sometimes forget that everybody has a boss. So, *cut the Old Man some slack.* I suppose I will, but very little, until I can (if ever) find out what was behind the chats and treats. Highly unusual and inappropriate in my view, but I will concede the possibility that the act was part of a PSYOPS or CA plan (psychological operations or Civil Affairs).

New General Beauregard, I believe, has potential. I read his opening address to the detainees, a sort of letter of introduction, traditional among Army officers when becoming attached to a new command. He told them about his appointment to head the detention operation, told them a little about himself and that the rules for the determination of their status had been set. He also told them that for their own safety and the safety of the guard force, discipline problems would not be tolerated. He did not make any specific threats, but with LTC Grosse in charge of the Joint Detainee Operations Group now, the detainees had better lighten up. General Beauregard's words were measured and firm, but although businesslike, were friendly. Kind of like "Hey, you, this is me, and I'm in charge. Be patient and cooperative and things will work out. Mess around and you will be dealt with." Kind of like T. R. Roosevelt's "walk softly and carry a big stick," only Beauregard didn't mention the stick so much, yet.

NPR is talking about the legitimacy of a fight against Iraq right now. Allies and Arab nations want us to wait until the United Nations can explore all possibilities with regard to getting Iraq to allow weapons inspectors back into the country. Iraq kicked out the inspectors, calling them spies, during the waning years of the Clinton Administration. Clinton blinked, and did not have the political fortitude to deal with it or to discipline the Iraqis, led by the evil and indiscriminate Saddam Hussein, especially during a personal scandal and his own futile attempt to leave a legacy of conciliation and friendship among former enemies and possibly earn a Nobel Peace Prize.

Yesterday, I was part of a briefing party for three three-star officers: One Navy, one Civilian equivalent and one Army Lieutenant General Peak, the Army Surgeon General. Accompanying General Peak was South COM (Southern Command) Surgeon, Colonel Jones. Colonel Jones made a point of seeking me out after the briefing. We spoke several times for a few moments, both during his tour of the Navy Hospital, the site for the briefing, and at Camp X-Ray. He asked me how things were going. I told him, OK, but we're not getting the cooperation, continuity, and support we need. The higher-echelon experience and limitations of the Navy Hospital Staff are not acutely sensitive to the Echelon I medical mission. We have only E-4 and below medical support where the troops live, and no pre-positioned evacuation assets at either the FAS or JAS. The bus schedule was changed over a week ago and excluded the hospital as a regular stop and ended runs through the major housing areas, forcing troops to wait in the dusty motor pool between the two housing developments. Ill or injured troops have to trek to the hospital or motor pool bus stop on their own. Command Sergeants Major made the decision about the new bus schedule without a Navy Chief or medical person present. Navy CAPT Phillips said he would "fix it," but it is not fixed. So, I was compelled to address these concerns with Colonel Jones.

I also gave Colonel Jones copies of my lessons learned and Joint Warfighter questionnaire, plus attachments. He wants to chat with me later, by phone, as he left after his and the three-star's six-hour tour at Gitmo. I hope I did not overstep my bounds. But hell, the Navy is concerned with the Navy medical mission. They are a bit arrogant, especially Navy CAPT Hartman, and they are a bit sensitive to not being able to meet Army expectations. They try, but they just don't get it, and apparently neither do the people who should get it, CSMs, Army-type.

I will enlist the assistance of the new JTF Command Sergeant Major, from the 89th MP Brigade, headed by COL Johnson, who is now the JTF Chief of Staff. CSM Mitchell made a tour of the JAS with the outgoing CSM, Marine-type. Seems she wasn't happy with the appearance of the facility (which is actually a lot better since I arrived six weeks ago). I have made my intentions to discuss soldier care with her obvious to COL Johnson. I popped into her office at the JTF HQ yesterday, she was absent, but I left her a note. I will thank her for her interest in the JAS, and in soldier care, and then enlist her support. I will discuss the operational necessity of having SSG David in operational control of the JAS and FAS. I will emphasize the need for evacuation assets at both facilities. I will ask for her assistance in getting the bus schedule changed back to servicing the Windward Loop and East Caravella housing areas and to the hospital. Anything less will be inadequate. I will enlist her help in getting the base safety officer to hoist heat index flags at CXR, the FAS, and the JAS, and to raise the international symbol of medical facilities (the red cross) above the FAS and JAS. I really believe she could help.

My mother in-law wrote me recently about Harrison's trip to a "Rescue Heroes" program at the library back home. She and his grandpa took him there, where he listened and watched the presenters talk about the firefighters, police officers, and EMS workers who help keep us safe. Harrison stood up, was invited to the front of the room and said, "My daddy is a hero, too. He is in the military in Cuba." He then showed everyone the medal I gave him before I left. He likes wearing it places. For a three-year-old, he is a man in my eyes.

31 March 2002. Happy Easter! I spoke with Sandy and Benjamin today. Harrison and Theodore were napping. Great boys, all. Benjamin had a lot to say about toys and candy and friends; such a sweet boy. Sandy and I are experiencing some of the same things: loneliness, longing for touch, reassurance, and love. This long distance stuff is not cutting it. I told her and Benjamin that my dream was to meet them at Disney World at the end of June when the boys would be out of school. Benjamin said he didn't want to stay so long next time, and that nine days was too much last time. He asked me how long I would like to stay, and I said at least ten days (the maximum amount of leave days allowable under the new leave policy). I told him I wouldn't mind living there at Disney. Sandra and I had taken the boys to the new Animal Kingdom Lodge at Walt Disney World. It had opened in the spring of 2001, before the world changed. We were there in August of 2001 in sweltering heat. But the heat gave us an excuse to return to our resort at noon each day for a swim and a nap. By dinnertime we were back in the parks. But the really magical thing was waking up and finding the boys on our veranda, watching the African animals feed only several dozen feet from them on the savanna. Sandra and I would just watch them from the room and enjoy their marveling at the animals and the specialness of it all.

I witnessed the two detainees getting intubated this morning with LTC Grosse. I hadn't seen it in person before. Detainee #44, hunger striker for over a month, got his tube first. Not much of a problem, but lots of people around, nine medical folks and three MPs. Detainee #217, more of a baby, took less time just because the group knew what they were doing and had all their equipment together. He resisted a bit, but his head was held by five hands, four from two MPs and one from the intubating nurse, a male Navy lieutenant. Detainee #44 was intubated by the Arab-speaking doctor. The interpreter, Navy lieutenant junior grade Dellmore, spoke with each detainee before the procedures, and attempted to get them to eat, or at least drink the cut Ensure they were about to feed them through the tube. No such luck.

They were both resistant, but in words only. They cooperated reluctantly, and did not resist physically. The Navy medical folk were incredibly patient, but also insistent and firm.

I spoke with Commander Carol James, Chief of Nursing at Fleet Hospital 20, where the procedure took place, and she said that she and her staff have had experience putting tubes down people who didn't want them in, such as drug addicts, drunks, or people in accidents. It could get messy, she said. But philosophically, one could disagree with what we were doing, but we have to do it. We're not going to let anyone die; it's not what we do. We help people get better. We heal.

I also spoke with Captain Romanov about his original mission, which included good guy care, but had changed once Captain Phillips, the JTF Surgeon, decided that all good-guy care would come from the Naval Hospital. Captain Romanov said his folks were ready to support the good-guy care mission, but were told to stand down from it. He came here with one hundred and fifty personnel, and is now down to one hundred and nine because of the lack of work for his people. The Army units were so haphazard about who they brought that they had very few medics and no preventive medicine guys with them. This added to the confusion about whose job care of U.S. personnel it is.

Speaking to Captain Phillips briefly, I mentioned to him, in front of Captain Romanov and LTC Grosse, that Colonel Jones, South COM Surgeon, was not happy when I told him our Freedom Heights first aid station (FAS) did not have the capabilities of a Battalion Aid Station (BAS), nor did the JAS have any routine or urgent evacuation assets. Something I had asked Phillips for weeks ago. I had also asked Dr. Blount, but never got a "green" (Army) ambulance or anything else.

I'm now poised to sit down with CSM Mitchell, the new JTF CSM, and not only ask her to give me SSG David to manage the JAS, but to help me get the bus schedule changed so that troops who are sick or injured don't have to *walk* to the freaking hospital. Of course, having a green ambulance with a red cross on the side would be nice, too, but I gotta start somewhere. Wish me luck.

4 April 2002. There is still no transportation for the Joint Aid Stations. But, I am officially the Operational and Administrative commander of the Joint Aid Stations, at Windward Loop, and soon-to-be Camp America, the sea hut city being erected by the local Seabees, whose motto is: "We Build, We Fight!" Five advanced party personnel will be coming in tomorrow from the 4th Infantry Division. 196

will be arriving on Saturday, all at once. Staff Sergeant David will be in charge (NCOIC) of the Camp America JAS. An additional mission will be for him to set up some tail-gate medicine until the JAS structure, two connected sea huts, is complete. The Seabees and the contractor's construction crews have been running 24/7 to get things squared away. Time is fleeting. Original completion date was 14 April. We'll have two hundred personnel out at Camp America by Monday, April 8. Doesn't that beat all?

One detainee, a guy supposedly with a birth certificate from Baton Rouge, Louisiana—born to Saudi nationals twenty-two years ago but who left the U.S. when he was a toddler—is being flown out tomorrow. LTC Grosse knocked on the bathroom door early this morning and asked me who I could live without for two days—1LT Tiva or SSG David. Well, I needed David to get started with the planning for Camp America JAS, so it was a no-brainer: he could have Tiva.

The mission ended up being a flight to the U.S. to cover medical needs of the Baton Rouge Saudi on his trip back to his birth country. Tiva couldn't legally give restraint medications in flight, so they took Air Force captain, Dr. Weld. Dr. Weld and six colleagues, who had been flying over from Kandahar with the first detainee waves, had been sequestered here a month ago, supposedly until the flow started again. None of them wanted to be here, but so goes life in the military. (Oh, by the way, who *does* want to be here?) So, I'm sure that the six left behind will be plenty jealous. They'll all be out of here soon anyway. More bad guys cometh by the 19th of April or so. Before that, all bad guys will be transferred, in one furious day, to the new detention camp at Radio Range. The new bad guy holding area will now be Camp Delta ("D" in civilian-speak). Camp America (formerly Camp Alpha) will house the U.S. personnel, mostly guards, some medics, and other support personnel, but all Army.

Yesterday, at a meeting at the Navy education center behind the hospital—and nearly at the end of an all-branches medical capabilities briefing—Captain Phillips announced that the Freedom Heights First Aid Station would soon be standing down. In fact, I learned today at the JTF Medical meeting that the whole of Camp X-Ray would be closing down when the detainees are moved to the new facilities. I would be in charge of the two JASs, Navy LT Daniels would be the clinical supervisor for the JASs, and Dr. Blount would be the overall clinical supervisor. I will still report directly to the JTF Surgeon, Navy CAPT Phillips. HM1 Wheatly will be the NCOIC of the Windward Loop JAS, which will have operating hours between

0700 to 1600, and will be locked when not manned—no more residents in the JAS. Camp America JAS will be a 24/7 operation until we decide differently.

7 April 2002. There is a lot going on, planning-wise and personnel-wise. Two hundred infantrymen and nine medical personnel hit the ground running yesterday. They came in at thirteen-hundred in full battle-rattle and looked a bit tired but ready to go. I hooked up immediately with the medical platoon leader, 1LT Muhammad Anderson, Medical Service, Occupational Therapist. He's prior Navy (seven years), so he can help translate Navy-speak for me; I'm here a few months and it still baffles me sometimes. He brought two E-5 91W20s, one of whom is prior Special Forces, 18D (Special Forces Medical Sergeant) qualified. The other, an E-5 (promotable) is a licensed paramedic as well as an Army medic. The others, E-4s and E-3s, are all 91W10 (Combat Medic/Medical Specialist) and EMT-qualified. We set them up in sea hut number A-1108, Camp America. Dr. Daniels sent an Air Force med tech as provider, both yesterday and this morning. By 9:00 a.m. there were at least three 4th ID soldiers with nausea, cold sweats, fever, etc. Immediately they asked about the water being tested. I told them that according to the Camp Commandant, CPT Kent, the water was tested by Army engineers, who said it was potable. I've requested Navy preventive medicine to take another look at it. It may actually be potable, but have some microorganism that doesn't agree with some of the 4th ID folks.

I got a call from CAPT Phillips yesterday regarding the JAS chain of command. He told me Dr. Daniels would be in charge. I'll be the S-1 (Admin.) for the JASs. That's just to keep track of the personnel. Dr. Daniels will be the operational commander for the JASs. Furthermore, Dr. Daniels is insisting that Navy corpsmen man the JASs and supervise them. I thought we had been down this road before—that Army folk should be looked after by Army folk, for the most part. The Windward Loop JAS was an operational disaster, and they realized it only after an alleged sexual assault took place upstairs in the JAS during off-hours. They came down hard on the medical personnel, who obviously had nothing to do with the incident, kicked out the corpsmen living there (it was a bad Navy idea from the start to have them living there), took out the washer and dryer, emptied the cupboards, etc.

I was asked to fill the obvious leadership void, but when I went for it and began to assert my responsibilities I was quickly relegated to administrative duties only, no operational duties. MAJ Erickson and I were in complete agreement about having only Army providers at Camp America, but that does not agree with Dr. Daniels' comfort level. So, the Navy is there. I believe they see the joint aid stations as clinical extensions of the Navy Hospital Gitmo. Fine.

10 April 2002. The days are flying by, with little time to write. It has been a day in which many things happened—some significant, some not, some just irritating, but also something wonderful. In my mental calendar of significant events, the tenth is the day I met my wonderful wife, in August of 1985. And I will never forget this year, 2002. My third son, Theodore was born (23 January), and on the day I was to report to Fort Dix, New Jersey, for in-processing.

The just irritating stuff includes two of our three Humvees being deadlined for nearly the same thing. On one, the alternator bracket broke. On the other, the teeth on the alternator belt drive became stripped. Neither truck was probably maintained properly. Mine? Well, my Hummer had a problem yesterday, and spent half the day in maintenance. The parking brake cable broke yesterday. So at the end of the day, I was informed that we would be giving up our only remaining Hummer to the 115th so that the 4th ID could do a dry run rehearsal for detainee transfers. Poof! Hummer number three, gone. I gave it up to the J-4 (Joint Task Force Logistics) folks this evening (they need it by 6:00 a.m. tomorrow, and will keep it most of the day). Of course, I must be at Fleet Hospital by 8:30 a.m. (good luck to me), and to the Navy Hospital to escort the skipper (Navy CAPT Phillips) to Camp America to meet the 1/22 4th ID medics! Confused? It gets better. I'm also supposed to be at the Navy Hospital at 1600 with 1LT Anderson and a meeting with the JAS NCOs and Navy LT Daniels. On top of that, 1LT Tiva needs to see me about the next detainee move. Sound like a full day? It would be par for the course if only I had a vehicle. Bizarre, how a little old 10-person unit comes up supporting a mission involving about 300 infantry and MP soldiers. Ah, the infantry's trucks are (drum roll, please) on the barge!

Of course, there are reports to write, SOPs to rescue from the Camp X-Ray Medical Facility, clothes to pick up, running to do—ah, heck, am I complaining? I shouldn't be. Life is good, just hectic and crazy and ever-changing.

The really great news is burning to get out. Pauline and Lee came into the office with cheesy grins. Lee hasn't smiled in nearly two months, even when he laughs; he does it without actually smiling. It was before the Humvee debacle, and I was somewhat clear-headed.

Pauline said, "Guess what?" Without skipping a beat, I said, "What? We're going home?" *Bingo!*

Turns out Colonel Johnson got a call from FORSCOM who told him the 455th BLD was scheduled to redeploy (go home) between June 3 and June 9. *Wow!* What a light, happy feeling it was to hear that. Lee was ecstatic. He actually held onto his smile and became talkative. He talked to me more in that hour or so after the news than he had in total for the last few weeks. Pauline was relaxed and talkative as well. I was in a slight state of shock and disbelief. Ironically, I was in an e-mail to Sandra. I called her immediately. I got through quickly. It was about 2:30 p.m., and I awoke her from a nap so she sounded sleepy (read: "sexy"). I told her she sounded cute. I told her the news right away with the old "good news" lead-in without a pause. Pauses can really be deadly when giving good news to Sandra; she has no patience for them.

She sounded relieved. I agreed that it seemed like a great weight had been lifted from us. It was a physical as well as an emotional feeling. I physically felt myself sitting up straighter. I immediately thought of my wife, and then my children. We talked about them. Benjamin would probably be the best off through this, but we worried about Harrison. I was a middle child, and remember the littlest getting the most attention, and the oldest having the responsibilities, and me, getting ignored. I feel for Harrison. I yearn for him. I want him to feel loved and special and like a big boy. I miss him terribly.

We talked about Theodore not knowing me when I get back. But, before I got into feeling too sorry for myself, it occurred to both of us that he would not know me, but he would get to know me quickly. We agreed we would never know the affect on him, good or bad. Benjamin would probably be OK, too. Harrison might have some behavioral issues. But I'll be there. I will love him and be there for him. I want him to be my little buddy, especially when Benjamin's in school. I can't wait to get home.

Rumors and Politics

"There was things which he stretched,
but mainly he told the truth."

—Mark Twain

13 April 2002. Max relayed a nasty unconfirmed rumor recently, that LTC Grosse or LTC Hendricks were pushing to get us extended beyond or projected de-mobilization date. I hope that's all it is, a rumor. Going home will happen when it happens.

I really feel like it's an effort to concentrate sometimes. As we get closer and closer to moving the detainees and troops down to Radio Range, people are getting more and more stressed. That includes me, and not necessarily because of the move but because things are not getting better as I thought they might. I got a call this morning (my third day off in two months) from Don Tiva, who continues to impress me with his professional, caring, and on-target aggressiveness, who at yesterday's battalion 1600 hour meeting touched base with LT Daniels regarding the First Aid Station (FAS) at Freedom Heights. He asked LT Daniels, at my request, whether or not that operation should stand down. Dan had already made out a schedule and gave me a copy before the meeting. I told Daniels about Dan approaching him and Daniels told me, minutes *before* the meeting, that his plan was to "stand down" the FAS. "Fine," I thought. "It's your show, might as well do what you're going to do. The skipper even said his plan was to stand it down eventually." So somewhere between my chat with him and Tiva, Daniels had a change of heart. It probably happened when Dan stared him in the eyes from about twelve inches away and said, "Who's going to take care of the troops on the Hill [Freedom Heights] before they all move to Camp America?" in his firm and convincing Special Forces way.

121

Daniels is maybe five foot six, blond, mustache, and has a California twang and a little paunch by Army standards. Navy standards seem to allow for a little more excess than the other services, although you find the occasional overweight person in every service (except the Marines). He has a touch of the Napoleon complex, a bit overbearing, but quite reasonable in a planned meeting or face-to-face. I have found him to be lacking two key qualities that really make the difference here: follow-through and attention to detail. Dr. Blount suffers from that complex as well. When we hit the ground here eight weeks ago, there was complete discord in the Aid Station set-up. Don Tiva was beside himself because of the disorganization, and is now just more exasperated. And now, even after all the meetings, organizational charts, e-mails, conversations, phone calls, etc., it's still fly-by-night. I think that if Dan and I were left to run the thing, especially since SSG David and 1LT Anderson are in the mix, we would definitely kick ass and take no prisoners.

Daniels told me that he would appreciate it if I could approach CAPT Romanov regarding the release of his Independent Duty Corpsmen (IDCs) from Camp X-Ray infirmary duty. They have to go out and do sick call at the camp for the detainees and they don't like it, and he feels they are needed at the Joint Aid Stations. Daniels also asked me if Don Tiva would mind taking over the detainee sick call mission. I told Daniels that I didn't think Don would like that at all. When I broached the topic with Romanov, his reaction was predictable; wide eyes, but only for a moment. He exudes emotion, but is not "emotional," if that makes sense. He is naturally compassionate and empathic, but does not wear his emotions on his sleeve, nor does he whine, raise his voice, or interrupt people, even under stressful or potentially upsetting situations. He does, from time to time, express frustration and consternation, but never dwells on the negative or expresses himself inappropriately or unprofessionally. So, Romanov let slip a sly, one-second upward curl to the corners of his lips, and said, "message received." You could tell he savored the information. He and Daniels had already had a face-to-face when Fleet Hospital 20 hit the ground here. CAPT Romanov told me that when he arrived, LT Daniels told him how medical care would work out at the Fleet Hospital. Well, Romanov described how he dealt with the "little twerp," extending his right arm at crotch level, grabbing an imaginary "pair" and twisting. So, no love lost there. I imagine CAPT Romanov holding that information for the right time, or confiding in CAPT Phillips. Either way, I think Daniels is up the creek. If this is a truly "joint" mission, why is the medical piece so Navy—not just by design, but by ego? There are plenty of "joint" service medical people to stand up the "good-guy" care element with minimal Navy Hospital interference. When the Army goes to a training site, no hospital medics or caregivers come out from the Medical Treatment Facility (MTF); they don't need to. We establish communication and coordination with the nearest facility, establish evacuation routes and routines, and then go about our business. Here, the Navy Hospital has its tentacles in every detail and every aspect of the operation, as if they need to micromanage something they know little or nothing about. We are capable of taking care of our own people, especially out at Camp America. But what the Navy planned and will stand up is a mini friggin' hospital. So, since it will look and feel like a hospital, it should be staffed with some hospital folks. "Comfort level" was mentioned a few times. Having one or more of his IDCs out at Camp America will give Daniels his necessary "fix" of a "homie" in the "hood," as it were. He doesn't trust us.

So, the Army (read: 1LT Tiva) comes to the rescue again. Don will make sure there is coverage at Freedom Heights until the last U.S. Army soldier moves to Camp America, while Daniels will take the credit for having the Hill covered. Question is: Will I mention this to his boss? I have been invited to the skipper's residence this evening for a get-together of medical folk, and it should be interesting. Hope I don't drink too much and say something I shouldn't (grin). You know the exciting thing about life, and the reason I really like sports and the TV reality show *Survivor*, is that you never know what's going to happen. And sometimes it seems the more you attempt to control things, the less likely things are going to turn out the way you want them to. In the Army, the more you plan, train, analyze, and revise, the better your end product is likely to be. The Army builds in this incredibly lucid element: the element of the unknown. They teach us to "plan for the unknown." To the non-military person, that may seem a bit batty. But what it means is, "be flexible, don't put all your eggs in one basket, and plan for contingencies…expect things to go wrong." That's good advice no matter how you slice it. It is a main adage in this business—sometimes written, sometimes not. And wouldn't you know it, it's the officers and soldiers who don't miss a beat when things get "f'd" up that turn out to be the best leaders. Don Tiva could have thrown up his hands at any minute during this crisis of organization, but never did. Even now, when he has more reason than ever to walk away and let the Navy people hang themselves, he won't. And neither will I, partly because he is setting the better example, and partly because it's the right thing to do. Admittedly though, I get pleasure out of fantasizing about the alternative, but the alternative is unacceptable because it might mean a U.S. person getting hurt. So, that won't happen if we can help it.

I'll make the attempt to be the good boy, but Phillips has a way of asking pointed questions, and I am getting more and more uncomfortable with his queries. My necessary responses are becoming more strained in my attempts to be politically correct and suave. I have some experience in this area of crafting politically friendly responses to pointed, direct questions, but I also have a record of failure in this area. When your boss tells you that it doesn't matter in the end if people say, "Monty Granger was right," but it *does* matter if people say, "I like Monty Granger," that gets your attention—especially if you've been professionally trained to believe that being right is more important than being popular. And this is one of the wake-up calls I got over a year ago back home. Before that it was Tony Serpa's School District Personnel class at the State University of New York (SUNY) at Stony Brook, where I earned my advanced degree credits for a school district administrator's certificate. Tony, who is the Assistant Superintendent for Personnel at a Long Island school district told us about a candidate he felt was right for a job. In fact, he *knew* this person was the best person by far. He was called by a school board member and told whom to select to put forward in the hiring process, and it wasn't the person he knew was right for the job. He told his boss, the superintendent, about the call, and the superintendent told him to go with whoever the board member wanted. The purpose of Tony telling the story was to answer a classmate's query as to how far you go to fight for who you think should get a certain job, and there are many levels to this answer. Tony was expert at having us answer our own questions. "What do you think?" was indeed his favorite line. And it drove us crazy sometimes, as most of us were used to the traditional egomaniacal teacher who needs to be the source of all information rather than a facilitator or coach.

So, "What do you think?" ruled the day at Gitmo as well. "You have to go with your gut," said one classmate. "You can't back down," said another, all of us staring at Tony, waiting for his response. He was good at the dramatic pause, although he insisted he was thinking. He did a lot of that, "out-loud" but without making a sound. And it paid off. His visual musings caused us all to think about it, too. He was a master teacher. So, we all chewed on the question some more, and we refined the question as well. "How far should you go to back your candidate?" It came out that occasionally you will work for a boss who lets you give him two or three candidates, sometimes asking you to rank them, the theory being that if the hiring process and your good judgment are of a high enough quality the superintendent will, of course, select the same person. This assumes quite a bit: First, that you are looking for the same qualities in a person, that you share or are at least aware of the district's hiring philosophy if one exists; and second, that there are no political underpinnings attached to the candidate.

For example, was it wise for me to even gently push a candidate for consideration, even though I had hired him at a previous school district? He had not received a permanent position there and was suspended—unfairly, in my view—from coaching because of a potentially violent incident—it probably was not. I had already been accused of hiring too many folks from my former district, even though there were no candidates from the current district. Later, it turned out well that I didn't push harder for the candidate, because he became involved an a nationally exposed news story wherein he was physically assaulted by a rich bratty daughter of a publicity firm mogul's Mercedes Benz while he was moonlighting as a bouncer at a Long Island nightclub.

Tony prodded us further, always refusing to answer our questions. "What's the most important thing here?" he asked. We all agreed that the most important thing here was hiring the best person for the job. No. That wasn't it. Theoretically or philosophically that was the correct answer, but Tony's further anecdote illustrated the real, inside story answer.

When told to do something immoral or unethical by your boss, (though not illegal, though some will argue they are not separately assumed), you should consider the possible and probable consequences. And, depending on your status (i.e., tenured or not tenured), make the decision that is best for you, not necessarily what is best for the candidate or the professed philosophy of the organization. The organization is a necessarily political entity. Denying that or pretending it doesn't exist in an effort to uphold some personal moral or ethical standard is foolish and dangerous. Board members and superintendents are the ones who ultimately decide what is "moral" and "ethical" for the organization, not directors or assistant superintendents for personnel. Our goal is to remain employed, and take care of our families and our careers. "Loyalty" is at the top, or should be at the top, of every administrator's list of important characteristics of a good "team player" who wants to survive. This brings us to the ultimate distasteful reality of life. It ain't about what's right and wrong sometimes (too many times); it's about what's necessary to survive. The age-old mantra of our species is just this: Survival of the fittest, natural selection, law of the jungle, call it what you will, it exists. And sometimes people color outside the lines and they are crucified. Other times they are held up as "genius" or "bold" or "creative." It all depends on that unreliable dynamic called politics.

In "Leadership Secrets of Attila the Hun," the author explores the survival [leadership] techniques of a ruthless leader [ruler]. Some called him masterfully successful.

Heck, he conquered many "unconquerable" territories and won many victories and defeated many perhaps more powerful enemies, including those from within, by practicing a few basic principles, including Attilas' seventh principle: pick your enemies wisely—do not consider all opponents, or everyone you argue with, as enemies. These are accidental enemies. Choose your enemies with purpose. They may be people you have friendly relations with, and in fact, you should let them think of you as a friend, all the while never telling them anything, and lulling them into a state of complacence and acting prematurely. [Do not make enemies unless you mean it].

This is a great piece of advice, but difficult to practice. Enemies are usually a distasteful bunch, and it makes one's skin crawl to be around someone who you know wants you dead, or at least severely maimed. And unless you are in charge, you don't usually get the chance to keep them close anyhow. That's why it's so important to ally yourself with those who do have power and influence. It's also why it's important that—when your boss tells you to do something unethical or immoral—you state your reasons for your position, and then swallow hard.

Of course remember, it all depends on what your survival threshold is. If you're tenured, of retirement age, and just don't care, by all means, stick to your guns—but just keep in mind who you work for and what other influences they may have. In a Long Island school district, like the small military community of Gitmo, everybody seems to know everybody else. And if you don't play nice, or are not at least perceived as "loyal," you may find it difficult to get that boat loan, or get that permit for an addition to your home, or find yourself getting pulled over by the local police more often than you used to.

Being careful here is just as important as it is back home. Whatever dirty laundry is aired here among the leaders and the movers and the shakers will follow you back to your home station without you ever even knowing about it until it's too late and you wake up one morning, look yourself in the mirror and stare into the face of a loser. Leaders talk to each other. Branches don't matter much when O-6s (colonels or Navy captains) talk to each other. They all have an interest in looking good for this general and looking good for their general back home, 'cause they all wanna be generals themselves. And "shit rolls downhill" in the military just like it does everywhere else; colonels want to be generals, lieutenant colonels want to be colonels, majors want to be lieutenant colonels, etc. It equals more money, more prestige, and a bigger retirement package. Bigger retirement gets proportionally more important the closer you get to it, believe it. And the closer a colonel gets to that general's star, the more he smells it, wants to taste it, the more road kill there's going to be if he perceives anybody trying to mess it up, intentionally or not. Good people get run over just trying to cross the street. The answer is, always look both ways, and a second time to the left. Make it a habit, and never waver, for the first time you do, you could be next and never see it coming or know why.

I've already had a lesson in not talking to certain people here who ask seemingly innocent questions. The preventive medicine area is one in which I have some frustration. I don't have control over it, but I do have some influence. The Navy does the survey, writes the report, maybe does something about the deficiencies and hands the report to the commander; Army preventive medicine folks go out and fix things as they find them. When I described the difference between the Navy and the Army preventive medicine philosophies, a certain E-6 Navy IDC, took offense—although not to my face—and relayed it to the kind and helpful Craig Tomms, Navy LCDR type, who heads the preventive medicine department here at Gitmo. Craig confronted me with the rumor that I was bad-mouthing Navy Preventive Medicine. "No," I told him. He and I had even discussed the philosophical and practical differences between the services' approaches to preventive medicine in the field. We never mentioned his name, but we both knew who the traitor was. And now he's in charge of the Windward Loop JAS, so he's dangerous. He can't make a schedule to save his life, he's not needed, and he's too confident in his own abilities. Spreading rumors and inflicting innuendo to gain favor with superiors is perhaps one of the most despicable moral and professional crimes one can commit. In wartime there is little else worse than a traitor.

On the Carrot front, one of the Little Orange Ones threw the contents of his waste buckets on a guard. The Quick Reaction Force was called in and the offender put down. Three guards put him face down on the concrete floor of his cell, while two others put him in four-point restraints. First, two guards with shields put the detainee against the cells' fence; he was then taken down to the ground and shackled. He incurred only a few cuts, abrasions, and bruises. He was lucky. He got two stitches in the temple and one in the lip. LTC Grosse told the chief of staff that "when something like that happens, somebody's going to get hurt, and it ain't gonna be one of my MPs." LTC Grosse told me that he and the CoS (Colonel Johnson) have been asking General Beauregard to stay away from the camp. Every time he goes there the detainees become disruptive. The Carrots want the general to tell them about their status, about their new prison, and they want to complain about this or that. The general has a feeling to engage them in conversation, listen to their concerns; all the while the detainees know the game. They want to gain the general's sympathies, make him weak, and keep him distracted. The whole purpose in life for these detainees is to disrupt operations, to gain an advantage, and to somehow strike back at the enemy, *us*. LTC Grosse said he and COL Johnson asked the general to give no more "fireside chats," so that they could "get the camp back." Organized disruptions are commonplace, but not very effective. Tough measures by LTC Grosse have kept things in line. If a detainee throws things out of his cell, he doesn't get them back for a week. If they attempt to injure a guard, they are put down and put in four-point restraints. If they incite a riot, they are removed from the camp and put in the base brig or in the isolation cell in the medical compound. Once at Camp Delta, where there are 24 isolation cells that truly isolate the detainee from his surroundings, we anticipate very few problems. Also, the cells are less open than at Camp X-Ray. Detainees will only be able to communicate with those next to them or across from them, whereas now, they can conceivably talk to nearly everyone in their cellblock, some forty to sixty people. The new detention facility will force them to be more creative in their communication.

If these were actual POWs, they would be held together in a pen-style facility, with open barracks and free movement about the compound. They would be able to associate with the people who spoke their own language. That they are not necessarily placed next to people of their own nationality and language is a big source of frustration among many of the detainees. In SFC Stern's reports many detainees wish to be moved next to those who speak their language. Some complain that they are not near people they like, not near a relative, not near their countrymen. Gee, I think they should have thought about that before they got into their line of work, which carried with it the possibility of capture and confinement.

In my own recent visit to Camp X-Ray, there was a detainee who was given a children's dictionary, presumably by the Muslim chaplain. It had colorful photographs of everyday items in alphabetical representations. The detainee was happy to see us (a preventive medicine tech in the 4th ID group). He insisted on showing us every page of the book and speaking to us in his broken, newfound language of English. I was so stunned at first that I did not talk or move. My inclination was to ignore him and move on, but when no one else did, I stared at the man and his children's book. Feeling a flood of emotion over not being with my children, teaching them to read, and here I was watching this smiling, happy, excited detainee, sincerely or not trying to get us to communicate with him, share his joy, and engage him in conversation. None of us would. We coldly turned away. But he had his moment. He showed us every page of a book while we all just stared.

I had told the entourage before we entered the camp that some detainees would want to engage us in conversation, and that we weren't allowed to do so unless it pertained to gathering information about preventive medicine issues. It was hard to see this detainee joyously trying to share his discoveries and not interact with him, especially considering my training as an educator and coach. I did have the urge to pat him on the back, so to speak. I did want to smile and say, "Good, show me more. What do you know? Read to me." Then I remembered that this man could just as easily be showing me pictures of dead and maimed Americans if I were his captive. No doubt. This is as difficult a job as I have ever had, especially emotionally. It is extremely challenging. I fight back tears on nearly a daily basis. The stares from convalescing detainees at the Fleet Hospital get me going, and I send back hate in my glares. My glares are my attempts at showing the detainees that I am withholding their care and encouragement, and instead, am guarding and caring for our own troops. It disgusts me sometimes, even though I know we are doing the right thing. It is difficult still to rationalize the smiling and laughing and encouraging. You think that perhaps it is necessary for the healing process, and complications only make our job more difficult, but so what? What modicum of courtesy do we owe them or have they earned? None. And how long before one of them does something so terrible that we kill him? Will that happen by design where a troop just snaps or by accident? Will a detainee get the chance to hold hostages, kill them, or put himself in position for "suicide by police," where he appears so dangerous that there is no choice but to kill him? There are already five potentially suicidal and two actual suicidal detainees. They would theoretically do anything to get what they want. Are we being careful enough? I don't think so. Complacency rules at the hospital. They seem relaxed and friendly with the detainees, mostly the hospital staff, but sometimes the guards, too. *God, help us.*

I hope the move to Camp Delta happens without incident. We think that the detainees may be planning something. It will be difficult for them at best. They will be blindfolded by blacked out goggles, chained to the floor of the bus and escorted by two guards at all times. The move is being changed from a one-day move to at least two days. One day would have been too crazy; there would have been too much pressure to get it done rather than focusing on doing it the right way.

Last night at Rick's (Officer's Club), CDR Pitts introduced me to CNN's Bob Franken, who was on Gitmo to cover the transfer of detainees to the new facility. A slightly conceited man, he is big, perhaps 240 pounds or more, tanned, white haired. He was in the company of two PAO boys and two people from the Navy Chaplain's corps, one, a young, attractive female, lieutenant junior grade (LTJG), and the other a mature married Methodist minister. I think it's odd Bob would choose to be with these two, considering he was probably the leader of his local atheistic cult. I eventually engaged Bob in conversation. "So, Bob, what brings you back to Gitmo?" I ask rhetorically (I had met him briefly once before on the morning the New York City flag was raised over Camp X-Ray, and the Pentagon stars and stripes flew over Freedom Heights, on 10 March). Without skipping a beat, and with a pinch of contempt at the obvious softball, "I'm here for the detainee move." I nodded and asked if he thought he would get to see the move. He said he hoped so and that he was still in negotiations to be allowed to get some pictures. I told him there wouldn't be much to see, without going into any details, of course. He said it would be important to get pictures, that it was a lot better than just seeing his face and hearing his voice. Of course, I did feel some animosity towards him. I disliked what he stood for. He had a contemptuous, almost stalking quality about him that I found offensive. Rather than appreciating what we were all doing he considered us somehow to be the enemy, a roadblock to his goal. He couldn't hide it. I wanted to see it, so I was going to get that no matter what he said or did. I don't think he saw value in bullshitting me, but then again, I sensed a ploy. Later, he said that he had a theory about the move. He knew I was listening, and the PAO boys had left us with the chaplains. He said he felt in his gut that the new detainees would be brought in to be the first to occupy Camp Delta, and that the current crew would remain at X-Ray. He never looked my way, but I smelled the bait. He couldn't have been more wrong. In fact, the American troops were packing up for their move to Camp America as we were speaking. And the operations order for the 115th had been completed just that afternoon for the movement of all detainees.

Camp X-Ray would be emptied, lock, stock, and barrel. Renovations would be made to accept overflow from Camp Delta, if necessary. Barring that, Camp X-Ray would be used for additional housing—not ideal, of course, because it is not well protected against the elements, but improvements would be made. A "piss tube," for lack of a better term, was being considered, but Prev Med had argued against it. It needed a water source to flush it out or the urine would dry in the tube and become rancid and stink—and not just for the detainees, but for the guards as well. And who's to say they would use it and not the buckets? And who's to say they wouldn't stuff things down it, or try to use it as a toilet for number two? Too many problems associated with it, and it still wouldn't relieve the guards from emptying the waste buckets.

No, Bob was off base, but I suspect wanted someone to correct him. I did not oblige, and I doubt the PAO boys would have known or taken the bait had they been there. Bob and I spoke about LTC Grosse. He said he liked Grosse; that he was up front and spoke from the heart. He asked if I could get him to come down to Rick's. I said I would give him a call on his cell phone, as he was at a JIIF barbeque with 1LT Bay. I asked Bob if he wanted another beer and he pointed to his Miller Genuine Draft. I got us both a beer and returned after I called Grosse. I told Grosse that Bob Franken was asking for him. He said he'd be there in a few minutes. When he arrived, Bob and LTC Grosse acted like long-lost buddies. Grosse thanked him for getting him on CNN the other night and asked him how he did it. Bob said he knew someone and took care of it. Grosse thanked him again, and Bob sloughed it off, saying Grosse had given him a good sound bite. "That's what it's about, isn't it? Sound bites," said Bob. Yeah, Bob, that's what it's about. I hope I get another chance to speak with him. I think he'd run away. I missed my chance when he talked about running into some folks who "hate the press." I wanted to tell him why, about the shots of Camp Delta recently that showed the sea in the background, which tipped off the bad guys to where the camp is. I wanted to tell him that that is why some of us hate the press, because they deliberately put our lives at risk. They deliberately disobey the rules so they can look good. Are we on the same team or what? Don't they feel any loyalty whatsoever towards the common fighting man, or is it really all just about sound bites and getting the shot you want?

Bob and LTC Grosse spent the rest of the night saying mutually adoring things to each other between bouts of playful verbal sparring, with Bob trying to eke out bits of information about the move and LTC Grosse baiting and switching him at every turn. LTC Grosse could lull you into thinking he was a dumb country bumpkin, which tickled him no end. Those who knew him could see it in the increasing twinkle in his eye. Those who didn't know him mistook the twinkle for a sign he was about to fold and give in. LTC Grosse never did give in. He was as principled as the day is long, and could hold his liquor better than anyone I ever knew, including dedicated and practiced keg-guzzlers I knew in college. In fact, he only seemed to get more lucid the more he drank, which surely put this wannabe buddy of his, Mr. Bob Franken, at less of an advantage with every sip.

14 April 2002. Bob invited LTC Grosse to work out with him the next day. Grosse declined, saying he was working, which he was. LTC Grosse worked every day of two months but one. He was ordered to take a day off (a Tuesday as it turned out). He said he felt guilty. I did too, the first day I took off. Today and yesterday, "off" for me, I feel not the slightest twinge of guilt. I earned these days off, and the "con" (or "control") of the JASs belongs to the Navy—just ask them, they'll tell you. My boss knows I'm off, and in fact, told us all to take weekends off from now on unless we had something cooking. I have nothing in the fire. The more I think about it, the more I want my day with Bob Franken. I want verbal fisticuffs. I want him to understand the sacrifices we make, that our families make, the risk we face, the loyalty we feel. I want him to understand why we feel the way we do, that he does not represent any interest of the country or its service members, but he represents a media/entertainment industry, period. He doesn't have any claim to represent any interest except that of a business. If he had the slightest thought of anyone else but himself and the glory and popularity that come from others seeing

and hearing him on television, he wouldn't even want to see or televise or report on the movement of detainees from Camp X-Ray to Camp Delta. It's not in anyone's best interest for him to do so. The people of the United States will not be negatively affected if they don't see or hear about it until it is over, and televising it, especially if it is live, puts the lives of those of us who are involved in it at risk.

CNN does a critical intelligence service for the bad guys. The sooner they realize this, the better. Bob's pagan ethic of doing what is "moral" from his utilitarian point of view is in no way consistent with the Judeo-Christian ethic of doing what is "moral." Selective morality, based on a selfish, Machiavellian perspective is dangerous, unfair, and certainly not consistent with democratic values. "Free press" means "free from government control and editorializing." The government does not own any major news agencies, nor does it control major news agencies. Its interest in this context is to accomplish a mission and do it in such a way the there is as little risk to its personnel as possible. Taking close-ups of detainees here means close-ups of U.S. troops, which put them at great risk. Showing the ocean behind the newly constructed prison puts us all at risk. Bob Franken and the media must stop this nonsense or be expelled.

I went to CPT Phillips' house last night for dinner. One of his guests was Al Width, the State Department representative here at Gitmo. He interviews Cuban exiles and determines their status with the assistance of the INS. He also spoke about his and CAPT Phillips' role in Cuban-American diplomacy. He said that once a month for several years now he, the medical commander (Phillips has been on board for 18 months so far of a 30-month tour), and the base commander either meet with or conference call the Cuban military general on the other side of the fence. They discuss—politely, but frankly and directly—concerns about one or the other thing: Why did your guard shine a light at our guard last night? Why did your guard flip my guards the 'bird'?" The Cubans can easily see nearly every part of the base, mostly from a northeastern observatory post, which overlooks Camp X-Ray and most of the Windward side facilities. CAPT Phillips showed us a recent photograph of himself and other medical and diplomatic personnel on top of this observation post. Clearly in the background is the Camp X-Ray site and all of "Downtown Gitmo." Mr. Width explained how he works with the base commander and the medical commander to work up a monthly agenda to discuss with the Cuban commander. He passes the agenda through the State Department folks and others, and then meets the Cuban general at the gate, or they talk on the phone. Mr. Width said the Cuban general has his home phone number and has even called him at his Virginia home. This is indeed a unique diplomatic arrangement.

CAPT Phillips explained how in June of 2001, Gitmo and the Cubans staged a joint medical exercise, in which Cuban medical personnel "treated" American "casualties," and American medical personnel "treated" Cuban "casualties." It was a huge success, according to the captain. They have even arranged between them Washington-approved joint disaster plans which include mutual aid in firefighting and medical assistance. CAPT Phillips even took a trip to the closest Cuban hospital, in the Cuban city of Guantanamo, where he said they had mostly late-1950s facilities, but had a modern and "acceptable" burn unit. He said that it would be nearly a 24-hour trip if we had to evacuate a burn casualty to the States. Here, with the signed agreement with Cuba, we would be able to transport a U.S. burn casualty to the Guantanamo hospital quickly, probably saving a life.

I asked Mr. Width about the chances of lifting the Cuban embargo in the near future. His reply took several minutes, and skirted a direct answer. But he did say that until the Cuban government changes its policies on human rights and other areas of contention, the embargo would not be lifted. There is, however a plan in place which would allow the Cuban government to pay cash for medicine and relief supplies were it to suffer a catastrophe. It is difficult for someone like me to appreciate fully this position, with the exception of the medicine and relief supplies. No other country in the world refuses to trade with Cuba. That in and of itself is not a reason to lift an embargo, but it does say that Cuba is not suffering any perceived damage from our embargo. And indeed, Mr. Width conceded that the embargo is nearly completely principled, and does not have an economic effect on Cuba except for the loss of potential tourist and business dollars, which is hardly felt now that many European and other tourists are creating a boom in tourist income for the country.

Some of these controlling restrictions include the fact that it is illegal for a Cuban to own a fax machine. It is illegal for any Cuban citizen to own a personal computer. The government controls nearly every aspect of life on Cuba, and the Cuban people live in conditions that model the facilities in Guantanamo, 1950s style. We don't appreciate though, that they have a 97 percent literacy rate, and that their socialized medicine provides for every Cuban at least minimum medical care, free of charge. Good or bad, these are differences that not everyone would consider a disadvantage, or a perceived reason for a sea change in philosophy. Cuban-Americans can only make one visit per year to Cuba without permission from the U.S. government. Is this bad? Is it necessary? Perhaps at this point, with detainee operations ongoing at Gitmo, for security reasons, it is better left the way it is. We can gain no possible advantage, other than the placement of agents in Cuba (if we don't already) to assist in the security of operations here.

I went into work today in civilian clothes to look at e-mail and call Sandra and the kids. Harrison is so sweet. He told me he broke the Harry Potter glow-in-the-dark wand that came with the last coloring book I sent him. He asked for a new one, and the NEX was out. I actually considered buying another one for him. I want him to be happy. This feeling of being out of control, is so damn frustrating. I never liked the idea of drugs or drinking too much because I hate not being in control. Benjamin was great. He talked about a "Transformer" toy. It was great just to hear him talk about it. Harrison also thanked me for the book I sent him. It was a "Thomas the Tank Engine" book, and I had asked Benjamin to read it to him. Benjamin told me he did. I would have paid any price to have seen that. I miss them so, and their mommy. Sandra's a great woman. She's so good with them, and the house, and the baby, and, now, the taxes. I usually do them, but it fell on her this time around. I remember her waiting until the last minute at Columbia to do her papers. She was the quintessential procrastinator, and now, on the eve of Tax Day, she's still not done. But she's cheerful about it. Go figure, maybe it's the rush of being so close to a deadline. Who knows?

I don't know why, but I get so irritated with her when I talk to her on the phone. I never get a word in edgewise, it seems sometimes. And when I do, she talks over me. Then when I'm talking all alone, she won't acknowledge what I've said other than a, "Mmm-mmm." Then she'll start on another topic. It's damned hard to talk to someone on the phone. The last time I called, we ended because I couldn't stand the fact that the boys had gotten themselves ready for a bath and were upstairs waiting for their mother. I just couldn't concentrate on the conversation, which was mostly hers. I love her, I worship her, but I can't continue these conversations. It's too much. And it's so bizarre, because I don't talk to her but once or twice a week for 20 minutes or so at a time. I just have so much to tell her, so much to say. I couldn't tell her half of this stuff anyway. Were we like this before I came here? Did we not listen to each other then? This time, I ended the conversation when the baby was crying, she was trying to feed him, and Harrison was asking for help using the bathroom. What an existence. I wish it were me there.

While I was in the office, LTC Lennie Wellborn, the 115th MP BN commander, came in and chatted about the medical in-processing. His point, that a full physical exam is not "in-processing" is accurate. The Navy has no experience with this operation other than the past several months. This is what we do, what we train for, and what our medical folks train for. It's not clear if it is regulation, or if there is a regulation for it outside of FM 19–40, the EPW/CI MP unit bible. And it is not explicit about who does the in-processing. In the scenarios I have experienced at Range 12-C at Fort Dix, NJ, the Area Support Group (ASG) provides medical support as needed. Injured detainees would end up on a ward of an American hospital, at a level of care required by their injuries. We would not keep any injured or sick detainee who required more than 24 hours of care. We would use our medical folks to man an aid station for our own troops, and perhaps perform the cursory medical inspection of the arriving detainees. This part is not as clear as it should be. I bumped into CAPT Romanov in the commissary and we spoke briefly about it. LTC Grosse didn't get a chance to speak today, so, I was on my own. But I told him I had chatted with LTC Wellborn. I told CAPT Romanov that EPW BNs do this as a matter of course, the head-to-toe once-over of detainees. It's important; I told him that they get a quick look-over to complete the requirements of the regulations governing the in-processing. Medical is very superficial, and is only a basic survey to identify needed follow-up. The thorough exam, in this scenario, is performed by Dr. King and her crew, but not during the initial in-processing. The goal is to get the detainees off the bus, processed and into a cell as quickly as possible. LTC Wellborn suspects the Fleet Hospital people are concerned about repeating a process that they are going to do anyway, but that is not the point. The point is they need to know if the guy can go into a cell or not.

LTC Grosse told me that in a phone call from the general, the general said, "Who does Granger belong to?" LTC Grosse said, "Me." The general said, "Tell him to make an appointment to see me through my aide tomorrow, I want to meet with him." No agenda was given. So, tomorrow at 0800 hours, I will go to JTF HQ, and make my appointment. Pauline came into the office with the news as well and said, "Maybe the general wants you to stay?" How the heck does she know this? "Why do you say that?" I said. "Do you know something I don't?"

"No," she said, "just a thought." Then she left.

My heart sank and I cursed the air she left behind. Lee closed our office door and said he was in the room when the general called and was on the phone with LTC Grosse, and he didn't say why he wanted to see me. Whew! Then why the heck would Pauline say such shit? Speculation aside, logically, he could want to see me because of the current medical situation. Or, he may want to see me because I gave him a letter of introduction and a biographical summary, and told him that I was at his disposal, and was, by some strange twist of fate, his senior Army medical officer. For what that's worth, I have a habit of being the highest-ranking medical person (Army type) wherever I go. Wasabe? (What's up with that?) I need a mentor here. Someone who's been around the block and knows what he's doing. I feel like such a klutz sometimes, not being able to make sense of the way the Navy does things, yet being caught in their many-faceted web of medical intrigue. So much depends on so few to get things right. All I really have going for me is that I know Army regulations, and what I don't know I can look up quickly.

We never did have a formation with all the medics. Something Dr. Daniels said we'd do. He never considered the Freedom Heights FAS when giving instructions to his minions, and now, if it doesn't fly? Who gets the blame? Up front or behind the scenes? Don Tiva did a tentative schedule and I'll just have to see tomorrow who will implement it. Does this call for a trip to Freedom Heights?

The 115th moved out of the Pink Palace today. It will be lonely. And who will get our mail for us? Guess we'll have to do it all ourselves. No more CPT Ulysses barging in every five minutes. No more 115th staff officers coming in to chat or hang out, including LTC Wellborn, good people. They are all gong down to Camp America, their new digs. The rest of the companies will follow. LTC Grosse told me that the 1/22 4th ID are going to be separate from the 115th. Dangerous stuff. The reason? The 1/22 have been plussed-up to look more like a battalion because of the support they brought with them, including MAJ Steed, their BN S-3 (operations officer). LTC Grosse said they will report to him directly instead of through the battalions, who have LTC Wellborn in charge. So, unlike before, when a move is made, two phone calls need to be made instead of one. Recipe for disaster? Inefficiency? Ego tag? We'll see.

I got some more reports from LTC Grosse, written by SFC Stern. The detainee who was taken down for throwing the contents of his shit bucket said he did something wrong, but did not deserve to have the stitches and scratches and bruises. He said he had his hands behind his head and facing the fence when the MPs came in and took him down. He and others complained about the "tall, black Guard commander," saying he was too mean, and caused trouble. They complained about being disturbed while sleeping to take medicine, and asked to have it delivered with meals. They keep asking to see and speak with the general, because he will help them, not the mean Guard commander. I don't know this guy, but I think I'd like to meet him.

15 April 2002. Tax day. Sandra got them off, and requested a waiver for the $59 penalty for something or other, due to my deployment. She's a wonderful person—tough, beautiful, warm, and loving. She's also very capable and smart. She can figure out anything she has a mind to. She talked about going to see Thomas the Tank Engine (a real live steam engine) in Lancaster, Pennsylvania, in June. What a wonderful thought. The boys love it there and so do we. It's a perfect trip, one we've taken more than any other because of the people, the places and things to do, and the food—if you go to the right place you get it fresh, homemade, and delicious. And it's a wonderful and wholesome place for children.

The detainees in "F" block are refusing to empty their waste buckets. According to the Muslim chaplain, unless they are unshackled and allowed to empty their buckets "like men," they will refuse to empty them. LTC Grosse asked COL Johnson what they should do, and Johnson said they would let the waste buckets overflow. I said, "If that happens, we would have to hose down the area and disinfect it. The detainees might get wet, though." Nobody cared about that, not even me, really. They should not be playing games with us. They have no position of power here, not even over their own destiny. We won't let them even kill themselves by starvation if they want to. Sorry, justice will be served, whatever it takes.

LTC Grosse tried to disallow the Navy Muslim chaplain from talking with the detainees privately. The chaplain was found with a book of detainees' names and addresses of relatives and loved ones, so the LTC said. The book was confiscated by CPT Eisen, the 115th MP's S-3 (Operations Officer). CPT Eisen said he would turn it over to the J-2 (JTF Intelligence/Security folks). CPT Wolfe said that such a book would constitute a breach in security. Why is this Navy chaplain given so much room in which to operate? Is he a spy for us? Perhaps so. When the chaplain wanted to enter the camp tonight, LTC Grosse had insisted he be escorted and have with him a translator so that the translator could report back to LTC Grosse, making sure the good chaplain was not trying something on the side. Later, Grosse told me that Johnson told him he would not undermine his decisions, but he had to rescind his order that the chaplain be escorted. Apparently, the chaplain had complained to the general, and the general had told him he could proceed. Johnson also told Grosse that the chaplain could continue to collect names and addresses, in an attempt to catch more bad guys, I guess, or to help identify the detainee.

I met with General Beauregard at 1030 hours in his office. He was pleasant and inquisitive. First, he extended his hand, I reported properly and rendered a salute, which he returned, and then I shook his hand. He had read my letter of introduction and bio sum, and thanked me for them. He wanted to discuss a report I made from Fleet Hospital regarding the incident which led to three guards being relocated. I told him who my sources were, how I gathered the information and what my recommendations were and are. He seemed genuinely interested. I later told Grosse all that went on, and prepared a folio of previous reports I had made, which he may not have seen because I would give them directly to COL Johnson, highlighted to identify relevant passages.

The general asked if I had made any recommendations in writing. I told him I had: to include the notion that more supervision was needed at Fleet, that the guard NCOs needed supervision and representation by an MP officer. It turns out—after reviewing my notes which I read in preparation of LTC Grosse's packet—that I noticed I had asked for an officer explicitly twice in my reports. The first request came from LTC Wellborn, who suggested CPT Lopez, a registered nurse in civilian life, and an MP captain in military life. The general may be thinking about junior officers, but I told him I thought people who work at the Fleet Hospital should be special and hand-picked.

16 April 2002. At 11:30 p.m. last night, LTC Grosse got a phone call from CP1 at Camp X-Ray. I was finishing reading for the evening and was awake when I heard his phone ring upstairs. Whenever you get those late-night phone calls, they're never good. The detainees were engaged in a pre-planned "riot." There's not much they can actually do, however one detainee seems to have broken a weld in his cell and was moved. The big thing LTC Grosse walked into was many detainees shaking and kicking their cells. He spoke with COL Johnson, who spoke to General Beauregard, and both men approved his plan to put down the behavior. LTC Grosse would have his men go

into each cell and restrain the detainees that the cell block NCOIC identified as being an instigator. This is how Grosse told it: "I went down there. Johnson was in his civilian clothes and the general was there in uniform. I told Johnson what I wanted to do, and he said, 'Make it happen.' I went for it, block-by-block. Two of the guys wanted to fight us. I got this big guy in the IRF (Internal Reaction Force), this big [he gestures his hands into the dimensions of the doorway]. He's got a shield, Kevlar. He goes in there and this guy is in the corner of the cell, ready to fight. The IRF go in and put him down. The commands I gave were: 'Ready. Boys?' and 'Go get 'em boys,' over and over again. They learn. I go into the next block and ask who the troublemakers are: 'Who's next?' to the block NCO [Grosse gestures with his hand and arm, pointing to an imaginary detainee]. I would walk over to the cell and see if the detainee was going to comply with instructions. If he did, I would say, 'OK, boys, gentle if they cooperate,' and the IRF boys would do what I asked them to do. Cell block by cell block I would go in there, ask the NCOIC who he wanted, he would point them out and I would give the command: 'Ready, boys?' they would say 'Ready,' and I would say, 'Go get 'em, boys.' We had the dogs in there. The handlers asked me if I wanted them inside the cellblock and I waved 'em in. The dogs went right up to the fence. Shut 'em up. Them boys had fun. They were swaying back and forth and were banging on their shields with their batons. The detainees were lookin.'"

LTC Grosse was tired. He'd only gotten maybe three or four hours sleep. But he didn't show it. He was wired from the night's activities. He said he radioed Johnson after the camp got quiet and said, "I guess our work's done here tonight." "Yup," said Johnson, then, "meet me at CP 1." Grosse met him there and Johnson said, "we're gonna get this camp back. As long as the General stays away, we're gonna get this camp back." Grosse agreed then came back to the hooch.

17 April 2002. CAPT Romanov, LTC Grosse, CPT Eisen (115th S-3), myself, 1LT Tiva and SSG David had a medical meeting of the minds yesterday. We met to discuss the "medical in-processing" that will take place at Camp Delta when we receive new detainees. CAPT Romanov said he didn't care if we did it or if Don Tiva did it, but felt it was redundant. Don and James Eisen explained that the quick head-to-toe exam and body cavity search was to OK the detainee for confinement. James' report had to get to the Pentagon via secure network e-mail within six hours of signing for them at the airport. That's a tight schedule when you've got 34 detainees to in-process. CAPT

Romanov pointed out that Fleet Hospital 20 would have sole responsibility for detainee health care. James Eisen pointed out that the 115th had control and responsibility for the in-processing mission, which included the head-to-toe and cavity search. CAPT Romanov, a thoughtful, mature, and brilliant leader, saw that there was no way for him to walk out of a meeting with five Army folk with a Navy solution. He stated what was for me the obvious, that the "medical" in-processing described to him by Don Tiva and James Eisen, was in fact, an "administrative function." No one argued.

CAPT Romanov stated again that he didn't care who did the quick exam in the Army in-processing hut. I said that if he didn't really care, then the comfort level of CPT Eisen and the 115th be considered. He and I would both prefer Don to Navy folk in that situation. James said that a Navy physician might want to do more than just a cursory once-over. And the in-processing hut was not the place for it. His goal was to get the detainees properly in-processed and in cells as soon as possible. No dilly-dallying, no extra exam B.S. We left with consensus for Don doing the quick exam, and with the people he wanted and needed, Army folks. The Navy would take the con (control) for the overall medical mission, and would continue to provide medical coverage at the airport and en route to Camp Delta. It was a done deal.

The Navy resists the idea of a "joint" medical mission at every turn. It doesn't even consider itself part of JTF-160. It scares me, yet I have faith and confidence in CAPT Romanov. But how long will he maintain faith and confidence in us?

At the Fleet Hospital this morning I learned that detainee #70 was in from Camp X-Ray for an eye removal, but was having second thoughts. I went on the ward where he was being spoken to by the Navy chaplain and the Army interpreter, Navy LTJG Dellmore. I spoke with Dellmore about the situation and he said the other detainees at CXR were playing with his head by telling him the eye was OK. The chaplain was asking him at this moment if he could see out of the eye, and detainee #70 said "no" and shook his head. They got him to sit up. Two guards were with him and suited up for the operating room. Dellmore said the detainee said he was afraid, and asked him if he wouldn't be afraid? Dellmore said, "Yes, of course I would be afraid, but the eye is dead. It will shrink and be deformed looking." CAPT Romanov said a prosthetic eye would be inserted, and then later, a painted shield put over it, to look like an eye. Detainee #70 looked tired, afraid, but resigned. He let the guards gently lift him to his feet, and he shuffled, shackled, to the operating room.

18 April 2002. Detainee #70, as it turns out, never went under the knife, still has his non-functioning eye, and in the words of Chief Nurse CDR Carol James, "changed his mind fifty times," and eventually settled on no operation. He said all his friends at Camp X-Ray told him his eye looks fine.

The press is out *en force*. New York's NBC and Fox affiliates are here looking for New Yorkers to interview. I met up with a Major Leon Reyes, a friend of Charles Gordon, a card shop owner from my hometown. Leon is from Selden and has known Charles for a long time. I was heading to the Navy Hospital to see CPT Phillips and saw some of our folks talking to the press and being interviewed on the lawn outside the hospital main entrance, and Leon came up to me and introduced himself. He seemed friendly, but then again, he is a PAO guy. He told me Charles said "hello." That's pretty cool, a guy from where I live coming over. He's with the 77th RSC out of Fort Totten, New York, and was actually in the 423rd MP Company out of Uniondale for a while and even attended Hofstra University, which is across the street from the 800th MP BDE headquarters. Go figure. Leon invited me to have some Ting, a non-alcoholic grapefruit soda from Jamaica, at the Jerk House (a Jamaican eatery) with him and the press, he said they'd like to talk to me. We'll see. *Survivor: Marquesas* is on tonight, you know?

Reap What You Sow

"Make it a point to do something every day that you don't want to do. This is the golden rule for acquiring the habit of doing your duty without pain."

—Mark Twain

20 April 2002. The crap buckets are filling up at "F" Block. LTC Grosse told me to stay out of there when I told him I should probably do a preventive medicine inspection. I asked about the smell for the guards and he said they're wearing protective masks. I'm not sure I believe him, but obviously he's intent on not giving in to the demands of the detainees—to allow them to "freely, like men," empty their waste buckets. That would be impossible, and the detainees know this. If they don't know it they are seriously out of touch with reality. Which may actually be the case, I don't know.

What I'm about to say next is the truth—as is all the other stuff, but this is going to be so funny you won't believe it, so hang on. The Muslim Navy chaplain is leaving us soon (*darn*). He is being replaced by an Army Muslim chaplain named Murphy. I kid you not. The kid is as Irish as a leprechaun; red hair, pale skin, boyish looks; Opie Taylor in uniform. I saw the guy last night at General Beauregard's first Officer's Call. He was smiling ear to ear as he met people. *This is going to be good.* The outgoing Navy Muslim chaplain, who is of Arab descent, with bad English, and according to the interpreters, no Arabic language skills to speak of, will not be missed. He was politely arrogant, especially for an O-3. He made demands in a vacuum, and was generally thought of as a traitor because of the things he said about how the detainees should be treated and what we should have done—all based on religious tenets. But get a grip, buddy, these guys are killers first, religious human beings second. That's why they are in prison. They are dangerous and not to be trusted. This guy has private conversations with them, gives them confidential information and apparently took the liberty of taking down the names and addresses of detainees' contacts back in their home countries. I spoke briefly with Navy LT Gibbs, the SPRINT coordinator and psychiatric nurse, about the outgoing Navy Muslim chaplain. She said she had received numerous complaints about him from soldiers. But she added that the point was probably moot now that he was rotating out. I have an idea; why not give him his own cell, right there with his buddies? He'd probably like that.

Apparently, another detainee came in last night. LTC Grosse and LCDR Montpellier were both drinking Coca-Cola last night at the O-call, which is highly unusual for both men, and when I pressed Gene Montpellier, "Hey Gene, why are you drinking Coke? He 'fessed up like a kid threatened with no TV for a week. "We're getting a new Carrot in tonight," he said. "Oh, really?" I said, "So you don't tell your buddy anything any more, eh? I guess he's alright then?" "Yes," Gene said. "He's in good condition."

Gene continued, and told me that Pauline Peterson had mentioned something about an in-coming detainee in the Pink Palace earlier in the day. I didn't hear the words from her that Gene did, as we were sitting about six feet apart at our desks, but he heard something that made him shoot to his feet and yell, "What did you say?" Down the hall he went after Peterson. A short, private (or so I thought) argument ensued, in Peterson's office. Last night, Gene told me that Peterson was mentioning the receipt of the new detainee, in the open, in front of several people who absolutely didn't have a need to know, and she was now questioning Gene in front of Specialist Java, of all people. Peterson claimed, according to Gene, that she had a "right to know everything because" she was "the unit XO and when she doesn't know things" she "looks stupid." 'Nuff said. So, Gene and the LTC left for parts unknown early in the morning, about 0130, and returned later this morning, after receiving the "package." I'll find out more later, according to Gene.

1LT Anderson received a blow yesterday. He was told that his paternal grandfather had passed away. He was being given emergency leave to go home for the funeral. Very sad to see such a big, healthy, strong soldier completely deflated. I know the feeling, the helplessness, and the sorrow. I offered whatever I could do, notified the skipper (an alternate Navy title for the commander), and asked if the skipper would follow up on the transportation for 1LT Anderson. We all later met at the Officer's call and 1LT Anderson's flight was confirmed for today. *God bless him.*

At Fleet Hospital yesterday, SFC Snodgrass caught me just as I was leaving the detainee ward on my normal survey. He asked to speak with me outside and began to tell me about a Navy nurse who had on at least two occasions that morning corrected a guard for his behavior (i.e., off-color comments) toward a detainee. The nurse did not notify the sergeant, which was standard operating procedure, but instead ended up telling his supervisor, CDR Williamson, that he had had to correct a guard. He also said that he informed the guard NCOIC, which he had not. I found this out after my conversation with SFC Snodgrass by speaking immediately with CDR Williamson. I asked SFC Snodgrass if he felt comfortable talking with CDR Williamson about this, and he said "Yes," but since I was there he thought he would inform me. I also relayed this information to CDR Williamson to ensure she understood the sergeant would go to her if I were not there. Apparently there are a few guards who are new to the Fleet Hospital, and are a bit aggressive, which is not necessarily the personality type you want working in the "healing zone." The detainees, of course, were testing the newbies by trying to befriend them, and act buddy-buddy with the guards. This annoyed the nurse, who chided the guards for their behavior. Again, according to SOP, this is the job of the NCO, not the nursing staff. Each group is to correct and discipline its own troops or Seabees, unless a potentially life-threatening or serious injury could immediately result. This was not the case, even though SFC Snodgrass admitted that the soldier was more likely than not at fault. CDR Williamson promised me she would correct the situation. SFC Snodgrass told me he thought the nurse was having a bad day; that he had worked with him before and had no problems. CDR Williamson confirmed this perception, and said that it wasn't like him to overreact.

CDR Williamson and I continued a conversation about the emotional and mental difficulty of the job down at Fleet Hospital. She agreed that it was especially challenging in those areas. I suggested the possibility of having a group decompression session once a week or so, so guards and medical staff could talk about their experiences and feelings in an open and supportive environment. She agreed that it would be a good idea and encouraged me to speak with LT Gibbs about it, which I did. LT Gibbs said she could work with the Fleet Hospital 20 folks to arrange it, but she also told me that according to the "out-briefings" she'd been conducting, the guards are in far more need than the Fleet Hospital folks. She said the guards have very hostile feelings toward the detainees and carry that with them. The guards are supposed to relieve themselves from block duty if they are feeling overly hostile and think that they can't control themselves, but this is not always recognizable, nor willfully controlled by the guards; hence my observations through the reports I read regularly which may indicate allegations of abuse on the part of the guards.

What kind of abuse? Things like waking up detainees on purpose for no apparent reason. Putting on handcuffs and shackles too tightly, roughing up the detainees when moving them, making fun of their religious practices, name-calling, etc. The kinds of things immature, less-than-professional kids would do. Some of these guards have no outside experience with detainees or prisoners. Some of the guards have extensive experience in law enforcement and incarceration of others. If you get a bad or questionable guard who has experience, the guys without experience will follow his lead. And, as was the case two months ago down at Fleet Hospital, if you have a bad NCO, who is ignoring inappropriate behavior on the part of one of his guards, you have a recipe for disaster. A confirmed case of abuse at this point would severely damage our attempt to keep the press and the international community off our backs so we can do our jobs, which is difficult to do under duress and scrutiny. We are the "good guys," and whether we like it or not we have to hold ourselves to a higher standard of conduct. Find Chapter 18 of an al Qaeda training manual in Appendix C, where you'll discover that "the Brothers" have been duly challenged to teach each other how to behave in prison.

I told CDR Williamson about my feelings towards the detainees and the people who care for them, after she asked me how I felt about what goes on at the Fleet Hospital. I repeated my mantra about how proud I am of those who work there all day every day, putting themselves in harm's way the way they do. I told her it was difficult for me because I am trained to heal, yet every time I look at a picture of my wife or children, I am filled with anger and hatred towards the detainees, because they are the reason I am here and not with my family. She said she understood.

I told SFC Snodgrass and Oaks about my conversation with CDR Williamson before I left Fleet Hospital 20 that morning. They appreciated the follow-up. I told them I would not include the incident in my morning sit-rep, and would not include certain things unless they requested it or CDR Williamson requested it, or unless I deemed it necessary, in which case I was more likely than not to tell them. I didn't want to undermine their authority here, but I will also not keep LTC Grosse in the dark about things he needs to know. I want these NCOs, as does LTC Grosse, to "handle" things at this level if at all possible. But I did tell CDR Williamson that I still thought an MP officer, who came by for the staff meetings in the morning and was appointed as supervisor of the guard force, would be a welcome addition. It's still uncomfortable for a field grade officer to interact directly with NCOs. It's not the way things should operate. But, you also don't want the wrong person down here barking orders and getting in the NCO's way. A delicate balance of competence, personality, and experience is needed here. This incident was minor, and should be handled easily. In the future, I still believe there should be a screening process for those who work in this challenging, complex, and emotional environment. There just aren't enough MPs to go around for that to be possible.

LTC Grosse came home at noon today. He was up all last night. The CIA flew in a new detainee at 0300 this morning. He was supposed to be in at 0200. The detainee was big compared to the others: five foot eleven, one hundred and seventy-five pounds, and, according to the agents who brought him in, a boxer. He had been beating up other detainees at his previous location, which LTC Grosse said he didn't know about. He could have been African, as the detainee was dark-skinned with cornrows in his hair. They put him in Camp X-Ray, and when they got there, there was another "riot" going on. Several detainees in "D" block this time, the "good" block during last week's ruckus. This time they had to put down four detainees, three the hard way: "Ready boys?" "Go get 'em, boys." And one the easy way because he complied with requests to go to his knees and put his hands behind his head.

The new detainee could speak perfect English, and asked LTC Grosse if he could speak to his lawyer. LTC Grosse said "f**k no."

"Who can I speak to, then?" the detainee said.

"Speak to yourself," was LTC Grosse's reply.

He was brought in on a Lear jet. LTC Grosse went on to the jet to sign for the detainee and said to a CIA guy, "Can I sign the paperwork and I'll take him off your hands?" There was no paperwork. "Here," the CIA guy said. "He's yours." And he turned him over to Grosse. Grosse said he got to thinking later that, gee, if they'd wanted to take him into the bushes and shoot his ass, all he'd have to say is: "Detainee? What detainee? Show me where I signed for this detainee?" I guess the Company Boys just got tired of playing with him. As a welcome present, they put him near Wild Bill (who spends a lot of his time sedated these days). This should be interesting.

22 April 2002. I looked at the photos Sandra had posted on the Internet. Theodore looks so big at three months old. He has a sweet cherubic face, huge saucer eyes, and a cute little body. He's smiling in a few pictures. He looks like Harrison in the face but has Benjamin's coloring, blonde hair, blue eyes. Benjamin looks tired, he also looks huge! I'm so afraid my children will look differently than when I left them. What a foolish thing to say: Every day they change, and I've been away from home for over three months, so what do I expect? I'm missing Theodore's babyhood, I'm missing Harrison's little boy-hood, and I'm missing Benjamin's little boyhood; such are the sacri-fices of war. Never thought I'd be here. Never wanted to be here, but I gave consent, didn't I? I gave consent.

CAPT Romanov said that the powers that be want to send all 254-plus detainees from Kandahar as soon as possible. They fear fratricide on the part of other Al Qaeda or Taliban. Fratricide was a top concern here when GEN Lehnert was briefed on Air Defense. "They'll die try-ing to kill their brethren rather than allow them to talk to us." Since we don't believe in torture or unconventional methods of interroga-tion (we give them cigarettes and McDonald's food), I don't see us getting much more out of folks than they want to tell. Then how much do we trust what they say? How long does it take, and how difficult is it to corroborate the information they give us? So, if they send all two hundred and fifty-four-plus, as fast as they can, we're looking at the possibility of thirty-four per planeload, at least every other day. That's nearly two solid weeks of deliveries. That includes at least eight hos-pital/litter cases—two of whom, we're told, are "dying." Yes, things are going to get more interesting very quickly.

At the Fleet Hospital, tensions are rising. For the last nine days or so, the MPs, for some ungodly reason, have been rotating four differ-ent and completely new guards into the Fleet Hospital on every shift. The guards are not necessarily well-suited to the environment or task, and the medical people are beginning to wear thin on patience. Four of the eight detainees currently in the Fleet Hospital could be returned to Camp X-Ray soon. LTC Grosse wants them back into the Camp so he can free up some more guards, and to re-acclimate the detainees to camp life. Two of the four who could return soon are amputees. CAPT Romanov discussed the height of the "beds" in the new cells. The beds are about thirty-six inches off the ground, and the half-inch thick steel plate is welded on two sides to the cell walls, which are actually tight mesh with steel tubing framework.

LCDR Lewis, the Fleet Hospital (FH) training officer, had a lot to say about why the "new" guards should be oriented and trained before they go on the ward. The guards are assigned only about twenty-four hours before their shift starts, so the desired training seems impossible. They are getting on-the-job training, but it is slipshod and not effective. The job requires a personality and disposition type that is not prevalent in every MP. My Joint Warfighter suggestions included the selection of certain troops for duty in the Fleet Hospital, but that was ignored. LCDR Lewis said she did not feel comfortable with the fact that the Army was creating a dangerous situation because the numbers don't add up. Well, somebody's got to make a schedule, and it's got to make sense. I can't believe it myself that they can't get a certain number of guards to be consistently at FH. LTC Grosse says that if they send four detainees back to Camp X-Ray, they may be able to stabilize the guard force. LTCD Lewis is convinced, and I'm not sure I disagree, that this glitch in our scheduling—allowing untrained, arbitrarily selected MPs guard these detainees—could be a potentially very dangerous proposition.

The 1/22, specifically CPT West ("Ring Knocker"—graduate of West Point) and MAJ Steed (BN S-3), are resisting giving OPCON of the medics who came with them to the JTF Surgeon. LTC Grosse sent an e-mail to the two of them yesterday, which said, among other things, "all medical personnel are OPCON to the JTF-160 Surgeon...and are assigned living quarters and are supervised by SSG Will David." The e-mail couldn't have been more explicit. Grosse let me read the e-mail before he sent it, and I thought it was a good, strongly worded statement, which it needed to be. SSG David moved them all to Windward Loop, and then had to move them all back because these two didn't like it. Tough shit! Where are the Marines when you need them? The Marines would have said, "Three bags full, Sir!" and would have taken it in stride. These two guys are so wrapped up in an enigma that they can't see the medics for the soldier. Grosse gave me a printout of their response, which on the one hand states that they "understand" the OP CON, but still believe they have "ultimate responsibility for health, welfare and discipline" of their medics. Ludicrous! They said their soldiers weren't mature enough to live on the Loop (their NCOs would be there, too, so I guess that includes them in the "immaturity" charge. They said they wanted to do PT (physical training) with them on their days off. SSG

David and the other NCOs can more than handle the PT. I suspect these are all excuses, and I told that to Grosse, Phillips and Porter today, but I left a message for Steed and West so that I could have a face-to-face with them and see if I could get them to tell me what's really bugging them. Maybe Grosse knows and he's not telling.

23 April 2002. I dream about going home when I look at pictures of my boys. I dream about holding Theodore in my arms like the day I left home, just the way I look in the photograph I keep above my dresser in my room that's actually the den of our condo. I dream about hugging Benjamin and Harrison so tight it almost hurts. They're such good boys. They're so far away. I miss them so much I'm afraid to think about them for very long for fear of "losing it."

LT Gibbs reported at the JTF meeting today that she's had three JTF 160 patients in the last twenty-four hours; one of them homicidal towards "his captain." Gee, I wonder who that might be, West perhaps? She said she had 15 detainee patients, some "on drugs." One detainee, #225, chewed a sharp object from his plastic canteen and cut his wrists.

On a visit out to the camp today with LCDR Tomms, specifically to "A" block, we asked a few detainees about the bug problem. They say they still have problems with mosquito and spider bites, but not as badly as before. The standing water problem is worse if it's anything. There are drainage problems, and still soap and shampoo bottles on the shower floors, and standing water in the shower drain channels. Once the rains come X-Ray will be pretty much a disaster. One detainee, on our way out, kept calling to Tomms and me. I ignored him. He kept calling after us, "Hey, excuse me, sir! Excuse me, sir!" Once in the sally port, I turned to face the man, a tall, strong looking, fully bearded Arab, speaking pretty good English. "Excuse me, medical. Excuse me!" He must have noticed the caduceus on my collar. I looked at him, and this he noticed quickly and said, "These things, mosquitoes, they keep biting," as he took one hand, bent his fingers as if they were the proboscis of five mosquitoes and tapped them on his forearm. "When are you going to fix this?" He said emphatically. I just gave him a thumbs up, his slight tone of arrogance catching my anger for him and his brethren: "When?" he said, "Tomorrow, this week, a month?"

LCDR Tomms and I walked away. We examined other things in the camp, including the waste bucket situation in Foxtrot block. Earlier, in Tomms' office, he showed me a commercial waste bucket system that included a disposable liner, plastic holder with cover for the toilet paper, a lid, rubber gloves, hand wipes. He had just come back from one of his public health conventions. We talked about getting these things for X-Ray. We also discussed what to do in the camp with the proposed "piss tubes." Tomms had a brainstorm right there in Foxtrot. The drain for the urine could be combined with drainage tubes for runoff, or at least run side-by-side. The current situation is that every block but Foxtrot has one detainee empty all the buckets. He is rewarded with extra food, candy, etc. In Foxtrot, they claim the Navy Chaplain said they should be allowed to have someone (or all of them) empty their waste buckets unshackled. *Yeah, like that will ever happen.* The detainees who do it in other cellblocks do it in shackles.

25 April 2002. I joined LTC Grosse at Camp X-Ray this evening. He went to check on #2, the seventeen-year-old, one of the hunger strikers who's having a relapse. He was so out of it he was hallucinating and having conversations with people who weren't there, like his mother, children, etc. The detainees in the cells around him called for medical to come and get him. He struggled and had to be held down in order to for the medical personnel to give him IV fluids. They got one and a half bags in him. He gained rational thought after the first bag. As they returned him to his cell, he defiantly told them he would not let them take his pulse the next day. The nurse on duty shrugged her shoulders and said, "So, we'll just do it all over again tomorrow." *Fine.* A detainee in the brig began the self mutilation/suicide gesture stuff again, banging his head against the concrete floor. "Blood everywhere," is how Grosse described the scene.

Grosse told me they had started moving 16 detainees at a time over to Camp Delta. Completely under the radar screen! Everybody, including O-6s, had been saying the move would be over two days and begin this Sunday. Then, the word was 24 hours more before it would start. Then Grosse tells me the detainee who was brought into Fleet Hospital last night and released today was telling detainees back in X-Ray that the move was going to happen on the 28th. Great OPSEC, eh? So, we've already begun to move them. That's real good. I did want to see the look on the face of the first detainee in, but, hey, you can't always get what you want.

Camp Delta Is Born

"Never tell people how to do things. Tell them what to do and they will surprise you with their ingenuity."

—GEN George S. Patton

30 April 2002. The actual move took place on Sunday, April 28, 2002, from 0700 to 1900 hours. It went smoothly, without incident or injury to anyone. I saw nearly every detainee step into every new cellblock, most cheerfully so, some somberly, some with fear. The Navy chaplain—there at the base of the stairs of every cellblock, along with GEN Beauregard, the general's aide, and a corpsman—told me that a few of the detainees were "sad, because they see this is a permanent structure, so they think they will never see their families again." Gee, maybe they should have thought of that before they went out and started playing cowboys and Indians for real, and against the wrong group of hombres. Others feared they were being taken to be executed. Interesting, but where on earth would they get that idea? Perhaps they feel that way because in their culture it is an expected consequence for their deeds.

The day was hot, but with intermittent clouds that gave welcome but brief relief from the intense Caribbean sun. Cooling breezes in the shade bathed the sweating brow and sent momentary shivers down the spine. After 0800 hours the "chalks," or groups of detainees, began to arrive. Flashbacks of three months ago became vivid in my mind's eye. The sound of the bus tires moving through the thickly laid gravel, the working dog barking with excitement, low conversations about the operation, the silence of the new Carrots. Everybody was present—GEN Beauregard, COL Thomas (in the guard tower near the internal sally port), LTC Grosse, LTC Wellborn. I stood with GEN Beauregard and his entourage by the entrance to each cellblock as the detainees were brought in, their red travel bracelets cut off, their cell block numbers checked and double checked, called out by the escort team to the MPs inside holding open the detainee's new cell door, and then escorted up the stairs into the cell block, into their cell. CLANG! Not a more beautifully justified sound in the world. *CLANG!*, indeed. Some of the guards must have been purposefully slamming the cell doors closed. No one said a word.

I did get to see the first detainee placed in Alpha Block, cell number one. He was brought in without his "blindfold" goggles, which had their lenses covered by the Army's olive drab version of duct tape. He was shackled at the ankles; the restraints had a chain just long enough to allow the detainee to climb stairs adequately. His wrists were similarly bound, and those shackles were attached to a leather belt that limits movement by keeping the arms close to the body.

He was escorted up the steep stairs without incident, as were all 300 detainees on this day. (Some were carried, like amputees and those who may have had acute orthopedic problems.) At the top of the stairs a guard cut off his red ID bracelet, called out the detainee's number, and allowed the escort team to put him in his cell. This one did not smile or speak with the Navy Muslim chaplain upon entering the cellblock, nor did the chaplain smile at him or speak to him. However, the chaplain did smile and converse with approximately 60 percent of all the detainees as they entered the cellblocks. Not once did I see him approach the general to tell him what a detainee may have said to him, but I noticed the general occasionally looking at the chaplain as if to say, "Well, what did he say?" I wonder if the tone would have been different were the chaplain Army? The Carrot was told to get on his knees with his back to the cell wall. He complied. The wrist and leg cuffs were unlocked, and the detainee was left in his cell, the guards having departed quickly, and the detainee having been trained that he must remain in that position until the door is slammed shut. He paused longer than he needed to—a precaution on his part perhaps. He sheepishly looked up, toward his one mesh window. He had a corner cell, so the wall to his left was the end of the cell block, which faced the perimeter fence of the cell block area, about 10 feet away. He stood slowly, turned around and took in the space, slightly smaller than his eight-by-eight cell at Camp X-Ray. Delta was indeed a maximum security prison. At least eight locked gates separated him and all detainees from the front (and only) entrance. He took things in for a minute or so, and then hoisted himself onto his "bunk," a steel slab welded to the three walls on the interior side of his cell. He sat there and looked at me, the general, and the chaplain, expressionless.

The first detainee in his cell at Camp Delta, Guantanamo Bay, Cuba, was in shock—mildly so, but in shock nonetheless. He didn't speak to his block mate, just released from his shackles and exploring with his eyes the surrounding six-by-eight foot space, much of which was taken up by the bunk. I thought the floor toilets and the sink with the pressure-release spigot would be a point of instant interest, but it was not the case.

Most of the detainees entered their cells the same way, slowly rising, turning around, sitting on their bunk, looking around. Later, they began to explore their personal comfort items: a sleeping mat (the same kind that I use three mornings per week to do sit-ups on in my hooch), except with the ties cut off, two acrylic blankets, two towels, a wash cloth, toothpaste, finger toothbrush (used so that detainees could not whittle standard toothbrush handles into a weapon), plastic cup, soap, and a medical face mask for hanging up their Qurans. They tied the four ties of the surgical mask to the mesh screen, and then placed their texts in them, keeping them from the floor.

They slowly began to touch things, move things into their individual comfort positions. Each detainee had developed a habit associated with his few items. Missing now were the five-gallon buckets used for waste and washing water. Gone were the canteens.

In "C" block, the second detainee in, a stocky, Caucasian-looking man with wiry blond hair and a full, thick beard the same color jumped up on his bunk, raised up on his knees and looked toward the Caribbean and began to sing repeatedly, "I have a sea view, na, na, na-na, na!" LTC Grosse happened to be coming out of the cellblock towards me, smiling at the childish but accurate lyrics. The blonde detainee got his next-door neighbor to get up on his bunk and look out as well. I told COL Grosse that we should charge extra for the view. He laughed. Oh, the blonde detainee? David Hicks, the Australian who joined the Taliban.

This process went on all day. Four busloads of detainees at a time, at one-hour intervals, but with each chalk, the time it took to unload and place the detainees into their new cells got shorter and shorter. The original plan was to move four chalks of four buses on Sunday, and then two chalks of four and five buses, respectively on Monday. After the third chalk, word began to spread that we would do all six chalks in one day. The escort guards, all of the 401st MP Company out of Fort Hood, Texas, and led by CPT James Mercado, were working harder and faster with each chalk. By the last two, they were running—and some sprinting—back to the buses after delivering and de-shackling their charges. Some crashed down onto the thick gravel after leaping past the steps on the stairs from the cell blocks, each one hundred and sixty feet long; four forty-foot converted shipping containers, end-to-end, on each side of a six-foot wide hallway, topped by eight motorized air-flow "mushrooms" on a center roof ridge vent.

LCDR Tomms, the public health officer, said the air exchange in the cell blocks was so good that you could weld without the need for a mask. Amazing! It was fairly cool in the cellblocks, with good breezes created by a carefully designed structure that functioned almost like a wind tunnel.

Two days later, the general asked to see only LTC Grosse and me. He was concerned about the water accumulating in certain spots in the cells, and about how the detainees were going to clean and sanitize their cells. Craig Tomms was available after lunch, so I asked him if he wouldn't mind coming with me to check things out. He and I took a brief tour of the facilities.

Delta block was the closest to the main sally port, so we went inside to check things out. Sure enough, there was standing water already in some cells. One puddle had already begun to cause rust. We took it all in as most detainees either prayed or slept. We looked outside and found leaks at almost every joint where the plastic drain-pipes met brass fittings, and there was lots of grass growing underneath the units because of this.

3 May 2002. The second group of new arrivals flew in today. The first group of thirty-two was in-processed without incident—just a few speed bumps, according to the guards and medical folk—as the escorts were let go after 2000 hours. There were still eight detainees yet to go through medical. The medical folk pointed this out and the situation was fixed, and did not happen again today. Today set a new record for in-processing. By 1900 hours they were nearly done with the same number of thirty-two detainees; a whole lot of cooperation and hard work got it done faster.

I didn't witness the first load of Carrots on the first of May; I was on a clandestine mission to repatriate Wild Bill. Today, I was seques-tered in the Pink Palace due to giving up BLD 1 (the Humvee I usu-ally drive) to the K-9 patrol due to the fact that BLD 1 has a covered bed in back, and the K-9 truck is just a regular pickup with nothing to protect the dog carrier from the sun. When detainees are picked up at the airport there is a long (at least one hour) delay on a completely unsheltered tarmac, which would be cruel for the dogs to have to endure. *Ever heard of a tarp or a tent?*

Oh, the clandestine mission! We had weapons and bullets, and did some sneaking around. I got a heads-up a few days before that I would be involved in a mission, hinting at the repatriation of Wild Bill. We'd had enough of him and his antics, clinically induced or otherwise. He was no longer of any intelligence value, and it was time for him to go. The Fleet Hospital had finished an out-processing protocol and the word was given by Washington that he could be repatriated. He would go to a mental health facility in Saudi Arabia, even though he was Afghani. Who knows what the Saudis would do with him, and who cares?

The day of the repatriation was 1 May 2002. The crew consisted of me, LTC Grosse, LCDR Montpellier (now the BLD XO, since MAJ Peterson was "repatriated" to Fort Dix for being "nonessential"), CPT Bay (he had finally received his promotion from 1LT), LT Gibbs (the psych nurse who used to head up the SPRINT team, but was now fully devoted to detainee care), MSG Singer, and an interpreter. We were armed. LCDR Montpellier and MSG Singer were packing 9mm pistols and had several clips of ammo each. CPT Bay and I had modified AR-15s, the old "M-16" type rifle that was modified to shoot semi- or full-automatic. The M-16A2s we qualified with were too deep in the armory to worry about, so we took the AR-15s. Bay and I each had a loaded 30-round clip.

We received a rules-of-engagement briefing from LTC Smith, the Staff Judge Advocate (SJA), and Max's boss in the JAG office. We were authorized to use lethal force if necessary to protect our "package," Wild Bill. He was in shackles when we picked him up at the Camp Delta Medical Facility. I was the designated driver, and so anticipated possible glitches in the driving. I made sure I was always pointing in the required direction, was double- and triple-checking the mirrors and blind spots. I was not going to make a fool out of myself here.

Wild Bill had been medicated before we picked him up. LT Gibbs said she gave him one and a half times the regular dose. She also said the flight surgeons that would meet us before they went on the plane would have a three-day supply of the antipsychotic drugs. Wild Bill was as docile as a purring cat. LT Gibbs even said that he is a "completely different person" than when he got here. No trouble from Bill.

After we picked him up in a Humvee with a tall back and cover, we transported him to the Windward Ferry landing, Marine escort in tow. I drove onto the ferry, with COL Thomas standing on the boat waving me aboard. Once on the other side of the bay, a minivan with some Secret Squirrel types got out and spoke to LTC Grosse, who asked me to follow them after he got back into the car. They drove slowly so as not to draw attention to themselves. The gun truck was left at the Leeward Ferry Landing for the same reason. The press was at Leeward on a hill overlooking the eastern end of the tarmac, waiting for the new detainees. We took a road that went behind that hill, out of their line of sight.

We traveled for only about five minutes or so, at no faster than 20 miles per hour. About a quarter mile or so behind the pink aircraft hangar, where nearly three months ago I landed with my unit to begin this experience, we turned away from the hangar and towards an abandoned hospital about a third the size of the Navy hospital on the Windward side of Gitmo. As we approached the white building with a few large, faded red crosses, a three-car, three-sided garage appeared on the northwest side of the hospital. The minivan pulled off to the side of the back driveway leading to the garage and motioned for me to pull into the garage. I turned the Humvee around and backed into the middle of three slots.

We got out of the vehicle—all of us but Wild Bill, who sat expressionless and glassy-eyed, seemingly OK with the world, in the back of the Hummer. We pulled security around the garage, with Montpellier and Bay exploring the abandoned hospital, which was open, but completely empty, not even a chair left inside. The plumbing didn't work, so we were looking at country latrines if we or Bill needed to go. Singer and I looked around the garage, which had good lines of sight in all directions save for the other side of the hospital. But the only approaches by vehicle were well sighted. Across the street to the southeast were a field and a playground, and then what appeared to be an abandoned housing area. There were several trees on the field, one which had an old tire swing.

We all had loaded our weapons on the ferry, the same procedure as the Marines. Ammo was in our pockets prior to that. Now, although not locked, we had inserted our magazines in our respective guns or rifles, and we were on duty to protect our "package." This was a bit surreal. A Navy "future OPS" officer, newly promoted to executive officer of an Army Military Police liaison unit (Montpellier), a newly promoted captain Quartermaster (Bay), and me, a Medical Service officer, all with loaded weapons, guarding a flippy Afghan Taliban or Al Qaeda.

Wild Bill was quizzed by those in the back of the Hummer during the ride over, the interpreter translating questions of the crew, such as,

"What line of work were you in before being captured?" Answer: "I was a heroin addict living in the street." I naively asked how he got the money for the drugs if he had no job, but I knew the answer. LT Gibbs gave me "two guesses." "Theft and selling his body for money" came to mind. Heads nodded. Bill said he liked Americans, and even invited Bay to his family's home in Afghanistan. Bay couldn't make up his mind to be angry, disgusted, or both. He laughed about it later, but at the time he seemed a bit insulted.

Our wait would be over two hours, but there is a calming, almost therapeutic quality to waiting in the military. Things were usually "hurry-up and wait," the common military way of life and so we were getting paid, had weapons and ammo, and no worries. In fact, the mission kicked off a couple hours earlier than anticipated. We did get a bit of a warning by getting the FRAGO (fragmentary order, which amends a previous order, is also considered a "warning order" and is quite common once things get under way) about 30 minutes before we actually had to leave for the ferry landing, but the warning order was vague, and I was caught in the middle of eating an MRE. I quickly scarfed down what I had already opened, and I stuffed the remaining food, some of which was in the process of being heated, into the cargo pocket of my combat uniform pants. I finished the meal in the Hummer during the ferry ride.

LTC Grosse left in the minivan and returned about twenty minutes later with a five-gallon water jug with ice water, cups, and two cans of Pringles potato chips. Near the end of the contents of the cans, Colonel Grosse suggested we give some chips to Wild Bill, who did not have lunch. Bill agreed and scarfed down about five or six Pringles in two bites. He seemed to enjoy them.

Bill was watched mostly by MSG Singer, who looked at him with calm resolve. Bay watched Bill a lot, too, sometimes staring at him with mild hatred in his face. I looked at Bill occasionally too, wondering how I felt about him. It wasn't too hard to despise him, thinking of him as a terrorist junkie. Not a lot to like there. I don't think I liked the idea of treating him so casually, but the man was shackled, ankles and wrists to a waist belt. He wasn't going anywhere, and didn't seem too concerned about things. But the thought did creep into my mind, on several occasions, that I had the means to kill him if I wanted to.

For the first time since September 11, I had the means and opportunity to end a suspected terrorist's life. It was a strange feeling. I had had weapons before and even fired them, but there had never been an enemy in my line of fire before. My previous experience with firearms in the military had only been instructional, for target practice or qualification. And now, here I was, a Medical Service officer, the senior Army Medical Department officer in Joint Task Force 160, loaded AR-15, and just several feet away from a possible or actual murderer. What role did he play in all of this? Was he really a Taliban or Al Qaeda mastermind, foot soldier, wannabe? Or was he innocently swept up in a dragnet; unjustly captured? It frustrated me not to know. I wanted to kill him if he was a terrorist. His innocent brown eyes, glossed with medication, looked back at mine. His boyishly round face of about twenty-five, covered by a two-inch growth of thin beard, could betray a sinister, murderous background. The whole Wild Bill persona could all be an act to get him kicked out of Camp X-Ray, which in effect it did. He was leaving. The interpreter said Bill thought he was going to be executed, just like some of the other detainees told the Muslim Navy chaplain when we moved them from Camp X-Ray to Camp Delta. No, Bill, you're not going to be executed—not yet, at least.

I saw myself shoot him, on full automatic, in my daydreaming fantasy. That was almost as good as actually doing it. I got some satisfaction out of it. It felt good, and I suppose I should probably feel guilty about that. I don't. After watching Guantanamo Bay/Camp X-Ray vignettes on the Internet at stickdeath.com, I have become a bit numb to such grotesque images. He should die. Why not? We don't need him anymore. Why should we spend one more dime on him? There were actually two planes on the tarmac for Bill. One was flown here especially for him, full crew standing by, and the other, which flew in the newest group of detainees, was at the ready in case there were problems with the first. The people, the money, the planes, all there for one guy—*ridiculous!* But I guess the price of democracy and doing the right thing outweighs common sense sometimes.

About an hour from repatriation, an oversized navy-blue pickup pulled up. My rifle was at the ready and my fingers ready to chamber a round, when I asked if anybody knew these guys. LTC Grosse said "yes," so I relaxed. I recognized the vehicle as the staff car for the Air Force commander. A big Air Force NCO got out and began to explain the details of the mission. I would follow the vehicle, which would return in about an hour, onto the tarmac, right up to the waiting plane. The signal that things were going to move would be the engines of the plane warming up, which we could easily hear from the garage.

Wild Bill had to pee, so Montpellier and Singer lifted him down from the truck and led him outside to the back of the garage. Bay and I went out too, to pull security. We could see clearly to the horizon.

The ocean to the south, the hangar to the southwest, mountains and Cuba proper to the west; this was my line of sight. Lee Bay had the other side. Wild Bill was done before I could imagine hoards of Cubans, or a CNN correspondent, pouring over the hills to get a look at or an interview with the Gitmo Crazy Carrot.

The last hour passed quickly, and we heard the engines of Bill's plane start up. The big truck came twenty minutes later. We all loaded into the vehicle, and I kept my rifle loaded and close. This ride was much faster than the first. Quickness was now on the priority list. I made 35 to 40 M.P.H., keeping up with the truck. News cameras at the ready by the east side of the hangar missed us completely, and we were out of sight of them by the time we drove up to the waiting plane. The side hatch was open, staircase down. Two MPs emerged from the plane to take custody of Wild Bill. He was still feeling nice, so he was not the least bit troublesome. The MPs searched him thoroughly, and then escorted him onto the plane. In less than a minute I was following the Air Force staff truck off to the side of the tarmac, waiting now for the plane to take off.

LTC Grosse phoned COL Thomas, who told him to wait until the aircraft wheels were up then call him back. As soon as the wheels left the tarmac, LTC Grosse phoned in: "The package is being delivered, wheels up." He then put the phone in his pocket as we all watched the plane drift powerfully up, and then turn out over the Caribbean, taking a Taliban/Al Qaeda to his destiny, which will be quite different than the rest of our Carrot/Pumpkin friends.

5 May 2002. Sandra said she's been reading a book about raising boys, and that the book says a lot about when babies and little boys and teenagers need their daddy the most. Guess when? Right, between three and six years old. Made me feel *great*. Babies recognize the difference between their mother's and father's voice by the time they're three months old. Theodore missed all that. She said our children will be forever deprived of certain things because I'm away. I asked her if she was trying to make me feel better. No answer on that one, but she did tell me Harrison asked her if Daddy was going to die. Her sympathy for that was to tell me to get someone to videotape me. Then she tells me Benjamin said on the way home from the church variety show fund-raiser that he wishes I were home. He rarely says anything about how he feels. Harrison says he's going to be so happy when I get home that he will "bock my head off." I guess that's three-year-old speak for, "I love you, Daddy."

I can't stand being away. I imagine myself seeing them all again for the first time, hugging them, kissing them, holding them. I want it to be now. I don't want to wait till the end of June, if that is indeed when we're going home. It's just not right, a father being away from his wife and children. The cost is too great. But how do you protect a nation, with eighteen-year-old conscripts? We tried that already and f**ked up a generation. I can see how they got f**ked up and I haven't even had to kill anybody yet.

Today we got the last load of the recent push of detainees, twenty-one today, thirty-two each load on May 1 and May 5. I went to Leeward this time to watch, just like I did in February. This time there were more folks along—hangers-on, people who weren't around in February, and the merely curious.

The infantry does things a little differently than the Marines when pulling security, but not much. They were tighter around the plane, a C-17 out of Andrews AFB, they got the buses closer to the plane, too. The mission went exceptionally smoothly. The MPs lifted the new Carrots gently into the buses this time, not like in February when they literally threw them in. GEN Beauregard was in the weeds micromanaging as he came over on each trip, got close to the action, near the entry to the buses. He was just watching, not really talking too much to anyone.

I loaned BLD 1 (my Humvee) to the K-9 guys again. This time they had Rex, a healthy German shepherd—but *damn,* these dogs walk funny. One of the two handlers would tease Rex near the off-load area around the tail of the aircraft to make him bark. The detainees were very cooperative. They came without coats this time, so there was less to do when they got off the plane. There were no medical concerns, really—just a nosebleed and some guy with old war wounds, but nothing serious, no litter patients.

Once at Camp Delta the new detainees, in orange prison uniforms, orange slip-on sneakers, blind folds (white opaque plastic safety goggles, with tape over the lenses), were taken one by one to be processed. One old guy stood up during his wait, but the MPs gently had him sit down. Other MPs would go from man-to-man and make sure the head gear and face masks were on properly, and Army SSG Lester went around making sure the detainees were OK. He and SPC Hastings would give out cold water in cups, soothing the bad guys if just for a moment, helping them lift the cups slowly and gently to their lips, waiting for them to take their fill before taking the cup away, saving grace.

Daily Grind and Freedom
of the Mind

"Human felicity is produced not as much by great pieces of good fortune that seldom happen as by little advantages that occur every day."

—Benjamin Franklin

10 May 2002. There was "Forced Fun" today at Windmill beach for all who worked in Camp Delta/Camp X-Ray. I cooked at 10:30 a.m. Everybody was signed up for something. I'd rather stay home and read, write, or sleep. I'm not as interested in cleaning the hooch as I was when I got here. There was little help from most in the house. LTC Grosse was the neatest and most conscientious, CPT Bay was somewhat aware of common areas, and CPT Wolfe acted as though he were in a four-star hotel, not lifting a finger. Petty I suppose, but after three-plus months, you begin to notice the little things.

As I tick off the days on a tiny calendar, it occurs to me we are getting significantly close to our potential leaving date, somewhere around the end of June. It's exciting. I dream about kissing and hugging my wife and boys when I get home. I go to sleep dreaming about cuddling with them again. A loving family must be the most wonderful, powerful thing in the universe, for the idea of it consumes me.

Not long ago, I received a book from Hugh Davies, a social studies teacher at the high school back home. He's a coach and good guy who became my friend. He was orphaned at a young age through the early death of his parents, and was raised by grandparents who are also gone now. He grew up in the town as well, graduated from the school where he now teaches and will hopefully earn tenure. He's the kind of guy who says, "Coach, put me in wherever you need me, but put me in," which is indeed what he did when he came to me over a year ago and asked for a coaching job. I told him I was looking for cheerleading coaches and an assistant girls' track coach. He became an assistant girls' track coach. He never complained, and, according to the girls and the head track coach, does a tremendous job.

I've always believed that if students believe you truly care about them as a person, they will do whatever you ask them to do. Hugh projects that to kids. And now he projects that to me. About a week ago, I received a book from Hugh. He must've gotten the idea to send me the book from our many conversations about our historical interests in World War II. I told him about a novel I've been writing about a German farmer with a wife and child, and how he is finally drafted near the end of the war. The book he sent me is called, *With Our Backs to Berlin*. It is the personal and composite retelling of these last few weeks and days before the fall of Berlin. Riveting and revealing, it is an exciting and pulsating book. I am grateful to the former German soldiers for sharing their stories, but especially to Hugh for being so generous. My feelings are that the average German was not necessarily sympathetic with Hitler and his ideals, and that especially near the end of the war there were many who regretted assimilating with the Third Reich. Germans are people, too.

I've recently gone to the hospital for dental and optometry services. My teeth are a bit stained from coffee and I need a current eye exam for the renewal by mail of my driver's license. I couldn't get a cleaning straight away because my dental records are not here. This is difficult to fathom because so much time and effort was put into having our dental records perfect before our deployment, including panographic X-rays. *What good does any of that do if they never make it to where services will be rendered? Insane.* So, the appointment had to be for an eye exam. The cleaning will have to wait till next Friday afternoon.

The eye exam was the most thorough I can remember ever having. Even my pupils were dilated with eye drops so the doctor could see my entire retina and optic nerves. I walked out of the hospital with a new pair of eyeglasses as well, with frames I picked out from at least thirty choices. The glasses were delivered to me in the galley (cafeteria) of the hospital not twenty minutes after I left the eye clinic. I also ordered prescription sunglasses known as "BC" or "birth control," the standard issue, with brown plastic frames that make you so ugly no female in her right mind would come near you. My old pair of tortoise-brown prescription sunglasses had a broken frame from the rough handling I sometimes gave them. So the BCs will come in handy, should be sturdy, and should offer some laughs. The bad news is if I want clip-ons for my new pewter-colored metal frames, I have to order them online and pay for them myself. I gave Sandy the information and asked her to visit the Web site herself to see what she thinks. Polarized clip-ons are $40, non-polarized $30, plus $8.95 if I want them shipped to me here, which may not arrive until after I am returned to the U.S.! So we'll see what she says.

I've been trying desperately to call home these past few days, by calling the "888" number to Westhampton Air Field, Long Island, NY, through the DSN telephone line. It's very frustrating. I'll get a busy signal, then call right back and the phone will ring dozens of times with no one picking up. I really want to talk to Benjamin. Sometimes when I do get through, he is at school. I need to talk to my wife and children at least once a week. I miss them so, and I know they miss me. We need each other to be a family!

No success on the phone. Again, just "busy" or ringing. I e-mailed Sandra to tell her, and to ask her to call Westhampton Air National Guard Station at the Westhampton Airport to see if there was something they could do on their end. Maybe offer a different DSN number that I could reach on weekends. I could've sworn I called successfully on a previous Sunday. If they man the phone only during drill weekends, we're cooked because that's just one weekend a month. It wouldn't be so bad if they picked up the damn phone during the week!

LTC Grosse may have his new boss coming in soon, a "bird" colonel, MP type. It will be interesting how things play out. The new guy will have big shoes to fill. The new guy will have a lot of ground to make up as well.

Recent e-mails from Dennis Jones, a boyhood friend from Santa Cruz, California, and my younger half-brother, Andrew Franks from Riverside, have been interesting and uplifting. Both are supportive and sympathetic. Although I share some views with both of them, there are some things we disagree on. Both are more liberal than they are conservative, and I tend to lean more to the conservative way, having been a registered Libertarian (I don't like the name much and like most of the leaders even less), but I am so fed-up with both mainstream parties trying to look more and more like each other and not addressing what we need to be doing.

Andrew seems to have some reservations about the guilt of the fellows we have here, although he didn't come right out and say that, he did express doubts about them being the "bad guys" I described to him in my e-mail. No word on why he felt that, but we can fill in the blanks safely, I believe. There are those in many walks of life who probably feel there may be one or two "innocent" characters here. Perhaps Wild Bill was one of them. Perhaps Wild Bill was a fake, or a high level Taliban or Al-Qaeda who was also a drug addict and psychotic. Perhaps we'll never know. But how much does it really matter at this point? Shouldn't we give ourselves an acceptable margin of error? We have now three hundred and eighty-two detainees. Of these, could one or two be simply regular citizens, non-combatants? Sure. But they sure were in the wrong place at the wrong time to be so involved, weren't they?

Dennis was far more specific, and angry, about his convictions and opinions. He had harsh words for President Bush's policies. I agreed with some of his arguments, but not with others. He felt the whole waffle on the Middle East was bad news, and made American policy seem "rudderless." I had to agree. Either we're an ally of Israel and we support them, or we're brokers of peace and we maintain neutral efforts of reducing violence and reaching long-term agreements which foster a new order of security that promotes safety and prosperity for all (*fat chance*). Dennis said that what we have done in Afghanistan—the decimation and destruction we've caused there, and the bombing, invasion, and occupation—is what we should have to expect from our allies in other theaters of war. His point was that if we are the "parent" or only superpower, we set the example for other democracies (or our "children") to be more aggressive towards their enemies. Aggression unchecked is aggression unleashed, however, and so, I believe, we must sometimes defeat the aggressor before he can do permanent damage. Perhaps that's an over-simplification. I believe it's simply an observation.

Dennis and I disagree on the blame game when it comes to the causes of September 11. Dennis wants to blame the military; I want to blame Clinton and his dismantling of our intelligence infrastructure, including the CIA. Although I haven't heard back from Dennis since we last discussed these issues, I'm not sure if he agrees, but if you are not vigilant, especially in peacetime (pre-9/11), how can you expect to prevent an attack, or a war? Instead of protecting us and making our prestige so impervious to cheap shots from the peanut gallery (third world countries who hate us), the Clinton policies simply exposed our weaknesses for our enemies to exploit. A pre-World War I Wilsonian isolationist, I would have bolstered my Special Forces,

Civil Affairs, PSYOPS, and intelligence during the "lull" between major conflicts. Instead of drawing down (or "right-sizing," as the PC crowd called it) the military in the 1990s, I would have better equipped it, tightened our strongholds against threats (mostly identified as terrorist), dealt severely with other countries through back channels, and reassessed aid packages and trade agreements for those who insisted on turning a blind eye to terrorists and their machines.

I would have focused on the banking and monetary system back home, alternate forms of energy, education and welfare reform. I'd have let the Secret Squirrels do their thing, and maybe even have started up an American Foreign Legion, modeled after the French Foreign Legion, our own group of soldiers of fortune; killers for hire. Let them man some of the front lines of the war against possible terrorist attack. A peacetime "Dirty Dozen" could hunt down terrorists, infiltrate their organizations, perform stings, kidnappings, and assassinations to keep the business of terrorism at least unglamorous and unprofitable.

With the Special Forces, establish many urban, suburban, and rural "fire bases" around the world, even similar to known terrorist entities that create small groups of operatives, or "cells," from which quick strikes of many varieties could be launched in clandestine ways. Each fire base or cell could have detachments of Civil Affairs, PSYOPS, and Special Forces "A" teams in training modes for their target areas. Significant operations could be conducted with the cooperation of host nations, which could greatly impact the effectiveness and viability of terrorist cells or even larger organizations, and defeat their purpose. My hunch is that this is being done now. It should have been plain to see, as the warning signs were all over, that the world was full of unhappy but wealthy and capable foes after the fall of the Berlin Wall and Communism in Eastern Europe; those events left far less stability than there was with the Iron Curtain in place. I had no doubt myself that the Soviet Union would stay put and that it would keep its satellite dogs at bay and on a leash if they tried to tempt fate by attempting to destabilize our allies, neighbors, or strategic areas.

The multi-polar world in which we live is significantly more hazardous than it was 20 years ago, when the world was arguably bipolar—just us and the Soviets in a Cold War and everybody else vying for the attention of one or the other, or staying ubiquitously neutral. We have to reassert ourselves. Isolationism in this world means death. Wilson was right to enter us into the Great War, even though he promised not to. What choice did he have? Sit back and hope the rest of Europe and England could take care of themselves? And if they did, lose their friendship for not aiding them? And if we didn't, eventually face their foe as ours, but possibly on our own soil? It only took eighty-three years for the snake of terror to find us sleeping.

Americans are not used to blood on our own front porch. It shocks the senses. We crave normalcy and we want to "put things behind us." Is it wise to attempt to heal the wounds of terror so quickly? I remember watching television into the wee hours of the morning in my youthful summers, and a picture of the Stars and Stripes waving in the breeze would come on the screen and the "Star-Spangled Banner" would play, and then the screen would go into a test pattern for the rest of the night until programs started up again in the early morning, when the scene would repeat itself. I'm thinking we need an instant replay of the terror of 9/11 every night and first thing in the morning to remind us that not even on D-Day or at Pearl Harbor did more death and destruction by an enemy of liberty and freedom happen on one day.

Don't we need to remember the horror so that we are constantly motivated to not let it happen again? Where are we going here with this idea that all we have to do is go back to work and everything will be OK? Over eighty-three thousand Reservists are in the shit right now. That's eighty-three thousand productive citizens who can't go back to their normal lives just yet. What about them? And the "them" is us. This is not as simple as going back to work. And the news media is so confused about what their role is. They think they have a right to see, hear, and report on whatever they want, regardless of the consequences to the "good guys." For crying out loud, there were news organizations that, after the terrible tragedy of 9/11, forbade their employees from wearing U.S. flag pins on their lapel for fear it would project a "bias." If this isn't a blatant attempt to embarrass patriotic Americans, I don't know what is. The policies were retracted, but not immediately. I'm sure a poll or two had to be taken first to confirm that keeping the policy would mean lost revenue. I've never been polled for anything, but I'll tell you, it would have been fun to give someone from *USA Today* (one of the offending employers) a piece of my mind on that one!

It seems as though, through the eyes of the media, what other countries are doing is more important than what we're doing here, and in Afghanistan, Kuwait, the Philippines, and other places. It could be our own fault, though, combined with the well-earned mistrust of the news media. We don't trust each other, but it's our ballgame, and the media have to play by our rules—at least that's what we tell them. But the media don't like rules, or they like to make them up as they go along—anything to their advantage—and to hell with the welfare of the troops. All they seem to care about is story, story, story; sound bite, sound bite, sound bite; photograph, photograph, photograph. That's what it's about, and the shorter, the better. *Oh, you don't have a fresh photo? Here, use this one from five months ago, no one will know (or care). Can't tell us what we want to know? You guys must not like us. You're unfair warmongers. You're hiding bad things from us. You're not letting us do our jobs.* All battle cries from the media. What else do they really want from us, unlimited access? Perhaps, but I think we've learned our lesson there, don't you?

These are echoes of Vietnam being heard now—the wartime correspondent wears the deceit of those times on his sleeve as openly as a soldier wears his stripes—and the sound is that of distrust and speculation. Since the wartime correspondent has been trained to not believe everything a government official tells them, they must assume something else is the truth, so what ends up in print or radio or television is some conglomeration of truth, half-facts, and fabrication, all in the name of keeping the government from lying to us. But what ends up sounding credible is so far from that, we may never believe the truth when we hear it or see it. We tend to believe what's on TV, or in the press, or the radio because it's there, and we rarely think critically anymore about what we see and hear because of how masterfully it is manipulated and presented, often with talking heads that God-like commentators voice over with verbal pictures of whatever it is they want you to believe, regardless of its relevance to the truth.

The tragic reality here is that the real beginning of the Global War on Terrorism (GWOT) started on November 21,1979. The media were the culprit in the agitation and escalation of male Muslim extremist behavior against the West, and, specifically against the United States. First, was the taking of American hostages at the U.S. Embassy in Tehran, Iran on November 4, followed shortly after by the first casualty of the Global War on Terrorism, CPL Steven J. Crowley, a United States Marine, was shot once through the skull, just above his left ear, at approximately 1:10 p.m. local time, while guarding the American Embassy in Islamabad, Pakistan, on November 21, 1979. CPL Crowley, a chisel-faced, six-foot-six-inch, nineteen-year-old from Port Jefferson Station, N.Y., a chess enthusiast and cross-country runner who graduated from Comsewogue High School, was pronounced dead in the embassy vault at about 3:25 p.m., after medical oxygen that provided his threadbare connection to life ran out. There was no way to get him to a hospital because of the siege by radical male Muslim student protestors, who were later to be funded by Osama bin Laden.

Steven selflessly defended his post against the first skirmish in the GWOT by radical male Muslim extremists, who literally tried to cook Steven and approximately one hundred others in the American embassy in Islamabad alive, setting a fire in the building below the Americans who were in the security vault on the second floor, and while Pakistani Army troops and police balked at a rescue and were nowhere to be seen.

Eventually, over four hours after sovereign U.S. Embassy territory was invaded, the Pakistani Army and police disbursed the crowd of bloodthirsty terrorists, who had arrived in buses together in a misguided attempt to show disapproval with the mistaken belief that the U.S. had seized the mosque at Mecca. In fact, it was a radical male Muslim extremist group within Saudi Arabia who had briefly taken control of the mosque, yet news agencies around the world perpetrated the lie that the U.S. had desecrated this holiest of holy Muslim sites. A few days after it was taken Saudi and French commandos stormed the mosque and routed the interlopers, but not before CPL Crowley was murdered in Islamabad, and great irrevocable damage was done to the tenuous peace between former crusaders and those who would restore Islam to its pre-crusade glory. Turn the clock back a thousand years and only the weapons and costumes have changed; death and distrust have unfortunately and chillingly remained the same.

While American hostages were being kept at the U.S. embassy in Tehran, with the threat of execution if we attempted a rescue, CPL Steven J. Crowley was being murdered in the line of duty. The war had begun, but we had just begun to discount our enemy's insidious ability to reach out and kill indiscriminately. Had the newspapers gotten it right—and had the American administration of Jimmy Carter heeded warnings that harboring an ill Shah of Iran in October 1979 would surely bring global Muslim reprisals—CPL Crowley might still be with us, living in a different world, and probably one without a Global War on Terror.

Never again should we sit and wait for death to come knocking down our door, or our buildings. A static defense is a losing proposition. By taking the fight to the enemy we ensure a safer United States, and if terrorists want to fight on ground of our choosing, so much the better. We will simply assist them in meeting Allah sooner, and follow their crumbs back to where they came from and seek out and kill the source of the male Muslim extremist movement—one bad guy at a time if necessary.

12 May 2002. *Happy Mother's Day, My Love! Every day should be Mother's Day, Darling. You are the best, strongest, loveliest, smartest mommy ever! I'm so glad I got to speak with you and the boys today. And thanks for trying to get Theodore to laugh for me. That was cute. Benjamin sounded great. He seems like a strong, with-it person, just like you. Harrison is "on board." He is with-it, too. If only he understood that I won't get lost, and that nothing bad will happen to me. He told me not to let the bad guys out. I told him not to worry, that the bad guys will be in "time out" for a very long time. He seemed OK with that, if only that were true for all of them.*

I feel like I've been burdened with a terrible secret. Lee told me last night, after he and the LTC got back from a Secret Squirrel barbeque that Wild Bill had been executed upon his arrival back in Afghanistan. Shot in the head. LTC Grosse corroborated the story this afternoon at the office. In between, I ran into LT Gibbs in the parking lot outside the Detention Hospital, and she brought the subject up to me. She said she heard the news from a medical person. I told her who I'd heard it from.

Though we can't be sure it's true at this point, and we will probably never know for sure. It seems all too credible. Wild Bill was not a problem to us, other than having to watch him round the clock and medicating him when necessary. He was actually getting better daily, but JTF-170 said he was of no further intelligence value. That's our number one mission here: gathering intelligence. There's no big rush to get these guys lawyers or give them trials, so I guess we just keep them here till we squeeze them dry then send 'em back where they came from and let their country of origin deal with them. An old Chinese proverb says, "Fool me once, shame on you. Fool me twice, shame on me." With that said, what do we do next time we are tasked with repatriation escort duty? If we directly assist in the transfer of a detainee we know may be executed on the other end of their "freedom" bird, are we then accessories to a war crime? Does it matter if the detainees are illegal combatants? Max says we can't assume after one (possible) incident that the next one wouldn't be welcomed home as a hero. Nor can we say they wouldn't be executed.

Of the thirty-three-plus countries that have citizens here, most would probably be quite brutal to—if not kill—the returning detainee.

There seems to be no legal problem with us giving them back, even if they were legal combatants and bona fide prisoners of war. Their home country can do with them whatever they please.

I'll tell you, it sure seems like these guys have it good here. They are safe, protected by the most powerful country on the face of the planet, well fed, and well looked after medically. They have it better than millions of Americans who work all day every day and struggle to put food on the table, clothes on their backs and the backs of their children, and can't afford medical insurance. The terrorists, I suppose, deserve what they get. Haven't I said all along that they should have thought twice before choosing their profession? We all make choices in this world. They made theirs. The get what they get, right?

LT Gibbs and I shared the silent moment of fear. Fear that we had unwittingly sent a man to certain death. A man who, despite his illness and medicated state, was in good spirits and talkative with us the day he left. We also shared the chilling thought of what to do about future detainees whose usefulness to the Secret Squirrels is no longer apparent. And we both realized that we would have little or nothing to say about it—not even Gibbs, the psychiatric shepherd of the bad guys. Her job is the mental health of the Taliban and al-Qaeda. Even she couldn't stop the deportation.

She's got a case right now: the guy who, unless heavily sedated /or restrained, hits his head on the first hard object he can find—wall, concrete floor, steel bed platform. Even shackled and restrained, he found a way to get off the bicycle helmet the medical folks bought to protect his head. He's self-destructive with a purpose. He is close to being sent back if he's of no value to the Squirrels. What then will become of him? We fantasized about Bill's fate, thinking that the Saudis would institutionalize him. For all we know, he never made it to Saudi Arabia. He probably hit Incirlik, Turkey, and then was flown to Afghanistan, where he may have evidently had an appointment with some projectile brain poison. (Excuse the grotesque.)

Lee, LT Gibbs, Gene, Max and I all feel badly about Bill's possible fate. It's one thing to catch a bad guy, incarcerate him, and then bring justice to him, in whatever form it may take, if fair and impartial. It's another thing to export a guy you know will get whacked. It doesn't feel good to know I may have risked my life to protect a guy who was being sent home to die.

14 May 2002. LCDR Montpellier and I went to the Detention Hospital at 0130 this morning, just to let the MPs know we still love them. CDR James told me that there had been some complaints from

detainees regarding the loud playing of a "radio," which she said was probably a DVD player; either way, it was inappropriate on the ward. SFC Giap is back on night shift duty at the Detention Hospital, so we got to say hello to him. He and I chatted for a while about things. Turns out that SPC Paul had an "incident" with a detainee, #75 (of course), wherein #75 was awakened by a guard, which guards are not supposed to do. When the guard touched #75's arm and shook him awake, #75 reached out and grabbed the MP's arm in retaliation. Perhaps a reflex on the detainee's part, perhaps a reaction rooted in frustration or anger, but the guards put him in four-point restraints for a time. Paul admitted to kicking the legs of the litter stand of #75 yesterday, after #75 threw his portable urinal and its contents at him. SPC Paul was carrying a 9mm at the time and got involved with the restraint of the detainee, which is not allowed. SGT Clark, a corrections officer on the outside, was instrumental in de-escalating the situation by bear-hugging the detainee until he calmed down.

SFC Giap said #205 ("Half-Dead-Bob"), now called "Willie" (short for "Will he live or will he die?"), was put into leg shackles for the first time because the guards saw that he was getting physical therapy for the legs (walking supported on two sides). That meant his freedom of movement needed to be restricted when not engaged with physical therapy. The physician quickly changed that requirement, saying #205 needed freedom of movement of his legs to aid the healing process. The shackles came off.

Here's a recent e-mail exchange between Sandra and me. It's pretty typical, but special none-the-less. I mean every word!

> From: Sandra Spears, Monday, May 13, 2002, 8:45 PM. To: Granger CPT Montgomery J. Subject: Nobody knows the trouble I've seen...

> "Today was probably the worst day of my life. Every thing was bad. I refuse to relive it by typing it. Some highlights—Benjamin threw up in the minivan (third row) BOTH going to and coming from the pediatrician. And there was a scary torrential rainstorm while we were out. He has a prescription for an ear infection. The nausea is caused by ear dysfunction. He probably shouldn't walk on any balance beams either. :)

> "The boys didn't have time to e-mail you. After getting the prescription, washing vomit off the boys (showers), the clothes (laundry), the car and feeding them dinner, I was already an hour behind schedule. Sorry.

"Oh yeah, Benjamin came home with a note written on his class work. Mrs. Spanos wrote that Benjamin was writing once again in a dead language, but not to worry, he had put a lot of effort into it. Basically, he had written his work in a made up language similar to that in the book *Weslandia*. I just don't know what to do with him. She apparently thinks he is a scholar in Mesopotamian culture. :)

Love, Sandra"

My reply:

From: Granger, Montgomery J. CPT (L). To: Sandra Spears. Sent: Tuesday, May 14, 2002 8:10 AM. Subject: RE: Nobody knows the trouble I've seen...

"Darling, I am so very sorry for your misadventures. The poor little man. He's so misunderstood. He has a very complex personality (don't we all, I guess). But with our children, I suppose we think we should know them better. You actually "called" the illness thing. You said Benjamin is reliable with regard to physical complaints. He did sound a bit weepy on the phone yesterday, probably not just about eating glue. I would encourage the Mesopotamian script—it sounds interesting and is probably a good indicator that he'll do well in math (abstract concepts and all). So long as he can distinguish between when it's appropriate for the English and Mesopotamian...what the heck?

"You continue to earn your stripes. I may be getting some (one?) awards upon leaving this place. Two general awards for all reservists have already been authorized: I get an "M" device (a little tiny "M") to put on an award I already have that indicates I've been "mobilized"; and a little star (to put on my National Defense Service Ribbon that I got during Desert Storm), which indicates I served during Operation Enduring Freedom. Anything else I may earn would be for individual achievement, so we'll see. In any case, you should be the one getting the awards. First, you get the large "M" device for being a "mobilized" Mommy, first class. And you get the big star for Operation Enduring Parent, for enduring all the dirty diapers, "accidents," vomitus, various illnesses and accidents, driving rainstorm trips, out-rageous-traffic-on-the-way-home-from-fun, meals "out," meals "in," baths, showers, squabbles, and tears. (I could go on, of course) AND, you get the Great Big Hug and Kiss award for being the best wife ever! It will be my pleasure to present you with these upon my return. ;-)

"Hang in there, Honey Pie. I will come to your rescue sooner than later. I am so very proud of you! Love, Me. xoxoxoox"

The Tunnel at the End of the Light

"Every citizen should be a soldier. This was the case with the Greeks and Romans, and must be that of every Free State."

—Thomas Jefferson

16 May 2002. Things are beginning to pick up. The momentum has begun to swell. We're entering a new phase. The turnover in troops is happening, and quickly it seems. The former Fleet Hospital, now the Detention Hospital, has had steady turnover, and is decreasing in size now. The new JTF staff has arrived, the 43rd MP Brigade headquarters staff, plus nearly one hundred personnel, replacing the roughly eighty personnel of the 89th MP Brigade of COL Thomas, which replaced the approximately twenty-five members of the 1st of the 2nd Marines of GEN Lehnert. Even the 1/22 4th Infantry is beginning to talk about "going home." It seems they just arrived. But sooner than later, it will be our turn. The 455th is scheduled for a commercial flight back to the States on July 1, which is not soon enough.

There are a lot of questions about who will replace whom. SSG David, who was awarded the Joint Commendation Medal from GEN Beauregard yesterday, will be leaving soon. He does so much; I'm sure we won't realize *how* much until he is gone. The 346th MP Company will train for the Detention Hospital guard mission on Sunday at 0900 at the DH. I will be there. Commander Gates announced this morning that the DH staff meetings would begin at 0845 every morning due to the time it takes for folks to get through the new security measures. One has to walk nearly a quarter mile from the DH parking lot, to the front gates of Camp Delta, then back to the now enclosed DH. It's a quick walk at a brisk pace, but it is tempting and easy to walk slowly through the thick gravel inside the camp, and now in the DH area, but I do it as fast as I can. Now, with 15 extra minutes to make it, I should have no trouble being on time.

Only three of the DH staff has not turned over since I arrived: CAPT Romanov, CDR Gates, and CDR James. LCDR King has been here the entire time, but she is leaving soon as well. And even CAPT Romanov hinted he may be leaving soon. He will be the Acting JTF Surgeon for a week as CAPT Phillips will be in Washington, D.C. It should be an interesting week. I'm going to enjoy interacting with CAPT Romanov as he will be the big boss and will have authority to make important decisions. Not that he would take advantage, but it will be interesting.

I had my teeth thoroughly cleaned at the hospital today. My mouth is sore from the opening, prodding, and cleaning that went on. I also had my prescription of Allegra refilled. I chatted with the new preventive medicine physician, Dr. Black, about the conditions of the cells at Camp Delta. I had just done a spot check in "C" block and found lots of rust around the sinks, and lots of filth in the toilet basins. I asked him if he had a proposal put together yet, and he said he had a report he would soon share with LTC Wellborn. When I asked for a copy, he said I wasn't on the distribution list. I asked to get a copy anyway, because it is my job to advise the JDOG Commander on preventive medicine issues, and if I knew what the proposals were I could help get them approved and follow up on them. He said he could get me a copy, but, for some reason, seemed reluctant. I'm curious why LCDR Tomms and I identified deficiencies some time ago and it's just now that a report is done. It is all too typical, unfortunately. Navy reports do not equal Army action. It seems the Navy is good at talk and writing reports, not so good at getting things done in a joint environment. It's as if the Navy's almost apologetic about its role. Preventive medicine has got to be proactive, or it ceases to be "preventive."

There was some interesting (if not serious) fallout concerning the Disease/Non-Battle Injury (DNBI) and STD categories in the last report I gave to CPT Phillips yesterday at the JTF Medical meeting. There were 11 sexually transmitted diseases (STDs) and over 400 injuries. The new chief of staff, COL Lebow, was in attendance and I gave him a copy of the report. He and CPT Phillips seemed concerned almost immediately with the STDs. I was pretty surprised, too. I later went to the Windward Loop JAS and asked Chief Presley what he thought about the stats. He and LT Porter and SSG Nolan agreed that the majority of the STDs were reported by half of the Marines, who left some time ago. The Marines had recently been to Okinawa. You can fill in the rest.

When I asked the crew what they thought about the injury numbers, they said they experience the greatest number of complaints beginning the week before an Army physical fitness Test. They are either lame ducks or hard chargers who aren't careful enough. The medical staff claims it's typical in Reservist and National Guard call-ups.

20 May 2002. The 452nd BLD will have no replacement for me. When I first heard that bit of news, I stopped dead in my emotional tracks, thinking I would be asked to stay on while the rest of my unit demobilizes back to Fort Dix. But everyone else, it seems, was thinking about who here would take on my duties. CAPT Romanov seems to be a big fan of mine. He's got great perceptive skills. He even insisted on seeing pictures of my children, which I promptly printed out from my computer and brought with me to this morning's Detention Hospital staff meeting.

CAPT Romanov allowed me to pick his brain this morning regarding the intrusion of CAPT Israel, the Navy Hospital GTMO XO, into JAS business. Romanov is interested because he supervises Dr. Daniels, my Riverside "homie," who is in control of the JASs. CAPT Phillips is off-island for a week and CAPT Israel is acting Skipper of the Hospital in his absence. I sought some advice from CAPT Romanov regarding CAPT Israel's perception that I am not sharing every shred of information about the JASs with Dr. Daniels. That perception is accurate, though—I have no authority whatsoever with the JASs. All I do is visit or call once a day, keep track of the people, and deliver a disease and non-battle injury report from time to time.

That is the problem, it seems. Delivering a document that indicated 11 sexually transmitted diseases to the JTF surgeon (CPT Phillips) and the new chief of staff, Army COL Lebow, was not such a good idea. Although most of the STDs were from before GEN Beauregard even arrived, but after the report went to CAPT Romanov, it also went to COL Lebow, who seemed interested in why there were "so many" STDs.

21 May 2002. Wild Bill lives! In an MSNBC online story titled "The One That Got Away," reporters Roy Gutman and Sami Yousafzai, in a "Newsweek Web Exclusive," former detainee Abdul Razeq (a.k.a. "Wild Bill" to us, but this nick-name was not printed), was repatriated to Afghanistan on May 11, and he is under guard twenty-four hours a day at an Afghani mental hospital. The report

says that "he is a schizophrenic, not a terrorist." Since when did schizophrenia become a mutually exclusive condition? Can one not hold a job or have a profession *and* be something else—like say, a schizophrenic? We were all pretty much happy about this, so shame on the Secret Squirrels for starting such a raunchy rumor in the first place about Bill's supposed execution. And shame on the rest of us for spreading it. Well, we'll know better next time not to trust things that come from JTF-170 sources. Only thing is, this may have been a ruse on their part. If so, it was very effective, I might say.

In the story, Wild Bill tells his story to the reporters that he was mistakenly taken by Americans after the fall of the northern Afghani city of Mazar-e-Sharif, and accused him of being a "foreigner." He insisted he was Afghani, but was not believed. He says he was first taken to a hotel and then to Camp X-Ray. He says he was given good food three times a day (obviously brainwashed), was interrogated a lot, that he had his own "Quran" and was allowed to pray at will. He was asked if he wanted compensation from Americans for arresting him. "No," was his answer. Liberal press. I'm curious why they would print that, it wasn't the answer they were fishing for.

They have a picture of Bill and there is no question it is the same man we guarded and delivered to a waiting plane twenty days ago. He looks to be in good health—even better than when he left on May 1. His hair and beard are longer, his cheeks are fuller, and he is sitting on a hospital bed, legs under covers and seemingly crossed Buddha-style. *Imagine that, Bill's alive and well and (though not living in Paris like Jacques Brel) being taken care of, for now.*

GEN Hill, the 800th MP BDE commander, hit the Island today, and we're all meeting him at the Jerk House for dinner, and then for breakfast tomorrow, probably at the Navy Hospital. He's been touring the camps with LTC Grosse today.

24 May 2002. The days fly by as I sit here alone in my hooch typing away, having just finished cleaning up a ceramic iguana for Sandra or Theodore. Only one of the two was molded when I got off work today, so I took the one and will get the other tomorrow. I just sent off two finished iguanas today to Benjamin and Harrison. Benjamin's is denim blue with white splotches from glazed crystal paint. The splotches look like little planets, with patterns like the surface of Mars. Harrison's is shades of moss green with large aqua splotches and tiny medium blue dots, planets, and stars; picture a Matisse garden on a six-inch long iguana. They both met my expectations. I have made the ultimate souvenir. They are only $1.50 each. The firing is

free, the paint a few dollars more. But the iguanas are priceless—made by my own creative hands—treasures of Daddy's time in Cuba! You know what's coming…if you had told me six months ago that I'd be making ceramic iguanas in Cuba, I'd say you were completely out of your mind. *How strange life is.*

LTC Grosse apparently insists on sending our three Hummers back to New York way ahead of time—next week to be exact. Current information on our flight departure date is 1 July 2002, and our barge is scheduled to leave 5 June 2002. We turn in vehicles next Tuesday, 28 May 2002. What's wrong with this picture? He says we need to have our vehicles back at Fort Dix when we get back so we don't have to spend a drill weekend going to get them after we return to Uniondale. I told him weeks ago that the 115th MP BN is having all their equipment and vehicles sent back directly to their reserve center after they get back to home station, and that we could do the same. Just have them sent back to Uniondale. No mess, no smell. He heard me, but he seems not to have changed his mind.

I don't see the benefit of going without vehicles for over a month just so we don't have to spend half a day getting them some time down the road. I will probably be most affected, so I am angry but trying not to show it. I attempted to reason with LTCDR Montpellier, our current XO, but he balked and wouldn't even listen to my whole argument. I doubt if he'll risk his relationship with Grosse by arguing with him about it. Hell, I wouldn't even go there again. I explained all this to Lee several weeks ago, too. He seemed to listen, but didn't push for it. Of course, he's going back home to stay about 15 days early because his wife is due with their first baby on 22 June. MAJ Elizabeth North is going back early to stay to see her son's sixth-grade graduation; nice for them. Meanwhile, I'll be expected to get to the Detention Hospital by 0845 every morning, without a vehicle; then go to the Camp America Joint Aid Station, without a vehicle; then get back to the Pink Palace, without a vehicle; then supervise the Windward Loop JAS, without a vehicle; eat, get groceries, attend meetings, and get home at the end of the day, all without a vehicle.

So, time to suck it up. They want to see what CPT Granger can do? I will stay at work every day until my work is finished, no matter the time of day. I will eat breakfast on Marine Hill, stop buying milk, paper towels, Kleenex and napkins, and stop cleaning the common areas, stop getting walked on. No help for me, no help for you, *Bubba*. And "Bubba" could be anybody who gets in my way. Look out for the angry young man (is forty years old young?)! Grosse said to me this morning, after I asked him if it was true that we were turning in the vehicles next week, "Yes. We'll survive." You'll survive. You'll have a freaking vehicle!

He's right. I'll survive. But I don't have to like it. Especially since yesterday Montpellier asked me to come to his office, that he had some bad news for me about the vehicle. He let Max have the pleasure of doing so. And yes, I do believe Max took pleasure in breaking the news to me, and can even see him asking for the privilege of doing so. He tried hard not to act like he enjoyed it, but he did. Singer and Bay were there as well, peeking at my reaction out of the corners of their eyes. I was the spectacle. I didn't get upset, because part of me suspected that they may have a conspiracy going. And even after my conversation with LTC Grosse this morning, I still suspected they were in cahoots. They would occasionally accuse me of "Bogart-ing" (hogging) the Hummer I drove (BLD 01). They would call BLD 01 mine and I wouldn't, at least not out loud to anyone. When I suspected they were getting sensitive about it, I said to them, "If any of you need the vehicle, ask." I guess they didn't like that because it wasn't fun. If they really needed it to go anywhere but to McDonald's, they could ask. I took care of it: cleaned it regularly, took it in to maintenance when something wasn't right, stayed on the maintenance chief about the new cover that was ordered for it back in February. All that, and I still get ribbed. Not surprising. I asked Max to turn off the kitchen light on his way out this morning, as he consistently leaves it on, and instead he turned on every light and fan in the house. He left it like that, which I discovered at mid-morning when I came back to get my iguanas to mail out, I turned everything off, and then when I returned this evening, after 6:00 p.m., everything was on again. Just before Max, the LTC, and Bay left to go out to Rick's to drink, I was sweeping the floor, and the LTC said he wanted the kitchen floor mopped, too. I said Max needs to do it for practice. I have never seen him do but two things on his own for the community of this hooch in four months, and both of those were taking out the garbage. The second time was this morning. I guess I'm pushing my luck with the light thing.

So, they just got back from drinking. They claim there is a replacement for me, a "Renfro." The newest member of the Army medical community, COL Salvatore Pinale, with the 160th MP BN, told me about him today. I don't recall his rank, but he's a former medic with the EFMB (Expert Field Medical Badge). He was working in the J-3 shop, and I am told he will be my replacement. I asked if he would start to "right seat ride" with me. The LTC says I'm "done." I said, does this mean I can go home? Bay said he was writing the "redundancy memo" right now. COL Fredericks, a nice man and rehab doc, said he's somewhat eccentric. The fellas tell me he's "an older guy." I can't wait.

We had a "forced fun" or "mandatory" free concert to attend last night at the local elementary school. The general had his aide send us all at least three e-mails since last week about how nice it would be if we attended. We went. The kids were really cute and typical. They were divided into younger and older groups. They sang, they danced, and they played percussion instruments. I laughed, I cried, I took some photos. They sang John Lennon's "Imagine." That's when I lost it. They reminded me of my boys, whom I miss terribly. I really can't stand being away from them anymore. It's too much. Send me home, please!

There will be more machinations of detainees coming soon, in another few weeks or so if not sooner. Troops in Afghanistan are taking more and more detainees. The J-3 was over tonight while the LTC was out and told me he wanted him to get back to him about "what if we had to receive detainees five days early?" I gave the LTC the message. CAPT Romanov said today that there will be several shipments in early June. He gave dates but I didn't take note of them because they are so likely to change it's ridiculous. The chief of professional services had to know dates so he could plus-up the work schedule. Hell, he could do that the day before they come. Where are we going? What else is there to do, for crying out loud?

My wife told me that she recently received a gift certificate for a local restaurant ($100) from the Suffolk County Athletic Administrators's Association. I am tremendously flattered and appreciative. It is such a nice gesture. I got a "thank you" card that shows an "educator" in front of a school building with an American flag flying, that says, "Thank you for being so nice," and on the inside it says, "This will go on your permanent record!" I like it because it has an education theme, an American flag, and mentions the permanence of their deed. I am truly honored.

My grandmother Tobias has been faithfully e-mailing me about once a week for the last four weeks or so. She reminded me that my great grandfather Merrick, her father, went through the vast majority of his adult life without a left hand after losing it in a farming accident when he was a young man. He never, ever complained about it. She asked me if I could have made the boy's iguanas with only one hand.

I'm crafting my answer. I have half a mind to tell her, with practice, I can do anything I set my mind to do. I also might like to ask her if Great Grandpa Merrick could go through college and graduate school at an Ivy League School without any money or major financial support from his family; probably, if he set his mind to it. What Grandpa Merrick lacked in physical completeness, I lacked in financial support. We are both made of the same stock, so who should be surprised?

29 May 2002. The new JDOG Commander, COL Salvatore Pinale of Albany, New York, has hit the Island. He made wheels down at 1100 hours. An ol' *paesano,* here with his New York *compagnos.* Nice. LTC Grosse is as happy as I've seen him, and gleefully told the story of how he stood up at the 1600 Command meeting and introduced his replacement. He asked the general if this meant he could go home, and the general promptly said, with a wry smirk, "No."

I haven't met the new colonel, but I will soon. I'm not in the office much; gotta get into a new routine, one without a vehicle. It is demanding physically, but, oddly restful once on the bus. On the way home yesterday I nearly slept going to the Navy Hospital for dinner. I walked back to the hooch, nearly a mile. Today I walked here and there between rides, drenched from sweat each time. I made it difficult on myself by leaving my CamelBak at the Detention Hospital this morning. I got up a half hour early to go in to the Palace with the LTC. I made eggs on fresh "everything" bagels (from the NX commissary, of course), then took the base bus to the NX from the Palace after checking e-mail. From the NX, I caught another bus to Camp America, visited with the troops out there for a piece, and then took the bus up to Camp Delta, walking through to the Detention Hospital for the 0845 meeting. COL Pinale was there along with the DH staff. CDR James went home today, so things were a bit solemn. She was a good, professional nurse who looked out for me, always shot straight, and was willing to listen to different points of view.

CAPT Romanov mentioned that the "policy" for Fleet Hospital 20 personnel inside the wire at the Camp Delta medical facility was that there would be no good-guy care except emergency care. In fact, this has always been the case, and is stated so in the JTF 160 SOPs. I've never thought otherwise. However, Navy medical people and Seabees are treated in the facilities, only Army MPs are excluded from care. Previously, MPs had been receiving clandestine treatment in these facilities as well as Navy personnel, with a wink and a nod from Romanov and his staff. Now, the good times are over. GEN Beauregard and/or CAPT Phillips strike(s) again. So, we must follow the policy. I wrote a two-page SIT REP to LTC Grosse this morning and copied it to CAPT Romanov (as usual). In it, I "respectfully" suggested for consideration that we follow EPW operational doctrine and allow the organic medical personnel to treat U.S. soldiers inside the wire, like any other U.S. Army detention facility.

Am I the only one who sees the absurdity in this? We have "unlimited" budget for the detainee medical mission. We have multiple medical facilities to handle their needs that exist inside the wire, but we have nothing for the MPs should they incur injuries, become dehydrated, or fall ill. *Stop, you have to go take the bus to Camp America, buddy, sorry, no ambulance, unless of course it's an emergency. You gotta get to the help on your own, Snuffy. Good luck!* It's been like this since I got here. No transportation to the big hospital—no transportation anywhere for U.S. sick or injured—unless of course you are an emergency.

COL Pinale can't believe it. He also can't believe he's fifty-four and a bird colonel and can't get wheels. They said it before he came. No one asked for him, he wanted to come, he's here, and now he doesn't like it. Whew! I get the feeling sparks are gonna fly soon. I don't think he's going to stand for this much longer. Wait till he finds out all the hospital folks (IDCs, Docs, corpsmen) have weekends and holidays off. Oh, boy. I can't wait. I've had five friggin' days off in almost five months, and these people just got off a three-day weekend! Welcome to Gitmo, the low-tempo gig.

30 May 2002. Harrison writes (through his Mommy of course) that he hopes I come home some day. *Break my heart, why don't you?* I wrote to him that I will come home and that Mommy will help him count the days on the calendar till I come home. *Lord, please let it be soon, and please let me come home safe.*

So, lots of rumors are floating around. An HM1 who works housing and bunks with some folks who run the detainee flights from Afghanistan were roused in the middle of the night and are gone today. MAJ Ericson put out at the 1500 JTF MED meeting that if Pakistan and India get into a shooting war, the airspace we needed in Pakistan and Afghanistan would be closed, so we'd need to get hundreds of detainees here right away. I got the PREV MED reports for Camp X-Ray and Freedom Heights and it ain't pretty. Lots of things were simply left behind: soiled waste buckets; feces, and urine on the "decks," or concrete floors. Ericson said we may have to double-up—in other words, two detainees per cell. The ICRC should like that.

Not a peep from COL Pinale today. Hope he's doing well. I wish he were around for some of the discussions I've had with people today about good guy care at Camp Delta. I brought up the transportation issue, and even made the suggestion we attempt to get some wheels from JTF-170. We treat their folks, why not? COL Pinale made that suggestion to me yesterday while we were "hoofin'" it around Gitmo, but he wasn't at the meeting. CPT Phillips actually wrote it down and said he would take it up with GEN Dunleavy. *Wow.* I emphasized the fact we didn't have the necessary transportation to complete our mission. It reminds me of a socialist distribution system (no, I didn't make this analogy, but thought about it later); the "state," in this case the Navy, decides what your needs and abilities are ("to each according to his needs, from each according to his abilities."). In the Army, we're Libertarian. We go by our doctrine. I did explain that when an aid station in the Army is stood up, we pre-position, as far forward on the battlefield as possible, our three ambulances, and our higher headquarters supports us with pre-positioned ambulances at our aid station. The combat medic is with the grunts on the front line, and they evacuate casualties back to our own pre-positioned ambulances. Here, the Navy seems to insist that routine or even urgent evacuation from Camp Delta or Camp America is not a priority. That the idea of treating U.S. personnel inside the wire is not the mission of the Fleet Hospital. Therefore, unless it's an emergency, only first aid will be given, if that. I'm sure Navy medical folks are afraid to even look at an MP now for fear of having to make the absurd choice between treating and not treating a U.S. person who needs care.

So, LTC Grosse is pushing me to write up a proposal to care for U.S. personnel inside the wire. He said he will present it to CAPT Phillips. I kind of like this because he's becoming more assertive on these issues. He and I are both concerned about the care of the soldier. The heat down at Camp Delta is brutal, the intense Caribbean sun beats down on you all day, and the light-colored stone serves to cook you, as they store heat, and the sun reflects off of them, hitting the MPs twice. Broiled from above, baked from below, they need people on the ground, checking them out, getting to know them, treating their aches and pains, kicking their butt to drink water, delivering TLC. The female MPs seem to be most vulnerable. It is typical on Reserve summer camp missions that females tend to look at it as an opportunity to lose weight, so they don't eat much, and if they do eat it's mostly carbohydrates. They don't drink the Gatorade because it has calories in it. The result is woozy female MP guards. Already one has passed out on duty, so we want to target them and have them start keeping nutrition logs, get nutrition counselling, and have their NCOs monitor this. So my plan will be to recommend that two medics work with each day-time shift of MPs. If needed, a third shift will be pulled at night, but that is not a critical need area at this time. The two medics—one enlisted, and one NCO—will play tag-team with their rounds and go from block to block, assessing the health and wellness of each soldier, keeping a log and making notations as necessary regarding those MPs who may require watching, cajoling, medication, or attention. Depending on the heat index work/rest ratio, the medics will rotate every half-hour to an hour. They will debrief each other at the switch and reevaluate soldiers as necessary. They should have basic supplies such as IV solution bags and IV sets, bandages, and other supplies as needed. Their main focus will be on potential heat injuries. They will survey soldiers to see if any of them are previous heat casualties, have allergies to any medications, bee stings, etc. They will debrief the next team that comes in, as well as the leaving NCOIC regarding the health and hydration discipline of the troops. This should be interesting!

1 June 2002. Happy 40th birthday to me! Whoopee! No, I don't feel 40. Now if only I can continue to say I don't "feel" my age as I go along, things will be great. I didn't get the birthday box from my family, although I did get the Father's Day box several days ago, which I'm sure was sent a couple of weeks prior to them sending out the birthday box. It is in the Twilight Zone, perhaps—or, should I say, the Gitmo Zone? Sandra had all three boys send me free e-cards through the Internet. It was very cute. Harrison's told a joke about not "lyin'" from a lion. Benjamin's had an animated photograph of a cat dancing. Theodore's—chosen, of course by his Mommy—was a big daddy bear playing with and hugging his little baby bear. Made me laugh, made me smile, made me cry.

I got back to the Pink Palace too late today to get the mail from down the hill, so if anybody sent me something recently, I'm gonna have to wait until Monday. That's the breaks. I tried to call home, but, as usual on the weekends, there was nobody at Westhampton to answer.

I've been working with Sean Ralph Kent, the Camp America Commandant, lately to get a phone in the CA temporary JAS in building A1106. He said he'll order the phone "put-in" today. He also said he ordered the paint for the red crosses to go on the new JAS, but won't put them on until it's ready to be occupied. He's a good, serious soldier. I thanked him appropriately for his help. COL Pinale is getting in people's weeds, even mine a bit. He asked me if I had gotten in touch with

J-6 about phones down at the Camp America JAS at the morning Fleet
Hospital meeting, putting me on the spot in front of the FH Staff and
guard NCOs; even his medical NCO was there. I answered, "Not yet,"
but said that this was CPT Kent's lane and that I had reminded CPT
Kent about the request. He asked who Kent's boss was so he could talk
with him about the phone, and I said it was the "BC, Battalion Commander." Pinale appeared stressed. He also appeared stressed yesterday
and I told him so, and said I thought he could use some stress release. I
told him I was going to the movies "tomorrow night" (that's tonight),
but he did not reply. I haven't been able to catch up with him since the
meeting. He seems on a mission to fix what was broken when I got
here, but he seems to be getting the same result I did, which he isn't lik-
ing. *More power to you, Sir. Best of luck—but if you isolate yourself,
especially from your own people, you're going to have a very tough
time of it. Relax, schmooze, and get to know people, build trust, and
then get frustrated. Heck, you only just got here.*

The new JDOG commander asked me if I wanted to go out on a
Coast Guard gunboat tomorrow morning. Sure! Sounds like fun. I
was gonna take tomorrow off, as I am really exhausted from my first
almost full week of hoofin' it around Gitmo, but I can always rest,
right? Besides, I think I'll knock off early today, go home, take a nap,
then freshen up for the movie, which is *Star Wars: Episode II—Attack
of the Clones.* I can't wait. I'm so glad there's something really fun to
do on my birthday. I don't really expect much, but I do like one or two
really fun things. Last night was the talent/fashion show and there
was not one fashion contestant; they were all talent contestants. No
one noticed. CPT Max Wolfe was the master of ceremonies, with the
PAO head, CDR Cyrus Washington, acting as the overall control person and organizer. Max did a very good job, was very natural, funny,
and spontaneous. He opened with his mechanical, musical James
Brown (a.k.a. "JB") impersonation, but the sound was too low on the
transfer to the microphone. He should have tested it out on rehearsal
night. If you can't hear JB, it ain't worth it. His best bit was when,
after intermission, he dressed up like John Travolta from *Saturday
Night Fever,* and threatened to take the audience back to the 1970s.
He had "Night Fever" by the Bee Gees playing, and did some of the
exact moves John Travolta did in the movie—very entertaining.
Then, after a few moments, he beckoned six elementary school girls
from the audience onto the stage and simply said, "Do what I do."
The girls followed him so well that it looked rehearsed! It was priceless. The photographers from the *Gazette* and the *Wire* were on hand,

so I hope to get a photo of that one. I was so spellbound by the act that I forgot to take a picture of it myself, even though I had my camera.

Max made two mistakes in my book, though. One, he attempted to embarrass me by playing a tape recording of snoring and telling the audience it was Monty Granger, "my roommate." It could have been me from Fort Dix, because I remember the tape from then. But I'm not his "roommate" now, I'm his housemate, and I know it doesn't bother him; if it did, he would complain and threaten to move out, just like he did at Fort Dix. So, I was fodder. Payback's a bitch. The other mistake was encouraging one of the acts, a high school girl playing electric guitar and singing, to play a second song. Some of the guys in the crowd encouraged her to play another song, and Max allowed it to happen, which tortured most of us and made other acts wait too long. Also, there were several unscheduled performances that lengthened the show. All in all, it was quite entertaining. Lots of variety. There was a Jamaican contortionist who danced on his hands while he folded his body over like a crab. There were also a local (born and raised) twenty-four-year-old man who works in the laundry/car rental shop who *yelled* poetry; an Irish guy who played a banjo and sang an Irish folk song; kids who sang; officers who sang karaoke style; and ladies who danced. Nice diversion.

Word is that the detainee flow could start again as soon as in one week. I stopped by the newly completed Camp Delta II on my way to Camp America from Camp Delta today. I was checking to see if "low beds," about eighteen inches off the floor of the cell, were installed in some of the cells. Camp Delta II appeared a bit smaller than Delta I. Delta II has one forty-eight-cell isolation block, one twenty-four-cell isolation block, and three forty-eight-cell open blocks. There were five low beds installed in the first left-hand cells in the first open cell block, and ten low-bed cells in the beginning of the second cell block, all on the left hand side of the buildings, facing the entrance.

3 June 2002. Yesterday's experience was a "Gitmo Top Five." So far, my other "Top Five" include touring the Navy ships (there were three that came during the last several months and I got to tour two of them, including a guided missile frigate—awesome!), wearing the plastic construction hats while driving a Hummer (our Kevlar combat helmets were way too heavy and hot for the mission and the environment, so Max obtained white plastic construction helmets from the Seabees for us), and probably singing karaoke the other night (I sang at least eight songs). But yesterday was near the top. COL Pinale invited Gene Montpellier and me along with him on a Coast Guard

PSU gunboat, a twenty-foot or so dual motor speedboat. The craft was waiting for us at the Windward Ferry Landing at 0700. LTC Grosse dropped us off and told us to call him when we got back and he'd pick us up. There were three Coasties (Coast Guard members) on the boat, which had a loaded .50-caliber machine gun up front, and two loaded M-60 machine guns mounted on either side of the boat near the stern. There was a sun canopy overhead and a control console in the center of the boat. The boatswain wasted no time getting under way, and the day was gray and cloudy, and would later, during the next two and a half hours, rain a bit on us, then suddenly clear a bit, letting the hot sunshine through.

We were taken out of Guantanamo Bay at speed, maintaining about thirty-five knots through what looked like from the shore, calm seas. Looks can definitely be deceiving. Once on the open ocean, we began to lift up and crash down onto the surface in jarring rhythm. My knees were bent to absorb the shock, but I really had to hold on! Soon we were along the windward shoreline, observing the lighthouse, Phillips Beach, two hidden beaches accessible only by foot or by boat, Windmill Beach, Camp America, Camp Delta (lights still on), and the old Migrant OPS sea huts. We saw an MIUWW Hummer (underwater warfare surveillance guys). I wasn't allowed to take close-up photographs, but it was still neat to see these places from the sea, about a mile out. The ride back to Gitmo Bay was a bit faster but just as rough, as we sped for the Guantanamo River mouth on the Leeward side.

Our boat crew was on for over their normal twelve-hour shift, so their relief offered to pick us up on our return from the river. We went up the river without making a wake so that we would not disturb the wildlife. The waters are said to have manatee in them, but we didn't see any on this trip. We saw a lot of fish-sign, fins and the occasional body of large fish coming out of the water quickly, in order to take a favorable angle on their breakfast. We saw hutia (banana rats), iguana, blue and red crabs, crane, blue heron, pelican, hawk, buzzard, many songbirds, and the like. It was like a safari—peaceful, quiet, and jungle-like in places, with mangrove vegetation on both sides of the river. At one point, the trees and shrubs gave way to savannah-looking territory with several abandoned vehicles that looked burned out and long-forgotten. We surmised that they must have been used for target practice. LCDR Montpellier said Gitmo used to be a training base for the Army's A-10 "Warthog" tank killer airplanes. An "ugly" plane armed with cannon and anti-tank missiles.

Finally, we arrived at one of two bridges across the river. A road bridge about 20 feet or so above the surface of the water, running parallel to the fence-line road, with a warning sign not to go any further. Gene took a digital photo of me standing by the 50-cal with the bridge and sign in the background. I've already sent it to my grandmother Tobias and others via e-mail. We cruised down the river and met up with our boat's relief, three fresh Coasties who took us to the water gate separating the U.S. controlled waters from the Cuban side. We got to see some guard towers up close. We passed by old moorings, which had long since been abandoned. Even cacti, grass and trees grew on top of these stubby monoliths to a grand age of the Navy. At one time dozens of Navy ships had huddled in these sheltered waters, moored to the giant pillars of concrete and wood, their crews scuttling off to enjoy a scintillating Gitmo Liberty. There were small islands, some with shelters, barbecues, and picnic benches; other islands had more burned-out cars and trucks that had apparently served as target practice.

We sped along the inner windward coast, taking in the scenery, getting a bit wet from some sudden rain, then just as quickly enjoying bright sunlight through breaking clouds and blue sky. Our new boat-swain sped to over 41 knots at one point, quite fast in a small boat, and too soon had us back at the landing. We thanked our crew and waited for LTC Grosse to pick us up after Gene called him. There was a man and his young (maybe five-year-old) daughter on the shore, searching for "just stuff," he said. The little girl was joyous and jumpy with everything she pulled out of the water, and sang and danced as she searched for new things. I picked up a few shells for the boys, small and perfect-looking. *I miss them, those cute little Granger ruffians. I can't wait to get them in the water again, beach or pool, it doesn't matter to me. I miss playing with them. I can't wait to get home. It was a great morning. June is here; my going home month? We'll see.*

7 June 2002. The general called all E-7s and above (sergeants first class all officers) down to McCalla Hangar for a briefing at 1630. COL Pinale, Lee Bay, Elizabeth North and I went down and filed into the bleachers. The general was announced by the chief-of-staff. GEN Beauregard told us there was an imminent threat from the air. Ten suspected Al Qaeda terrorists, traveling as nine Russians and 1 Briton, were either en route to Miami or already there. Three of the suspected terrorists were "known" pilots. The threat report stated that reliable intelligence said that there was a planned incident that would "shock the world." The general had his J-2 (intelligence staff officer) tell us

about the threat, and talk to us about how vulnerable we are. We have no known air defense, although my conversation with Air Force COL Alexander months ago comes to mind. It may be that F-18s are in Key West, or they are here. Also, the air defense briefing given to GEN Lehnert comes to mind, when the Air Defense Artillery LTC briefed the General on possible threats, and how easy it would be to hit Gitmo from the air, since we don't control the airspace around this tiny plot of land. It's scary. *I don't want to die. I can't, I just can't.*

John Wojohowitz, our new JDOG S-2 says that he has confirmation that everything we send via e-mail and telephone is definitely intercepted by the Cubans.

9 June 2002. It's Sunday, and LTC Grosse and I are taking the day off. I'll go into the office soon to do e-mail and such; he's going to "chill" for only the second time since 8 February. You can say what you want about him, but he's the hardest worker at Gitmo. And his work, aside from keeping watch over detainee operations, is full of taking care of soldiers. He knows just about everybody here. And most of the people who he sees and knows like him. He's a people person—fair, caring, and dedicated.

We just watched the Tom Hanks movie, *Cast Away,* on HBO at the hooch, just he and I. The movie validated a lot of feelings I'm having now, especially about being away from my family. My feelings are acute right now, but I certainly am profoundly affected by this deployment. At the same time, I feel a bit guilty for feeling sorry for myself. There are so many who have it worse than me. I know I've said this many times before, but if I must be deployed I do feel fortunate to be here rather than many other places where lives are in danger all the time. I'm sure we don't know to what extent we are in danger here. And from time to time I feel vulnerable. My fear is that we won't truly know how vulnerable we are until it is too late. We must believe those entrusted with our care and safety are doing their jobs; I just hope they are out there, somewhere. At the end of the movie, Tom Hanks' character comes back to his wife, and she's remarried, even though she tells him she never stopped believing he was alive. I think that told him she really had let go, because if she had trusted that feeling, she would have never remarried. I know I haven't been gone for five years, even though it hurts to be away from my familial commitments and obligations for even a day. And I should be constantly grateful for the fact that I'm not a POW, separated from my family for years and years in horrible conditions, but I still hurt. I still suffer the separation. I will try to give something back.

Back to my family, every day I am home. I am determined to follow my own advice, the advice I am giving to the student-athletes at this year's Spring Sports Awards ceremony next week. I'll be e-mailing a speech I've written to Tony Perna. Here it is:

"Good evening, and thank you all for coming here tonight to honor the achievement, commitment, and dedication of some of our school's finest students.

"I am extremely grateful for the loyalty, support and love shown to my family and me during this difficult time by the School Board, Dr. Wine, the Central Administration, my colleagues, teachers, coaches, support staff, students, parents, and friends. Special thanks go to Tony Perna and Diane Domke, for doing great work every day for our student-athletes, teachers, school nurses and coaches. There simply are no adequate words to describe how thankful I am to you all.

"My current experience is one that will shape who I am for the rest of my life. I am doing a distasteful yet necessary job—helping to ensure the health, safety, and wellness of suspected murderers and terrorists, in the hopes that information we may get from them may somehow prevent any more innocent people from being hurt. In my search for meaning in this new, uncertain and dangerous world, I realize I have been given the chance to see what really matters in life—my family. Leaving my amazing wife, Sandra, and three young wonderful boys; Benjamin, six and a half, Harrison three and a half, and little Theodore, five months, has been the most excruciating experience of my life. And missing the girls' basketball and boys' lacrosse championships, as well as missing two whole sport seasons of great effort and performance, are right behind!

"What I want to say to the student athletes out there is: never underestimate the love your parents have for you. Let me explain: imagine the feeling you have when you don't perform the way you know you can, or lose a game you know you should have won. Now multiply that feeling times a thousand, and you may begin to realize what your parents are going through in these uncertain times, with their hopes and dreams for your success and happiness.

"Never underestimate what your parents sacrifice for you—putting other things aside, important things, and things that put them at risk, for you. No, this isn't meant to be a guilt trip (although, if you feel a little guilty, that might not be such a bad thing), this is a love trip. Learn what family really means now, and you'll avoid the common pitfalls of those who would fight authority for no reason, and realize too late, what could have been.

"You have an opportunity, starting tonight, to begin giving more than you owe. And the best part is you already know how. Your parents have taught you already. Just do it, love them back—in your words, your deeds, in the way you carry yourself. Thank your Mom and your Pop and your coach, and other family members for 'being there' for you, even though some of them may not be here tonight, for they are 'there for you' every time there is a roof over your head, food in your belly, clothes on your back, and a shoulder to lean or cry on. Show gratitude and appreciation now for things you won't be able to take for granted when the bills start coming in with your name on them. And no matter how lonely life may feel, being part of a family means you are never truly alone.

"These high school days should be some of the best of your life. You have more people who care about you here, now, than you probably ever will again in your life. Take advantage of it. If you have a question, ask it. Teachers and coaches actually really like it when you ask questions; shows you're paying attention. If you need help, seek it out. If you see someone who needs help, give it freely and expect nothing in return, except the satisfaction that you have contributed to goodness in a world sorely in need of it.

"If you don't have a varsity letter yet, make sure you find out from your coach exactly what you need to do to earn one, and don't expect it to be easy. Nothing in life truly worth having is easy, and you might as well learn that now. If you received a varsity letter tonight, be proud of your accomplishment; get something to put it on and wear it around. You earned it, you fought for it, sweat for it, maybe even bled for it, and your parents paid for it with their love and support (okay, and with their school taxes).

"God willing, I will return to my happy, healthy, and loving family soon. You have yours with you now. So, what are you waiting for? Hug your Mom and Pop and those others that helped get you this far, and show them every day, in your own way, how much you appreciate their love and support, by doing your very best in all you do, by doing the right thing all the time, and by being honest when you make a mistake. In this way, you can all fulfill your dreams of success and happiness.

"God bless you all, congratulations, best of luck to the seniors, and I hope to see you all soon!"

I finally got my birthday box yesterday. I also sent away for five Medical Service Corps coins to give to people who have done me solids and who have done an outstanding job here: CAPT

Romanov, LTC Grosse, 1LT Tiva, CAPT Phillips, and 1LT Anderson. Good folk, hard workers and supporters of me and my work here. My birthday box was full of love, with cards, toys, fruitcake, words of kindness. It was mailed on 2 May 2002. It was obviously opened by customs, as the paper tape was cut, and the box resealed with clear tape.

14 June 2002. The replacement BLD is here. Full circle is around the bend. We have a confirmed date of departure, June 26—*12 more days and a wake-up!* We have a new roommate at Windward Loop 11 C, CPT Rick Robles of the 452nd BLD Adjutant/S-1. I haven't met him yet, but LTC Grosse just informed me that he will be sharing my space until Lee moves out of the upstairs room with Max, on the 19th. Obviously, a whole lot is going on, as detainees have been arriving every other day since a week ago through June 22 between twenty-four and thirty-four of them are on each planeload. There are no real medical cases. The Fleet Hospital has had only one detainee in it for over three days now. Funny, since two months ago they made plans and expanded the hospital to accommodate up to forty patients, and now they have nothing. They probably could have gotten away with just using the Navy Hospital Guantanamo for the whole thing, but the hospital people didn't want to mix detainees with good guys.

COL Pinale is now in charge of all U.S. troop healthcare, and Daniels is out. I asked for this to happen, but know others asked for it, too, so I can't take all the credit. Pinale answers to Navy CAPT Salazar, a real good guy.

I am getting "short" and feeling "short" as well. It is harder to focus, though I am putting more effort into things just because that's what's required. More to do, so much I can't do it all, so others have to pick up the slack, which is OK; it's time to move on. I am still doing the medical intelligence; reading Camp Summary reports and culling the medical and preventive medical info out. One detainee says he's throwing up trying to drink the tap water, which is potable, but warm and sometimes discolored. I gag on it too because of the temperature if I try to drink it from my hooch. But we don't want these guys to dehydrate, do we? The water lines here are all black above-ground pipe, so you can imagine how warm the "cold" tap water is. I went down to Camp Delta to speak with this detainee through an interpreter and, sure enough, he was very animatedly telling me about the temperature of the water. I told him nothing could or would be done, and that, whether he believed me or not, the water where I was living was just as warm. He actually seemed to appreciate my visit, saying "thank you" through the interpreter, but he was visibly upset and depressed-looking before and after my talk with him. *Sorry, buddy, we're both going to have to live with this one.*

There was a farewell potluck dinner for CAPT Romanov last night at the Seabee hooch. It was fun. I made a "Top Ten Differences Between the Army and the Navy" list for him, read it to the crowd, and used two hats, one Army and one Navy when I read off and acted out the differences, respectively. I framed the Navy captain's copy and he seemed genuinely amused. Here they are:

Top Ten Differences Between the Army and the Navy

10. Chivalry: Army—"Make a Hole!"; Navy—"By Your Leave."

9. What am I? Navy—Carnivorous Mollusk ("Squid"); Army—Guttural Sound ("Grunt").

8. Sleeves: Army—Practical (rolled so that at a tug, can come all the way down); Navy—Cool Not! (rolled like an old newspaper).

7. "Joes": Navy—"Smuckatelli"; Army—"Snuffy"

6. Dining Facilities: Army—Sounds like you need to bring your pet food dish ("Chow Hall"); Navy—Sounds elegant and relaxing, or some place you might find art for sale ("Galley").

5. Buildings: Navy—Think they're on a ship ("second deck," "Bulkhead," "deck plates"); Army—In touch with reality (use terms such as, "second floor," "wall," "floors").

4. Combat: Army—Do it ourselves; Navy—Get the Marines to do it for them, or the Seabees do it, before or after they build something.

3. Going Home: Navy—"One day and a bag drag"; Army—"One day and a wake-up" and oh, we carry our bags.

2. Toileting: Army—Honor our French allies with "latrine"; Navy—Insist on being anatomical with "head." I don't get it.

1. Affirmative: Navy—Again with the anatomy thing, counting the ocular organs in their heads, by saying "Aye, Aye"; Army—C'mon now, everybody say it, "HOO-ah!"

13 June 2002

For Navy CAPT Pete Romanov

In thanks and fond memory of our inter-organizational sharing

Your friend,

Army Captain Monty Granger

15 June 2002. "Fair winds and following seas." That's what the bull ensign's sign reads at the going-away ceremony for CAPT Peter Romanov. He made a short, grateful speech, shook every one of the fifty or so hands that were extended to him by his sailors in formation and the smattering of Army and Air Force folk there to say good-bye. He said to me, "Take care of yourself, my friend," and said to stay in touch, and to get his address from CDR Gates. I will. But even if he and I never see each other again, or never even communicate, he will be a friend for life, for he truly cares about every single soldier and sailor in his keep and in his realm. It was a privilege and a pleasure to have been associated with him. He will be missed.

16 June 2002. Father's Day. Very anticlimactic. I am brooding, feeling sorry for myself that I am not with my family. Not feeling like a very good father. I want to take my family and go far, far away, to the woods. I know I've said this before recently, but I can't get the vision out of my head. I'm tired of these Carrots, these people, these ridiculous problems with providing, or rather trying to provide, the care I know soldiers deserve…to *them.* I'm tired of messy, selfish hooch mates, of leeches, of people in general. I want to go home. And I'm finding it difficult to forgive LTC Grosse for not getting us home on the 21st. Elizabeth's son "graduates" from the sixth grade on the 24th. She's afraid if we went home on the 21st, she wouldn't be allowed to be there. *Tough shit!* Nine people should suffer so one can do something with her family? Don't the rest of us want to be with our families, for crying out loud? I'm sick of this convoluted and self-ish decision-making that makes no sense at all. And the Navy IDC's (Independent Duty Corpsmen) can't do the in-briefs because they're too busy. You know what? The next big brief is on June 23, a Sunday morning in fact, three days before I leave this rock. I wanted to take an on-island, four-day pass before I left. Part of that would be the check-out process. But now, I'm expected to do a brief on Sunday. I wanted to pack my uniforms and military gear and have that be that. Now I have to keep one set out. *Poor me.*

If I had to do this deployment all over again, I'd do it much differ-ently. I'd be more involved with my job much more quickly. Preven-tive medicine issues would have been number one immediately. Joint Aid Station issues would have had to be corrected immediately, and with no compromise. The things that went on before I arrived, and continued for months after, were unacceptable. And now, well now, COL Pinale has the "con" on JAS health care. Will he be any better? Or will he, too, succumb to the Navy Hospital way of doing business?

There is no way in hell that the Navy, even the supposedly talented IDCs, should be in charge of Army health care. They have been allowed to decimate everything we know and do in a field environment for our soldiers. We bring the care to the soldier, and constantly train the common soldier in self-protective and first aid skills. We monitor, 24/7, the health and wellness of the troops. And in this environment, we also do the same for detainees.

I know I'm too bitter. I am over-reacting to things I can't control. Will going home be that much different? A wife—a beautiful, loving, mothering wife, and a woman I chose to be my life's partner and mother of my children. She'll need to control things at home. That's not an entirely bad thing, but she'll want to control me within that environment. She's made a list of things that need to be put together, fixed, and done. I can't wait. The boys will need fathering, but not too much on the discipline at first, the experts write. I should not immediately try to take over where I left off; that wouldn't be fair to the kids. Hell, I'm assuming I make it back. They've caught two suspected Al Qaeda operatives in the U.S. and linked them to possible "dirty bomb" attacks, they say, against Washington. But COL Pinale said an attack was believed to be targeting Gitmo. Will I make it back?

I just want to be safe, emotionally, physically, and mentally. Is that a lot to ask? I hope not. I will be careful, am being careful. I just want my life back. And I want it back now. I'm tired of taking shit from people. I've got to let them know. There's not much anyone can do to me here now, I've got my OER (Officer Evaluation Report), I've done my PT test and weigh-in. I'm good-to-go. I won't be rude, but I swear, I'm gonna give back to anybody that does something stupid exactly what they give out.

20 June 2002. The saving grace is that CAPT Phillips said that my contribution to the medical mission here was "unique, extraordinary." He said it at my last JTF Surgeon's meeting at JTF Headquarters today. That made my tour. No award or coin or congratulation could ever match that. I hadn't thought of myself as that. I was just doing what needed to be done the best I could under the circumstances. I told him I could not have done it without his guidance and patience. He said our time together was not without its difficulties, but we worked through them.

There will be more detainees coming on Saturday. This is unexpected. There will be a lot more, 80 or so. We are nearly full in Camp Delta, having received detainees every other day from the 8th through the 18th—over five hundred now. There was talk at Fleet Hospital this morning about there being a contingency to separate part of the hospital (tear down the vestibules) and shackle non-medical detainees to the beds. First of all, that's probably in violation of the letter and spirit of the Geneva Conventions. Second of all, it would definitely close the door on any protection the conventions would give a medical facility. We were already suspect because of the guard tower near the east fence of the compound, and because there are no "distinctive red cross emblems" on the hospital. Therefore, we would have no legal protection from attack or hostilities. One detainee was put into the DACU (Detainee Acute Care Unit) at Navy Hospital Gitmo. It's a lockable isolation ward that is suitable for suspected TB cases, which is the reason for the detainees' placement there. He was suspect, and then began coughing up blood. He was recently returned to Camp Delta from the Detainee Hospital as a "rule out" TB case, so much for that.

I have been "right seat riding" with CPT Sherry Days, who is an Army Transportation Corps Officer with our replacement unit, the 452nd BLD from Tallahassee, Florida. She's the JDOG S-2 as well as taking over the medical liaison duties I had with the Detainee Hospital, the JTF surgeon, and the preventive medicine shop. She'll do fine. Tomorrow should be my last day in the office. After that, complete checkout, do two more in-briefs for newbies on Sunday and Monday, pack, chill, and get on that Freedom Bird on Wednesday, 26 June. Fly to Jacksonville, Florida, then to Philadelphia, on to Fort Dix by bus, two days at Dix, then H-O-M-E!

I have been e-mailing Sandra on other people's computers, as I have checked out of J6 and closed my JTF e-mail account and Internet access. When I went to the public library here (attached to the high school behind the Windjammer social club and restaurant) to check out (they had to initial and stamp to verify I did not owe any books or fines), I noticed their computer room. Bingo. Just like at the Fort Dix library.

I just got off the phone with my honey and my boys. They all sound great! Theodore was gurgling and squeaking, Benjamin and Harrison were both very talkative. Sandra sounded wonderful as we talked in code about my coming home: "D-Day minus six is still on. Tell Dr. Wine I'd like to come to work on D-Day, and D-Day plus one and two. The rest of the days I'd like to back-up to the first day of school." I forgot to tell her to notify Tony, my interim replacement, and Diane, my secretary and family friend, as well. And to tell Dr. Wine I would like to have permission to work Fridays in August, as football practice goes on Fridays at the end of August. It shouldn't be a problem, as I did pretty much the same thing last year. My fear is that during the first three days in July I will run into so many people and need to speak with them all that I won't get any work done! We'll see.

I hinted to Tony in an e-mail today that I'd be back the same day I had previously had Sandra tell him. I set up "D-Day" as July 1 with Sandy through print mail over a month ago. Tony wanted to know my status, vis-à-vis getting back and having to re-deploy in the fall. Joyce Bing, the current athletic director in a neighboring school district, is leaving to take a job with a school district in a neighboring county, and Tony is being asked if he's available to be the interim to take her place. I told him I'd love it if I could just put him in my hip pocket and take him out whenever I needed him, but I said that wouldn't be fair and is not realistic. I told him to take the job. The 455th is de-MOBing. We will not have another mission for some time, knock wood.

George Bush has stopped saber-rattling with Iraq. He has drawn the saber and is waving it over his head, saying that Saddam Hussein must go. Military leaders are saying it would take three months from the "word," or "green light," before they would be ready to invade Iraq. It seems inevitable. And if it is, you can bet my unit will be there.

I want to go to the Brigade Field Medical Assistant slot when I get back. LTC Grosse says he wants us to drill in early August, but he also said we all have "good" years (this alludes to earning a certain amount of participation points, usually four points for each monthly two-day drill, fifteen points for being in the service, and fourteen points for annual training. It comes out to about sixty-five points for a "good" year for retirement purposes. On active duty, you get one point for each day—for us, that will be about one hundred and eighty days/points—plenty). He hinted this way that if we didn't want to, we wouldn't have to drill again this year (through October, as the military fiscal year is from October 1 to September 30). I will definitely drill. Not a question. I just want to drill with the brigade. If I must stay with the BLD, so be it. I am wiser for this mission, but it would be better if I had been allowed to do the job I was trained to do.

CAPT Phillips has asked me to do "lessons learned." I will do so, and give them to all who may want them—namely, him—and at least to those whom I mention in the lessons [see Appendix A].

Home

"We make war that we may live in peace."

—Aristotle

26 June 2002. Leaving day. For the past several days, since I started to out-process on my own, things have begun to feel strange. I'm not as focused, not in a rush necessarily to get anywhere. That part actually began when I started having to take the bus everywhere. I had so much less control with things. And now it has snowballed.

I am sitting in a modified Hummer in back of the Leeward Hangar, waiting for the word to put our baggage into the hangar for our flight home. Flight plans changed somewhat yesterday. LTC Grosse called me while I was at the hooch, packing and doing my last load of laundry. He said, "Change of plans." There was a pause. My heart sank and I began to think about all the possibilities: an extension, no planes available, we're going somewhere other than back to Fort Dix. The last was ironically true and false. It turns out that we were going directly to McGuire Air Force Base. A C-141 was coming in from McGuire with a new MP Company, and was scheduled to return to McGuire empty. So, we are probably going on the C-141. There is a possibility that if there was trouble with the plane that we could still go on the commercial flight, they are saving seven seats for us. If there's no problem with the C-141, then we're in. It would be my first ever military aircraft ride except for two Huey helicopter flights. The first was during the third phase of Officer Candidate School in Camp Smith, New York. I was performing a leader's recon to a new platoon operations area and so went with a couple of TAC officers and some fellow OCs (officer candidates). The day was beautiful and it was crisp when we were aloft. The machine shook and banked more steeply than I had anticipated. Of course the side doors were open, so when the craft banked on my side, all I had to do would be to unbuckle my seatbelt, and *foosh!* Out I'd go. The second ride was while doing a make-up annual training with a medical unit at Fort Indiantown Gap in Pennsylvania. I was the safety officer and had to wear a gold armband with the word "Safety" on it in black letters. We were almost done with the tour and the unit was getting ready to dismantle the DEPMEDS hospital slice they had constructed and played in for 10 days, so I went to the airport, where a medevac unit was doing training in their helos. I went to the tower and signed up to go on a ride overlooking the site to take some photographs for posterity. They called my CP (command post) and got clearance for me to go up, or so I thought. As it turns out, the CP relayed to the commander that "someone" wanted to go up in the helicopter to take pictures of the site. The commander assumed it was his unit historian, so he gave the thumbs up. The CP told the tower it was all right and I went up with the medevac commander in his helo. He was practicing touchdowns and takeoffs from remote sites, so we did a few of those and then flew over the hospital site a few times. We got close on a couple of passes and evidently the hospital commander saw my armband, which I had not taken off for the flight. Heck, I was planning on going back to the site after the ride.

I strode back to the company area, just in time for a formation and met the XO on my way there, who pulled me aside and about tore me a new you-know-what. Seems the hospital commander was madder than a hornet that I went up there without his permission. I explained to the XO that the tower called the CP and were told that the commander did give his "OK." The XO said the CO didn't know it was me. I told the XO that I'd heard the tower folks mention my name to the CP, and that it wasn't my fault the CP didn't tell the CO who it was, nor that the CO gave permission without asking for a name. Nonetheless, I was given a letter of reprimand. I appealed to the CO through the chaplain, to no avail, and CO refused to speak with me about it until the day we left the fort. But I was given two days extra duty, guarding the exercise site overnight twice, so that I could not go out during the last two days, when everything was winding down and people were relaxing and having fun. I think the CO softened a bit, because when he finally spoke with me just before we left, he was supportive and almost apologetic. I never complained about the way he treated me, and I think that spoke volumes to him. I took my punishment and filed it under "lessons learned." Either read your CO's mind, or always get verified permission to do something before you plan on doing it. It stayed with me. I still feel I didn't do anything wrong, and that the CO had the responsibility for the details, but he said he didn't want something to happen to me when I was not engaged in official business. So he decided to tear up the letter of reprimand before I went back to my unit. That was the last helo trip I went on, and the last military aircraft I have flown in, until today. God bless this plane, her crew, and all of us on board.

I can't wait to see Sandra and the boys. I've been daydreaming about my homecoming more and more. It will be grand. I'm hoping we can de-MOB at Dix with speed. I'd love to go home Friday, but I am concerned about my boxes in the connex sitting now at Uniondale. I'd much prefer to get those boxes before going home. The plan now is for us to meet our families—at least those of us who need to go to Long Island—at the Reserve Center. The timing better be right, because there is currently no plan for anyone to be there who can open the place up. That sucks. I don't want Sandy and the boys waiting around for me. I might even wait until I'm there to call. I won't mind waiting another hour or so to make sure they are safe and not waiting around. I could pee in my pants I want to see them so badly. Soon enough, I guess, but not soon enough for me. Almost time to unload our stuff. I'll be back later.

It's later. 1105 hours. We're waiting for 1130 hours to load our luggage onto a pallet, to be placed onto our plane. It looks like it will be the C-141, though they will be a half-hour late. Not a big deal. I'm getting paid. I'm going home. I'm OK. I'm actually feeling better as time goes by. There is a sense of relief creeping into my psyche. There is a comfort zone that I'm entering, a peaceful place. I know I'm going home, and that calms me. Images of Sandra and the kids—smiling, laughing, playing games, building things, going places, and doing things together—dance in my head. It's wonderful. I just can't wait for that coziness on the couch, with popcorn, apple slices, and milk, snuggling and watching a movie. That's my ultimate comfort zone.

1356 hours. Airborne and cool. Earplugs in, and about two hours of batteries left on the computer. I prayed on takeoff. I prayed that we would make it home. That's really important to me right now. It's my new mission. If there is any way I can get home on Friday, I will do it. I'm feeling excited and exhilarated. I can't believe I just left Gitmo after one hundred and thirty-eight days on the Island. It doesn't seem real somehow. But I am so happy that it is a memory, and I can't wait for the rest of it to be a memory as well. As soon as the plane took off the air inside got cooler, and it is getting cooler still. Wheels up was approximately 1640 hours, and the estimated time of travel was three hours and possibly longer due to thunderstorms in our path. According to the flight chart in the airport waiting room, our route should take us over the Bahamas, cutting the south western corner of the Bermuda Triangle. Oooooh, spooky! Not. It's a typical Gitmo day—hazy, hot, and humid. The flight engineer who gave us our pre-flight safety briefing was dripping sweat. It was "H-O-T." He told us it was 96 degrees at McGuire. By the time we get there, around 1645 hours, it should have cooled off a bit. They had Armed Forces television network showing on the waiting room TV, and their "Town of the Day" for weather was Lake Ronkonkoma, New York—About eight miles from my house! Low 80s in the daytime, high 60s at night, with, of course, our trademark Long Island evening summer breeze. Ah, New York! Back home, where the love is. No love at Gitmo. Didn't expect any, didn't get much. And by "love" I mean, kindness, generosity, brotherly love. Nope, too high-stress for that. There were a lot of people doing a lot of work, 24/7.

Some of the JTF 160 coffee mugs came in last night. LTC Grosse, Singer, and I went to pick up ones that were ours. I ordered ten, but only five were ready. The balance will be sent to me. I ordered three with the inscription "TRUE PATRIOT" on them—one each for my three supervisors, Dr. Wine, Dr. Summers, and Les Winthrop, the school business administrator. I'm thinking about giving one to James Sinnott, the school board president, and one to Tony Perna. But I'm afraid I would offend the balance of the school board if I did that. They all really deserve a small token of my appreciation. But they did get the certificates from the ESGR. That should be enough. I bought six Gitmo coffee mugs from the gift shop yesterday, before we knew the JTF mugs would be ready—two green, two black, and two cobalt blue. They each have the Gitmo seal in gold, have a gold rim and have big letter "GTMO" on the reverse. A very nice gift, I think. I have an extra blue one I bought for myself in March. I bought the six thinking I would never see the JTF mugs. So now, I probably have just enough to offend someone who doesn't get one. This is the nature of gift-giving. It is stressful. I'll work it out.

I'm carrying a "Brave Heart" pin for Sandra. Red, white and blue stones set in silver to resemble the U.S. flag, in the shape of a heart, about the size of a half dollar, in 3-D. I think she'll love it. It will be her award for having the bravest heart of all. I love her so much. I hope she knows that. I have to show her how much I love her every day for the rest of my life. I want this feeling to last forever. I feel like sleeping this journey away. It's very comfortable in the plane now. It looks smaller from the inside. It has three sections of seating. There's room for 64 per section, each of which has double-row, inward-facing nylon jump seats made of solid fabric, the back having the cargo net look. Our bags were palleted and are in the section closest to the tail. The seats for the rear two sections are set up against the fuselage of the plane. LTC Grosse is crashed on several seats. I can't see the other five of us, as my back is to them as I face the starboard side of the plane. The flight crew in the back with us seem to be studying flight manuals. There's not much else to do. There are only four small windows, each one in the far two thirds of the plane and each one attached to a door. I can't see much from where I am sitting, but on liftoff I caught a glimpse of the Leeward side;—buildings, land, and then water. Then I saw the coastline of the Windward side. I would have gotten a great shot of the detainee camp if there'd been more windows. That's OK. I saw enough.

15 September 2002. I've been home over two months now. Out-processing at Fort Dix was surreal. Nothing seemed "normal." It all seemed foreign and strange. I found it hard to concentrate. I was obsessed with getting home. It was unbearably hot at night. I couldn't sleep, I couldn't write. I was terribly depressed. Going home day was a great day, though. I was told the day after arrival by LTC Grosse that I would be able to "get out early." He arranged for COL Ecke, the 800th MP BDE Deputy Commander, whose wife was my wife's recovery nurse at the birth of our third son, Theodore, some six months prior, would take me home. The next day, after breezing through out-processing, my dream came true. GEN Hill was at Fort Dix with COL Ecke, and when the general heard I lived so close to COL Ecke (he lives about fifteen miles east of me) he ordered COL Ecke to leave early from Dix, for which the colonel was very grateful towards me.

The colonel and I had a good time talking on the way back. I enjoyed the ride, seeing the sites that were once familiar to me, zooming back into memory. He told me the tale of his deployment to Kuwait, his brief stay in Guantanamo, and I told him about the operations while the 455th was there.

Basically, the colonel said we were preparing for prisoners in Kuwait. The Afghanistan mission was advisory in nature, but our duty in Kuwait was to build prisons and barracks for our eventual deployment there. He said his trip to Gitmo in December 2001 was completely useless. He was treated as a fifth wheel, and even though his presence there was requested by SOUTHCOM, Marine GEN Lehnert was less than welcoming, not so much of the man, but of his ideas, experience, and expertise. COL Ecke told me he couldn't believe the conditions and procedures when he arrived, not to mention the lack of transportation. He couldn't understand why they felt they had to shackle the detainees within the compound. Where were they going to go? Why agitate them unnecessarily? He said that prison psychology was such that one could expect less cooperation in interviews (interrogations) if they were mistreated or perceived themselves as being treated unfairly. He said he made recommendations, was told "thank you," and then summarily ignored.

COL Ecke asked if I didn't mind stopping at a car stereo place before dropping me off. Of course I said no. I didn't mind so much. I had told Sandy I would be home later, and I hadn't gotten a chance to tell her I was on my way due to the abruptness of my departure from Fort Dix. But I had told her that was a possibility.

I arrived to a beautifully manicured, lush, and splendid yard and house. The flowers were more vivid and plentiful than I had remembered; the grass thicker and greener, and the trees fuller and taller. It was like coming home to Tara before the war, only this war wasn't over, just for me, and just for now.

No one answered the door, and I couldn't open the garage to get to the concealed house key because I didn't have a remote control. Sandra had obviously hedged her bet and guessed I would be home when I said I would be, not earlier. COL Ecke almost insisted on staying until she arrived. I declined, thanking him profusely. I really didn't want to share my homecoming with anyone. I took my gear from his car, piled it up on the front porch, sat down in a front porch chair and waited, smile on my face, for no more than ten or so minutes. But it was a good wait, a fulfilling time, enjoying the pleasure of being home, not being dusty or tired or in need of going or being anywhere. I was right where I needed to be.

My beautiful sweet wife Sandra pulled the minivan into the driveway, noticing me at the last minute and doing a double take. *"It was me, honey!"* She smiled broadly and I could see the two older boys beginning to stir inside the car. I stood and she parked and got out. We embraced, kissed, such soft lips, beautiful almost shoulder length honey blonde hair and those hypnotizing ice green eyes. I was still in love with this woman. What a wonderful feeling.

Theodore was angelic and not noticing me in his car seat. Harrison looked at me with vacant, hurt, unknowing eyes. I expected something like this from him, but was still taken aback by the look. Benjamin was out of his seat, coming for a long, long overdue hug. He held me tightly for what seemed a very long time. I wanted to break the embrace only to see his face—a pale, sad, but happy look, a bit pained, but joyful nonetheless, with tears and a few sniffles. Finally, Harrison emerged, timid, not knowing this green-clad person. I knelt down to him and smiled. I said, "Hello, Harrison. I'm your daddy. Do you remember me?" And as if my voice and eyes had unlocked a secret memory, his face began to loosen from its perplexed tightness. He smiled ever so slightly his cockeyed smirk of a grin. It faded just as quickly and he let me hug him. I held him tightly for a moment then let him get another look. It was me. He smiled again, more broadly and more confidently that *yes, this was the person he once knew, and would know again.* I could almost see his defenses melt away, and the little boy I knew six months before was still there. He didn't grow an inch or change an iota from what I remembered. Benjamin seemed to have grown some, and Theodore was a complete stranger. I had no reference in my flesh and blood memory of him.

I was most afraid that he would not know me, cry when he saw me or if I tried to hold him. I was sure he would fuss. I was prepared for this, or so I thought. I was hesitant to pick him up. Sandra motioned for me to "go ahead." I got him out of his car seat, took a look at his face, so cherubic, so innocent. He scanned my face and found no stranger there. I hugged him quickly thinking he wouldn't have time to register my strangeness. But he was one with me. There was no whimper, no cry, no hesitation, twitch, or squirm. He melted into me as if he'd always been there, fuzzy head in the crook of my neck, nuzzled, safe and warm. A miracle, I thought, *a miracle.* My baby son knew me! Tears flowed from my filling eyes.

I didn't push it and let his mother take him. I was home, and soon the excitement began to fill the house with chattering children, a barking dog, a wife all aglow, and a baby needing attention. This was bliss.

Since my homecoming I have fought off tears many times, alone in my car, in the bathroom, sitting at my desk at work. September 11, 2002 found me at an athletic director's meeting thanking my colleagues for their generous gift (a $100 gift certificate to a fine restaurant for me and my wife) and for their support during my absence. My voice broke several times as I explained my gratitude, and at once I couldn't breathe, or hear, or think. I saw bowed heads, some tears, and some smiles. I remembered what I had wanted to say, but it came out differently, of course. The message was sent, though, and received. A line of them waited after the meeting to greet me home and say, "Thank you." The oldest among them shook my hand last and as we spoke I noticed a Marine Corps tie tack, and asked when he had served, and he said he was in the Pacific between 1943 and 1945—And he was thanking *me?* He described a recent trip to the island of Iwo Jima, and how he had gotten into a "six pack" (old Army lingo for a cargo truck) that took him and others to scenes from their violent and bloody past. He told me he regretted not getting out at a certain point to go look at the caves there. He repeated this several times, as though if he said it enough, he would be permitted to return. You could see him viewing an old movie of his life in his eyes, almost seeing the smoke and gun flashes and jungle in their liquid. He thanked me. I was stunned and honored. No ribbon or medal could compare.

Celine Deon sang "God Bless America" on the radio, and I could no longer control myself. My chin shook and my lips quivered uncontrollably. Tears fell as I sobbed, trying not to. I had told my colleagues, reminded them, that there were "about eighty thousand reservists currently activated," and that "we should remember them as well as the sacrifices of hundreds of thousands of active duty military personnel on this day."

25 September 2002. I made a presentation today for Bill Bodkin's American history class at the high school today. I came in uniform, as requested. Although I had not promised to do so, Bill said it would have a greater impact on the kids if I did. That was hard to do. I don't flaunt my military affiliation. For five days leading up to this event I had been suffering from an unknown ailment. It was mild but annoying, probably related to stress, and has manifested itself as a tightness in my gut, just below the center of my rib cage. Not indigestion, not heartburn, just a dull tightness, just tight enough to be uncomfortable nearly all the time. I thought about the presentation a lot. It kept me up a few nights, in anticipation. I tend to be unable to control my emotions at times over the pain associated with having left my family, at such a critical moment, and the knowledge that they suffered because of my absence, especially Harrison, who continues to have emotional distress related to my going to Cuba. He has only recently seemingly stricken the word [Cuba] from his every day vocabulary.

I prepared for the event by giving Bill, who also works for me as my lead crowd control chaperone for night games at the high school stadium, several handouts for the kids, including prisoner of war processing guidelines, my personal biographical summary, a map of Guantanamo Bay, Cuba (very generalized and crude, but clear enough to give them a reasonable picture of where I was). I also brought with me a few things to enhance the presentation. I brought the Philadelphia Inquirer article of April 28, 2002, titled, "For Detainees, Growing Despair." The article attempts to paint a bleak picture of life at Gitmo for the bad guys. Navy LT Gibbs is quoted several times in relation to the psychiatric patient detainees, all thirteen of them. Author Tom Hayes of the Associated Press tries to make the case that we were mistreating the detainees, a.k.a., murderers and terrorists. I read from the article and set the record straight with the students, all advanced placement seniors, as a demonstration of the difference between fact and liberal press innuendo.

I told them about the worst-case scenario regarding detainee discipline, describing what might provoke a severe response and what that response entailed: e.g., detainee spitting on an MP repeatedly and refusing to comply with instructions, leading to the Internal Reaction Force going in, subduing and then hog-tying the detainee until the detainee capitulated. I discussed the role of the ICRC and gave Bill my copy of their guidelines vis-à-vis the Geneva Conventions. Bill also teaches Law and other Social Studies subjects. I shared some photos of my time at Gitmo, including photos of my children the day I left. I mentioned that leaving my wife and children was the most excruciating time in my life, and that my wife, Sandra, was my personal hero, and that she had it much worse than I while I was gone.

Bill and the kids asked questions, which I felt I answered candidly and appropriately. Bill thanked me as the bell rang to end the all-too-short class period, but told students to stay as he asked one last question about the "switch" that had to be turned, going from civilian to soldier to civilian again. I told him and the class that the switch had not been fully turned yet. But that by being allowed to share my experiences with the class, it had helped me a great deal. I thanked Bill in front of the students by presenting him with a commemorative coin, one memorializing the strike on the Pentagon.

The day after the presentation I wrote Bill a thank-you note, and he expressed his gratitude, telling me that every single thing I presented was a home run. I told him how it made me remember how rewarding teaching was, and he told me how the rewards of teaching have kept

him going even after thirty years of teaching and passing up retirement to continue. We talked about how it would be good for administrators to teach one class per year, just to keep them in touch and to
have an opportunity for them to share their knowledge and expertise
with kids.

27 September 2002. Sal, from Plaques and Such, a trophy and
awards vendor, came over to my office for a meeting today to discuss
letters, banners, and award pins. After greeting each other for the first
time in almost a year, Sal presented me with a beautiful, acrylic free-
standing engraved plaque. It had red, white, and blue stripes on the
outside borders, with stars on the blue stripes, which spelled out:
"Presented to Montgomery Granger, in grateful appreciation of your
service and dedication to our country as a member of the U.S. Army
Reserve."

I was completely blown away. Sal said he had thought of me a lot
since receiving a call from me just before I left for Cuba. He said he
was grateful and wanted to express his thanks. He said he had a
cousin in the Italian Army who was being trained and will be sent to
Afghanistan. It was quite an honor.

Epilogue

"The summer soldier and the sunshine patriot will, in this crisis, shrink from the service of their country."

—Thomas Paine

During the American Revolution, soldiers who joined the Continental Army during the spring or summer but went AWOL in the fall or winter were known as "summer soldiers." Many of these "summer soldiers" were farmers, who would join up with the Army when their crops were planted, fight with them during the summer, and then go back home to help with the harvest. Others would stay with the Army through the harvest, but sneak off in the middle of the night once the weather got cold.

Meanwhile, the people who supported the revolutionaries when the revolution was going well—but not otherwise—were called "sunshine patriots." So, in the famous passage from "The Crisis," where Thomas Paine wrote the quote above, he was talking, literally, about the fair-weather friends of the Revolution.

Fair-weather friends of the Global War on Terrorism (against the United States) clamber for reasons we should be nicer to illegal combatants than we need to be because it is the "right thing to do." They are concerned about our global reputation for being above reproach when it comes to treatment of prisoners.

As I write this, we have Army troops in seventy-two countries worldwide (according to the 2008 Army Almanac), including countries we defeated in a war that ended over sixty years ago—namely Germany, Japan, and Italy. We also still have troops in South Korea, a country we helped defend in a United Nations "police action" over fifty-five years ago which only has a cease-fire agreement on the books, so the thought that we will ever leave places like Iraq and

Afghanistan is naïve and myopic. We are there to stay, in one form or another, for a very long time, and not as occupiers, but as friends and good neighbors—ones that can be counted on.

My experiences doing what I did at Gitmo, but in Iraq, will be the subject of a subsequent book. It will be about Iraqi detainees at Abu Ghraib after the scandal, Camp Bucca in the south, and Ashraf, near the Iranian border. The facility at Ashraf was filled with Mujahedeen el-Kaq, or "MEK," also known as the People's Mujahedeen Organization of Iran, or "PMOI"—Iranian expatriate nationalists who once did the evil bidding of Saddam Hussein, and whose current sole purpose in life is to overthrow the mullahs in Iran. Never underestimate the strangeness of the world in which we live, for you would be wrong if you thought the majority of people are "normal," which is a completely relative term. The MeK have only women leaders, and only men as the rank and file. They don't allow marriages, or even intimate relationships between men and women. And there are no children.

DAVID HICKS

David Hicks, the Gitmo detainee who was captured on the Afghan battlefield, was convicted of providing material support to terrorists, and in fact admitted to traveling to Afghanistan for the purpose of engaging in Jihad against the United States and its allies, including his own country, Australia. Hicks wrote a memoir titled "Guantanamo: My Journey," published in October 2010 by Random House Australia, and as of this writing is not available in the United States. I have not read the book, but I have read excerpts published in Australian on-line news releases, and I have read several reviews of his book, most notably by Australian journalist, Carolyn Cash at *http:// carolynmcash.suite101.com/david-hicks-guantamano-journey-a297407* who interviewed me in part for her article. Hicks' book is conspicuous in its absence of substantive information about his terrorist training. This is what we do know from his book. Hicks chose to become a Muslim, and then later renounced this choice. Hicks chose to travel from Australia to Afghanistan to train as an al Qaeda fighter. Hicks was rising in the infrastructure of leadership within the al Qaeda terrorist group. Hicks met Osama bin Laden. Hicks was captured on the battlefield, and then was transported to Camp X-Ray at the U.S. Naval Station at Guantanamo Bay, Cuba.

What we don't know is why Hicks feels he deserves special treatment after having been an unlawful combatant in our struggle against

Islamist extremists. David Hicks is a criminal and someone who cannot be trusted to tell the truth. Using an established law that prevents criminals from profiting from their crimes, the Australian government has decided that Hicks should not receive money from the sale of his book. This is just, fair, and appropriate, yet there are those who defend Hicks and feel he should be able to benefit financially from his book deal. The U.S.

Constitution calls giving aid and comfort to the enemy "treason," so what should it be called when Random House Australia publishes the writing of a convicted terrorist for profit? Random House Australia is as culpable as Hicks in the glorification of unlawful combatant activity which promotes the killing of innocent civilians. The Geneva Conventions were written to protect innocent civilians, not reward those who pretend to be civilians while they murder real civilians. Al Qaeda terrorists pretend to be civilians to try and claim extra-legal privileges; benefits legal combatants who earn the status of Prisoner of War are not even entitled to. Lawful combatant POWs who are not accused of war crimes may be released from custody at the end of hostilities, according to the Geneva Conventions and the Law of Land Warfare (U.S. Army Field Manual 27–10). So, given these facts, on what legal and moral basis can Hicks or any unlawful combatant ever held at Gitmo claim such privileges, such as a right to a trial or a right to Habeas Corpus? Even dry-foot German spies captured on long Island, New York, and in Florida during WWII were not extended the privilege of Habeas Corpus, which is a Constitutional guarantee to due process rights.

The Constitution allows for the suspension of Habeas Corpus during time of war, including "invasion" and "rebellion." Surely, Hicks cannot expect a reprieve, compensation, or sympathy. Yet, he has applied for redress through the United Nations Human Rights Commission, which is completely ludicrous.

It is the express goal of al Qaeda and associated terrorist groups to claim, at every step, extra legal privileges, and to claim falsely that their captors tortured and abused them in hopes of reaping monetary rewards, which undoubtedly would go to fuel the persistent Islamist extremist efforts to kill innocent civilians. David Hicks is a pariah in his own country, and a selfish utilitarian opportunist who is lucky to be alive, and should gain no profit or benefit from his illegal and immoral behavior.

OSAMA BIN LADEN

The struggle against Islamist extremists was never about Osama bin Laden (OBL). That idea was a media attempt to personify and simplify the conflict for consumption by a sound-bite public. The reality is that we are engaged in a chillingly similar struggle in the late 18th and early 19th centuries in our two Barbary (Pirate) Wars with the Islamist extremists of those times. So the reported death of bin Laden by members of the elite Navy Seal Team Six on May 2, 2011, although evoking a strange mix of celebration for killing the head of the terrorist organization that orchestrated the attacks of 9/11/01, and remorse for not having had an opportunity to try and convict him on terrorist charges, is, objectively, another tick mark in the tally of dead terrorists. The night I found out about the death of OBL was a very emotional time for me. I was alone, and just before going to bed while finishing a session on Twitter, I saw a tweet that mentioned a pending announcement by the President on television. I watched the announcement, which aired later than was initially announced, and then I began an emotional roller coaster ride through reliving the events of 9/11/01. The ride ended with an odd sort of satisfied sadness. It was good that he was gone, but how it happened was probably not ideal, and my fear now was that the masses would be led to believe the Global War on Terror, a.k.a. our struggle against Islamist extremists, would be over. In fact, I believe, these events should steel us to make an even bigger push. Like a shark smelling blood in the water, we need to continue our offensive or active defense, to decimate the ability and will of our enemy to resist or continue. So, in this sense, the death of Osama bin Laden should act as a catalyst to victory, in whatever form victory must take.

LEAVING IRAQ

As I watched the last American military vehicle cross the border between Iraq and Kuwait on television, I could not help but feel a sense of dread.

In a letter to the editor of New York Long Island's *Newsday* several weeks before, in response to the paper's editorial supporting the withdrawal, I shared my anger and frustration:

"Dear Editor,

"The nation's "longest war" started on November 21, 1979, with the murder of 19 year old Marine CPL Stephen Crowley, of Port Jefferson Station, when an Islamist extremist's bullet found its way into his brain while he was defending the U.S. Embassy in Islamabad, Pakistan, against blood-thirsty "students" bussed there to overtake it during a false media frenzy stirred by erroneous reports that the U.S. had occupied the mosque at Mecca, Saudi Arabia. There is a park in his memory on Old Town Road, not far from where he lived, and played, and went to school. Or, maybe the war on terror started when the Barbary Pirates, Islamist extremists of their own time, began to capture U.S. ships and crews and then hold them for ransom in the late 18th and early 19th centuries. We fought two wars against that tyranny.

"Or, maybe the "longest war," which sees us presumably leaving ancient Babylon and the land of the Garden of Eden (modern day Iraq) by year's end, started during some of our ancestors' participation in the (dare I say it?), Crusades, over a thousand years ago?

"What is certain is that our "longest war," as today's *Newsday* editorial postulates in a piece titled, "Time to leave Afghanistan," will not end if we simply pack up and go home from the two most popular of the 75 countries in the world where we currently have troops deployed. That's right, 75. And what about the 90-plus countries in which we have CIA operatives, or the over 200 countries in which we employ Diplomatic Security Service agents, shall we bring them home, too? You see, the "tip of the spear" in this Global War on Terror, is not in just Iraq or Afghanistan, it is in our clandestine operations, world-wide.

"Our military presence in Germany, Japan, and Italy (as well as other countries), over 65 years after we defeated them in WW II, allows us to project that clandestine, as well as overt power wherever necessary to protect and defend the interests and shores of the United States of America, against all enemies, foreign and domestic, so help him, God; our president's most sacred trust and duty.

"If you had asked me back in 2004–2005 if I wanted to go home from Iraq, I would have said, "of course I want to go home, but I have to complete my mission first." To a soldier, Marine, Sailor, Airman, Coastie, et. al., in our all-volunteer military, going home happens when the job is done, and not before, unless properly relieved. President Barrack Hussein Obama's sleight of hand in making the U.S. military disappear from Iraq by the New Year is nothing but an illusionists trick, calculated to endear moderates and his liberal base to his cause of re-election. In a recent speech, the President said "our strategy for bringing the troops home" has worked. The "our" in this statement is not the American People, nor does it represent our best interests. The "our" in the president's speech referred to his campaign staff. "Going home" has never, is not, and will never be a military strategy; defeating the enemy and removing his means and desire to wage war against us has been, is, and will always be the goal of our military.

"*Newsday* took the opportunity to also slip in the thing about leaving Afghanistan during this Iraq hullaballoo because they sense momentum building from it. The opportunist in the White House is organizing the community, you see? If you ask those coming home from Iraq if they are happy, they will say "yes." If you ask them if they'd like to go back in a few months when Muktada al-Sadr stages an offensive against the still weak democratic Iraqi government, they will say, "I'd rather not, but I'll do what I'm trained to do when I'm told to do it." How much blood on Obama's hands will it take before we realize that the struggle against Islamist extremists is not over, nor will it be over anytime soon?"

After the withdrawal, the paper struck again, basically calling the whole Iraq operation a failure, and again I lashed out in a letter to the editor, which they published after calling to say it had to be edited for length.

This is the full version of my response:

"Dear Editor,

"With regard to your editorial, "Tough Lessons Learned in Iraq," *Newsday*, Friday, December 16, to say our great sacrifices did not justify the spectacular success of Operation Iraqi Freedom is both myopic and cruel. We still have troops in Germany, Japan, and Italy over 65 years after the end of WWII, and we currently have troops in over 70 other countries, all because we and our unique way of life are under constant attack, verbally, culturally, and physically. The weak and appeasement-minded Obama administration could not (would not?) agree to terms in order to allow troops to remain in Iraq past the first of the year, sacrificing an important and strategic power projection platform from which we could assert persuasive influence over belligerent nations in that area of the world, effectively giving up the high ground and creating a power vacuum that may soon be filled with those with whom we fought. How dare you suggest that even one drop of American blood was misspent. The Coalition and U.N. resolutions, al Qaeda training camps and exiled terrorists (Abu Abbas), vicious dictator (Saddam Hussein), and grateful people, all are rational reasons to have done what we did, when we did it. Because Obama wasn't the president at the time of the invasion of Iraq is no reason to ignore historical facts: The Iraqi people are not only better off, for what our allies and we did, but they are free. The blood of Americans, British, Australians, Italians, and other of our allies has watered the Iraqi Tree of Liberty. Your opinion that it was a mistake insults every military person, their families, and every loyal and patriotic American. My feeling is that I and my fellow Global War on Terror veterans would go back in a heartbeat if asked in order to make good our commitment to Iraqi freedom, so insidiously disregarded by you and Barak Hussein Obama."

Clearly, the Obama administration has a different world view that I and many who think like me, that the best defense is an active offense. If we have the means to destroy our enemy before he can do us harm, then we have a moral, ethical, spiritual, and legal obligation to do so. Leaving Iraq to the Iraqi's is myopic and disingenuous. If we had left certain European countries to their own devices after World War II, then the Soviet Union would have happily filled the void. And then what? The Marshall Plan (or European Recovery Plan, ERP), set in motion in April of 1948, was devised and executed in order to aid a post-war Europe, and to guide them into a modern, peaceful existence.

The proof of success, now over 65 years after the end of World War II, is that the countries we defeated then, now make-up the most economically robust countries in the world. We restricted how much they could spend on their own defense (to no more than 1% of their Gross National Product), supplementing what was needed to deter an aggressive Soviet threat with our own forces, so that more could be spent on infrastructure, research, and industry. The result is the most impressive and successful reconstruction the world has ever seen. The military and strategic advantage was that we now held the high ground in Europe, which allowed us to project our power and influence into the surrounding territory, then mostly controlled by the Soviet Socialist Republics of the U.S.S.R.

To leave Iraq after over eight years of effort to establish a similar situation in the Middle East, borders on complete incompetence. Militarily and strategically, it will probably go down as one of the biggest foreign policy blunders in the history of the United States. Several days after the last U.S. soldier left the country, no less than 16 bombs were exploded in Baghdad, killing many innocent people. U.S. President, Barack Hussein Obama released a message in response: "Anyone trying to derail the progress in Iraq will fail." Astonishingly underwhelming; tantamount to a shrug in the midst of smoke, fire, and blood. The day after U.S. troops departed Iraq, the Prime Minister of Iraq, Nouri al-Maliki, a Shiite, issued an arrest warrant for the Vice President of Iraq, Tareq al-Hashemi, a Sunni. Al-Maliki had been preparing for this for some time by appointing non-Sunni Islamist hard-liners and Shiites to important cabinet posts, and by creating an internal security force who would answer only to him, and not the reconstituted Iraqi military. The groundwork is prepared for a bloody regression into sectarian chaos, with no U.S. military presence to keep the peace.

As much as I do not wish to witness the tearing apart of the peace won by me and my brethren, from April 2003 to December 2011, I am resigned to the reality that we may very well have to return. God, please spare me the pain of having my own children face this unnecessary burden.

§ § § § §

As a Christian, I'd like to believe I don't practice moral relativism. I'd like to believe I live a principled life and that there is no cognitive dissonance between what I did or didn't do in my official capacity at Gitmo and what the right, moral, and Christian thing to do was. I remind myself, as the ICRC doctors told me, "We are the best at what we do." And that is an absolute.

Now, as more and more soldiers and veterans who are serving and who have served in the Global War on Terrorism are committing suicide, I can see where they are coming from. Although I have never felt suicidal because of any experience I've had in the military, I can understand how others—more viscerally intense experiences or with fewer support resources with which to decompress and adjust—could feel suicidal.

In my preparation as a health and physical education teacher, and as a combat medic at the beginning of my military career, I learned that only about 8 percent of suicidal attempts are "successful" (end in death), and that only about 4 percent of those are what experts consider "hardcore" suicidals, where there is such a desire to stop the emotional pain that the victim chooses a sure-fire method of death. The 92 percent who are not "successful" in killing themselves are still out there hurting, suffering, and contemplating their existence. If you know any veterans, let them know you care. Sometimes just listening can be the best salve to a soldier's wounds. Help them seek assistance if they seem depressed or suicidal. Call the local VA for resource information.

There are Reservists with whom I served at Gitmo who did not fare as well as I did emotionally, mentally, or psychologically. After their tour, a few of them ended up dysfunctional, unable to continue to manage successfully in the military or in civilian life. Some lost jobs, some changed jobs, and some joined the full-time active duty Army in order to make ends meet and make sense of their lives which were changed forever by their selfless service.

Spouses change, too. They become more independent; the ones who stick it out are faithful and fight through the daily fear of the unknown. They resent their military spouse coming back and trying to take over where they left off. There is no "left off." It's a deep-to-the-roots change, a change that can't be properly defined because it is different for each couple, each family, and each community.

When I returned home from Iraq, I was selected "Man of the Year" by the local paper, for being "devoted to family, school (I was the District Administrator for Operations for my local school district), and country." But my feelings were those of guilt for having left my family, confusion over my new role as "returned veteran." Eventually, my job with the local school district was "abolished in order to achieve cost savings," and, as I was told by the new superintendent, I "wasn't [there] enough." I did almost immediately find another job, unlike many of my returning comrades who could not find new work when old jobs were eliminated. The Uniformed Services Employment and Re-Employment Rights Act (USERRA) does not protect reservists whose jobs are eliminated in most cases, the majority of the school board, members who were not on the previous board who gave me a new job and automatic tenure, agreed with the new superintendent, but they did so illegally.

In December 2008 I joined the Retired Reserve so that I could make amends to my family and employer for my absences. In June 2009 my job with the local school district, for which I had worked for nine years and was the senior administrator, was eliminated. They retitled the majority of what I did into a civil service job for less pay and bragged to the community that by eliminating my position they had saved the district money—my salary was one one-thousandth of a percent of the entire budget, and after they paid me my unused sick days (I had taken 12 sick days in 9 years, mostly for the birth of children and to take my father-in-law to Manhattan for cancer treatment), it actually cost the district $16,000 to "save money" by eliminating my job. Many politicians and service groups have implored public and private sector employers to hire unemployed veterans, and find ways to retain employees who are veterans, but not my employer. If I had remained in the Reserves I would have faced at least one more twelve to fourteen month deployment to Iraq or Afghanistan.

For many returning Reservist veterans it takes time for the ghosts and demons to rear their ugly heads. But for me, although I am very proud of my service at Gitmo, and proud of the service of 99.9 percent of my brothers and sisters at arms in this all-volunteer military, my ghosts and demons do come and go, and hopefully they will be less powerful as time goes by. Writing this book has been a journey of discovery and catharsis. I have re-discovered and reconciled some of the raw emotions I experienced at Gitmo, and I have healed somewhat during the process of putting this work together from my journal and notes. I only hope that my fellow brothers and sisters at arms can find similar healing and reconciliation.

I believe that as Americans we can all be proud of just about all who voluntarily put the uniform on every day. They are why we here at home are enjoying civilian life, and why we can hope. Remember, we are at war, and with an enemy who would destroy us and our way of life if they could. It is not a war in Iraq or a war in Afghanistan, it is a Global War on Terrorism, and those are military operations; Operation Iraqi Freedom and Operation Enduring Freedom, respectively. It is a war that will probably not end, but one we must fight to win every day. Phaedrus, a Greek fable writer, once wrote, "Aggression unchallenged is aggression unleashed." As we eventually did during the ending days of the Barbary pirates, we must refuse to pay the ransom of fear, and foster on in brave defiance of those who would chain us to our own terror.

When I returned from Iraq in late November of 2005, I marveled at—and was initially disgusted by—a civilian society seemingly unaware of the battles being fought every day in a faraway desert, both with bullets and bombs, and with ghosts and demons. I caught myself soon thereafter, and I remembered that this communal feeling of vast security I was witnessing was why I went in the first place. It is at least part of why any of us volunteer to put our lives and livelihoods at risk, especially Reservists and the National Guard. Our families don't enjoy the vast support network that active duty soldiers enjoy at bases, which are far and few between for most Reserve and National Guard families. Over time, and with multiple deployments, many of us find ourselves at career crossroads when we return from battle. The new "Operational" Reserve, in order to honestly take care of all of its soldiers, must address openly the daily tragedies affecting those of us who join the Retired Reserve, join the IRR (Individual Ready Reserve), or just plain resign or ask for a discharge. Because of today's challenging job market, and laid-off veterans leading other sectors of the work force in unemployment (over 11 percent at this writing), not enough is being done for these Citizen Warriors.

Reserve retired pay doesn't start until age sixty, whereas active duty retired pay begins immediately following retirement, which for some soldiers can be at age thirty-eight if they joined at eighteen and put in twenty "good" years. That's twenty-two years more earning potential than their brothers and sisters in the Reserve components. Is a Reservist's life so much less valuable? The monthly amount of retirement money is vastly different in favor of our Active Duty brothers and sisters, which is fair because Reservists don't work 24/7 as soldiers unless we're activated, so our retirement pay is comparatively far less and is determined on a point system according to actual time served training or fighting. So why the disparity in when we can collect? It goes back to the way Reserve funds are allocated and how they can be spent. To risk oversimplification, Reserve money for retirement must currently come out of the same pot it uses for training, supplies or "beans and bullets," and equipment. The Active Duty has a separate retirement fund. This needs to be the case for Reservists, and until it becomes a reality no speech, no program, and no legislation can pretend to make things "equal." There needs to be the same retirement opportunity for both components, and it needs to be retroactive to 9/11.

Most of us joined a "Strategic" Reserve, not an "Operational" Reserve. We trained for one weekend per month, two weeks each summer, and were available for major conflicts that required Reserve Forces. Now, in the Operational scenario, we find discrimination in the form of less benefits than our active duty counterparts, even though there is no questioning that without the strength, experience, and maturity of the vast majority of Reserve Forces we would not be able to conduct or sustain current or future operations. We are still second fiddle.

Only when all benefits are equal can we say with confidence that we are one force, and one nation, under God, indivisible, with liberty and justice for all.

Appendix A

Lessons Learned

23 June 2002

MEMORANDUM FOR CAPT A. Phillips, JTF Surgeon, Joint Task Force 160, Guantanamo Bay, Cuba.

SUBJECT: Lessons Learned for JTF 160 Health Service Support.

1. As per your request, I have prepared lessons learned from my perspective for the medical mission of Joint Task Force 160 and the Joint Detainee Operations Group.
2. The lessons learned follow normal Army format and include two previous lessons learned requested of me through JDOG command this past March.
3. The lessons learned include the following topics:
   a. Entomological services.
   b. Preventive medicine personnel.
   c. Geneva Convention, International Law and Army regulations pertaining to medical operations.
   d. Transportation for routine and non-urgent medical patients.
   e. Navy Hospital GTMO Emergency Room philosophy.
   f. General issues vis-à-vis Health Service Support for U.S. personnel.
   g. Holistic approach to U.S. personnel health care.
   h. In-processing and health care records.

4. I am grateful for your request of my opinions and insights. I anticipate your concern with regard to some of the information contained within my lessons learned. I assure you, at every turn, I informed the appropriate authority of any concerns I had at the time. Please understand that the nature of lessons learned tend to focus on constructive rather than complimentary aspects of operations, and that in no way are these comments and opinions meant to take away from the professional, quality health services provided by you and your Navy Hospital staff and facilities. Rather, they are intended to give my candid view and opinions in the hope that necessary improvements or at least meaningful discussion on these topics can begin.

Attachments: Eight Lessons Learned

Montgomery J. Granger

CPT, MS, USAR
JDOG MED OFF
cf: COL Pinale, LTC Grosse, CDR Gates, LCDR Tomms
LESSONS LEARNED
HEALTH SERVICE SUPPORT
JOINT TASK FORCE 160
JOINT DETAINEE OPERATIONS GROUP
GUANTANAMO BAY, CUBA

14 March 2002

OBSERVATION: Navy entomologist left GTMO after only 33 days (January/February 2002), and identified only "nuisance" vectors, but failed to identify envenomed arachnids in and around Camp X-Ray and Freedom Heights or to employ measures which would have deterred their invasion of living and sleeping areas or recommend personal protective measures. U.S. personnel and detainees are now experiencing increased cases of acute localized necrosis somewhat consistent with the known bite of the *loxosceles reclusa* (brown recluse spider).

DISCUSSION: An entomologist should be available during the entire operation, working with preventive medicine staff to constantly monitor ever-changing conditions in and around inhabited locations for the protection of the guard and support forces, as well as the detainee population. The physical and psychological health of U.S. personnel and retained persons should never be a matter of convenience or random circumstance, as new locations, changing weather and sanitary conditions are just a few of the variables which affect both the quantity and type of animals which may pose a threat to the health and welfare of the troops and detained persons. The possibility of enemy employment of biological (animal) means of threat to U.S. operations must be considered.

LESSONS LEARNED: Always retain entomological presence in field conditions where known vectors of disease or debilitating effects are present or a possibility, and enemy threat poses even the slightest potential for disruption of U.S. operations.

RECOMMENDATIONS: Immediately employ Army entomologist with Caribbean or Central/South American experience and retain such personnel throughout the duration of the operation.

Respectfully submitted:

Montgomery J. Granger

CPT, MS, USAR
JDOG MED OFF
LESSONS LEARNED
HEALTH SERVICE SUPPORT
JOINT TASK FORCE 160
JOINT DETAINEE OPERATIONS GROUP
GUANTANAMO BAY, CUBA

14 March 2002

OBSERVATION: 115th MP Battalion deployed without authorized preventive medicine Section personnel, nor were they supplemented with individual augmentees. (NOTE: As of 23 June 2002, the incoming 160th MP BN, replacements for the 115th, brought only one of four required preventive medicine MTOE personnel.)

DISCUSSION: Military Police battalions are authorized Preventive Medicine sections which, among other functions, provide sanitary inspections, assist entomologists and other specialists, and provide for the preventive health and personal protective training and educational needs of the troops. Although Navy preventive medicine teams are available and well-employed, they do not coexist with the troops, nor do they have the number of personnel to function optimally.

LESSONS LEARNED: Always deploy Army Military Police battalions with all authorized MTOE preventive medicine personnel.

RECOMMENDATIONS: Immediately employ Army preventive medicine personnel to co-locate and provide services for Army personnel in their living and working environment.

Respectfully submitted:

Montgomery J. Granger

CPT, MS, USAR
JDOG MED OFF
LESSONS LEARNED
HEALTH SERVICE SUPPORT
JOINT TASK FORCE 160
JOINT DETAINEE OPERATIONS GROUP
GUANTANAMO BAY, CUBA

23 June 2002

OBSERVATION: Medical personnel and facilities are not identified IAW Geneva Conventions and DA PAM 40–19 and DA PAM 27–1 with regard to the proper display of the red cross emblem, and a guard tower exists inside the perimeter of the Fleet Hospital, in clear violation of the Conventions. The current discussion of sheltering un-wounded detainees within the Fleet Hospital, were it to become reality, would also compromise the protected status of the medical personnel and facilities, and is in direct conflict with the spirit and letter of the Conventions.

DISCUSSION: "Under the direction of the competent military authority, the emblem shall be displayed on the flags, armlets and on all equipment employed in the Medical Service," so explains Chapter VII, Article 39, *The Law of Land Warfare.* The proper identification of medical personnel, equipment and facilities is an important element of quality health care of U.S. personnel, especially in a joint environment where subdued and unfamiliar medical identification devices may inadvertently conceal the identification of medical personnel in a critical situation. Proper identification of medical personnel, equipment and facilities, and following Convention guidelines regarding unacceptable practices, such as having a military observation post inside the compound and housing un-wounded detainees there, is paramount to providing efficient access to medical systems in times of emergent or urgent medical circumstance, and to maintaining the protected status of medical personnel and facilities. Secondary benefits to the proper identification of medical personnel, equipment and facilities through the wear and display of the red cross emblem, and otherwise maintaining the legal status of the medical personnel and facilities include, but are not limited to, the following:

Contributes to psychological well-being of U.S. personnel. Visible medical systems marketing equates with higher morale and better performance of the troops.

Legal protection of medical personnel, equipment and facilities.

Positive perception of the humane and fair treatment of detained persons.

International recognition of medical assets.

LESSONS LEARNED: Decisions regarding compliance with Geneva Conventions and Army publications, i.e., DA PAM 40–19 and DA PAM 27–1, should be made and planned for prior to deployment.

RECOMMENDATIONS: Immediately employ use of red cross brassards, placards and flags IAW Geneva Conventions and DA PAM 40–19 and DA PAM 27–1, to be displayed appropriately on all medically qualified personnel, equipment and facilities. Replace military observation post outside Fleet Hospital complex. Never house un-wounded detainees within the Fleet Hospital compound.

Respectfully submitted:

Montgomery J. Granger

CPT, MS, USAR
JDOG MED OFF
LESSONS LEARNED
HEALTH SERVICE SUPPORT
JOINT TASK FORCE 160
JOINT DETAINEE OPERATIONS GROUP
GUANTANAMO BAY, CUBA

22 June 2002

OBSERVATION: Routine transportation for injured and ill U.S. personnel from Joint Aid Stations was haphazard and/or non-existent. On occasion, transportation for urgent sick and injured U.S. personnel was haphazard as well.

DISCUSSION: Although JTF bus service from the Windward Loop Joint Aid Station (WL JAS) to the Navy Hospital Gitmo was available to injured and ill U.S. personnel through early March, the JTF bus route from the housing areas to the hospital were ended then and no new means of transportation were made available. Injured and ill U.S. personnel were left to their own means if appointments, follow-ups, medications, X-rays, etc., were required. Although recent changes in the JTF bus route included the living areas again, the hospital route was not reinstated, despite my adamant request since mid-March that such a route be reinstated in lieu of nonexistent medical transportation. Attempts were made by me to acquire transportation assets from the Joint Logistic Support Group/J-4. These attempts, although not falling on deaf ears, were met with resistance from lower echelons, e.g., maintenance duty driver was frequently unavailable or unwilling to transport U.S. personnel, stating it was the responsibility of the injured/ill U.S. personnel's chain-of-command to transport. Requests were made by me through the JTF Surgeon for such transportation, with no result. I also requested through the JTF Surgeon that JTF 170 "ante up" a vehicle for such purposes, again to no avail. Once Camp America Joint Aid Station (CA JAS) opened, transportation was unavailable there as well. However, for about a seven-week period, a field ambulance was made available to the CA JAS through the Fleet Hospital (even though such assets were designated for detainee care only). After seven weeks, for unknown reasons, the Fleet Hospital took back the ambulance, once again leaving the CA JAS without transportation for injured/ill U.S. personnel. A notional plan to have all individual units transport U.S. personnel to Navy Hospital Gitmo never materialized. After repeated requests by me through command channels for movement plans or a written FRAGO, no action was ever taken. Army Medical Department policy and practice is for transportation of injured and ill personnel be provided by the treating medical facility or aid station *to* the next higher level of care required and also state that personnel requiring transportation *from* hospitals or medical treatment facilities should be provided through the S-1 section of the personnel's unit.

LESSONS LEARNED: Routine and urgent medical evacuation assets are essential to providing basic medical customer service and good medical care, and must be available throughout the duration of an operation.

RECOMMENDATIONS: Required medical or other adequate and appropriate means of transportation should be made available for service to the Joint Aid Stations immediately and retained for such purposes for the duration of the operation.

Respectfully submitted:

Montgomery J. Granger

CPT, MS, USAR
JDOG MED OFF
LESSONS LEARNED
HEALTH SERVICE SUPPORT
JOINT TASK FORCE 160
JOINT DETAINEE OPERATIONS GROUP
GUANTANAMO BAY, CUBA

22 June 2002

OBSERVATION: Recently, anecdotal data revealed the perception that Navy Hospital GTMO emergency room personnel were not receptive to JTF ill/injured personnel on weekends and after hours of the Windward Loop Joint Aid Station (WL JAS).

DISCUSSION: Several and repeated conversations I have had with JTF personnel and non-Navy medical personnel, consistently revealed that JTF personnel who sought help at the Navy Hospital GTMO emergency room after the WL JAS hours (1630 and after) and on weekends (WL JAS is closed on weekends), were treated in a nonchalant and even dismissive manner by ER personnel.

LESSONS LEARNED: All JTF personnel, no matter the severity or slightness of their injury or illness, deserve caring, professional and attentive treatment, including proper bedside manner.

RECOMMENDATIONS: Education and training should immediately be made available and required of all Navy Hospital GTMO personnel who work in the ER. This training and education should focus on the readjustment of a treatment philosophy in the emergency room that accounts for the fact that routine and urgent medical care for JTF personnel is needed during WL JAS non-operating hours, and should be delivered appropriately.

Respectfully submitted:

Montgomery J. Granger

CPT, MS, USAR
JDOG MED OFF
LESSONS LEARNED
HEALTH SERVICE SUPPORT
JOINT TASK FORCE 160
JOINT DETAINEE OPERATIONS GROUP
GUANTANAMO BAY, CUBA

23 June 2002

OBSERVATION: Although many JTF personnel are enjoying quality medical care, many improvements can be made. The current basic philosophy seems to be, "Let the soldier, sailor, airman, Marine or Coast Guard person come to us for Echelon

I care." The perception persists, even among some of the highest-ranking medical personnel, that the health service support for detainees is better than that for U.S. personnel.

DISCUSSION: Many important aspects of health service support for U.S. personnel are either casually observed or not observed at all. Including transportation (see separate Lesson Learned), in-processing (see separate Lesson Learned), command and control structure, scope of service, standard operating procedures, discipline, administration, environment, supervision and accountability. These things seem to be well planned, thought out and executed for detainee care; sick call hours for detainees is at all hours of the day. "Rounds" are made to ensure their health and comfort, even though the Geneva Conventions require only once monthly medical checks. In the meantime, the very people who guard them and ensure our safety are relegated to only receiving first aid or emergency care inside the camp. This is contrary to U.S. Army policy and practice, and has directly or indirectly affected the health, safety and well being of U.S. personnel working in the detainee camp. Morale is something that more often than not only gets command attention when it is low. By then it is too late. Just like the health care that is only provided in a fixed structure, and offered in measured doses salving only the physical ailment, is only marginally as effective as it could be.

LESSONS LEARNED: Health services support philosophy should include the projection of services to those who need it. As per Army Field Manual 3–19–40, Army medical personnel should be inside the detainee camp promoting and providing the highest possible health service support for all U.S. personnel. Proactive health service support must be delivered to the personnel, not the other way around. If it is not, we face the risk of performing reactive medicine, which in the worst case could unnecessarily cost lives of U.S. personnel.

RECOMMENDATIONS: Immediately review and adjust level and frequency of detainee care in accordance with the provisions of the Conventions, while at the same time review and adjust the level of care for U.S. personnel at least to the level prescribed in military regulations, policies and manuals. Project care forward.

Respectfully submitted:

Montgomery J. Granger

CPT, MS, USAR
JDOG MED OFF
LESSONS LEARNED
HEALTH SERVICE SUPPORT
JOINT TASK FORCE 160
JOINT DETAINEE OPERATIONS GROUP
GUANTANAMO BAY, CUBA

23 June 2002

OBSERVATION: The following problems exist within the scope of a holistic approach to health service support for U.S. personnel: high incidence of preventable injuries; incidents of heat illness; improper buddy aid; substandard transportation services; infrequent impact awards and praise for deserving personnel; reactive rather than proactive medical, preventive medical and sanitary practices. All these deficiencies contribute to decreased or low morale.

DISCUSSION: Most soldiers seen at aid stations are complainants of preventable injuries. Heat illness is too frequent if just one person succumbs; it implies there are potentially many others who are near the point of illness due to dehydration, low sodium or improper nutritional practices i.e., skipping meals. Soldiers injured inside the detainee compound are not given appropriate buddy aid, as the inappropriate moving of a casualty who had fallen from a guard tower indicates. Buses are cramped (designed for children, not adults), hot, dirty, with loud and often vulgar and inappropriate music playing, and drivers who are less than professional, e.g., slouching, one-handed driving, speeding. While NAV Base GTMO buses are designed for adult passengers, air conditioned, clean, quiet, professionally operated and therefore offer healthy, safe and stress-free respite. The lack of impact awards and praise is often a main topic of discussion among troops, yet are intended to be a regular, effective means of promoting good morale and *esprit.* The lack of visible medical, preventive medicine and sanitary services that are aggressive and proactive for the benefit of U.S. personnel contribute to less than adequate health service support, and decreased or low morale.

LESSONS LEARNED: It seems that a contributing factor to the problems listed above is the Joint Command structure, which is not connected by staff planning and functions, and a mixture of Echelon 2 thru 4 providers in a decidedly Echelon 1 environment, which does not address the expectations and needs of the JTF personnel in the field. The combination of these factors creates an overall environment that is unhealthy, more dangerous than it should or could be, and that directly contributes to decreased or low morale.

RECOMMENDATIONS: Employ Army Medical Service Personnel (67A/70B series) at each level of command (O-5 at the JTF level, O-4 at the JDOG level, O-3 at the battalion level, O-2 at the company level, and O-1 at the platoon level) to ensure that a healthy, safe and positive environment exists for U.S. personnel, and that plans, policies and regulations are enforced, practiced and revised as necessary and needed.

Respectfully submitted:

Montgomery J. Granger

CPT, MS, USAR
JDOG MED OFF
LESSONS LEARNED
HEALTH SERVICE SUPPORT
JOINT TASK FORCE 160
JOINT DETAINEE OPERATIONS GROUP
GUANTANAMO BAY, CUBA

23 June 2002

OBSERVATION: Incoming JTF personnel are not consistently carrying medical/dental shadow records, and those records are not being quickly delivered to the appropriate Joint Aid Station. In-processing of incoming JTF personnel is not executed and managed by Navy Hospital GTMO administration.

DISCUSSION: Currently, non-Navy Hospital medical personnel are providing in-processing services for in-coming JTF personnel. Command emphasis is not used to ensure in-coming JTF personnel bring accurate, current medical records which should include medical, dental, shot and other important information necessary for us to provide appropriate and efficient quality care.

LESSONS LEARNED: Patient administration is a critical link in the chain of efficient quality health service support for U.S. personnel. The responsibility and authority for U.S. personnel health care begins with the Navy Hospital GTMO, and therefore should be expressed with aggressive interest in the collection of all heath records, information for CHCS enrollment, and environmental, medical and preventive medical in-processing.

RECOMMENDATIONS: Navy Hospital GTMO patient administration services immediately take command and control of the in-processing of in-coming JTF personnel, and make an aggressive effort to ensure that all in-coming JTF personnel bring with them the necessary and appropriate health documentation in order that the best possible heath service support is delivered.

Respectfully submitted:

Montgomery J. Granger

CPT, MS, USAR
JDOG MED OFF

BLD Duty Descriptions

STAFF DESCRIPTIONS and RESPONSIBILITIES
for
THE ENEMY PRISONER OF WAR/CIVILIAN INTERNEE
BRIGADE LIAISON DETACHMENT

1. GENERAL

    This appendix prescribes procedures for the deployment and use of the Brigade Liaison Detachment (BLD) during wartime operations.

2. SITUATION

    The BLD is employed when the brigade's assigned Enemy Prisoner of War (EPW) Battalions in theatre exceeds seven at which time one BLD will be employed on-site with every grouping of three EPW battalions. When U.S. EPW battalions are not used in theatre, the BLD is employed to provide supervision and command and control of attached MP EPW/CI processing and liaison teams. Historically, battalion staffs have focused their attention and resources on both managing internal Internment Facility operations and external logistical support operations. This need to manage both internally and externally has stretched the battalion staff beyond their staffing capabilities and manpower.

3. MISSION

The BLD augments the brigade to extend the commander's staff planning and coordination of operations for three U.S. MP battalions or provides staff planning and coordination link to indigenous prisoner of war command and staff, and command, control and supervision of attached MP EPW/CI processing and liaison team operations. The BLD will only perform one of the above two missions at a time.

4. EMPLOYMENT

   A. When the brigade deploys more than one EPW battalion to the same geographical area to form an EPW Camp, the brigade commander will appoint one of the EPW battalion commanders as the camp commander. This individual will typically be the senior EPW battalion commander. The BLD does not perform the function of the camp commander unless determined by the brigade commander.

   B. Unless otherwise determined by the brigade commander, the BLD will co-locate with the EPW battalion of the camp commander. The Senior EPW officer of the BLD, after consulting with the brigade commander, may decide to employ one or more members of the BLD at other locations (i.e. the BDE, ASG) in order to facilitate the BLDs coordination function.

   C. When the BLD is employed, the brigade staff, unless otherwise notified by the brigade commander, will continue to correspond with their counterparts at the battalion level with a copy furnished to the BLD.

   D. The BLD concept was designed to support the battalion staff by alleviating the responsibility to simultaneously manage both the internal and external support. The BLD will provide brigade level functional planning and coordination capabilities for transportation, logistics, medical, legal, and engineer onsite with the supported EPW Battalions.

      1) Battalion staff will manage the *internal* process. Specifically, the battalion staff will own the responsibility for managing all local, support and sustenance for Internment Facility.

      2) The BLD will support the battalions by coordinating and facilitating the *external* process. Specifically, the BLD will coordinate support for the battalions with

the Area Support Group (ASG), the local Transportation Groups (MCAs), and all other support agencies within the ASG footprint. As appropriate, the BLD will consolidate requests for like items from ASG agencies.

3) In the instance where ASG agencies cannot support BLD requests for assistance, the BLD will forward the denied request(s) to the appropriate brigade staff representative who will coordinate with Support Command.

5. EXECUTION

A. Senior EPW/CI Officer: Acts as the brigade commander's representative on-site to ensure EPW Operations in the theatre follow U.S. policy and published directives, international agreements, and U.S. policies implementing international law. Supervises the operation of the BLD in extending the capabilities of the BDE. When employed as a liaison link with allied or indigenous PW commands and staff, will command, control and supervise the operation of attached MP EPW/CI liaison teams.

B. EPW/CI Officer: Assists in developing operations plans, SOPs and directives for camp security, training, operational records and reports pertaining to the EPW/CI Camp. Serves as the subject matter expert to supported battalion commanders and their staffs for operations and logistical support within the theater of operations. Coordinates the accurate accountability of EPW within the EPW battalions assigned to the camp. Coordinates visits to the camp by such organizations as the International Committee of the Red Cross and other organizations.

C. Transportation Officer: Coordinates plans for the expeditious movement of EPW/CI to and from medical/dental units, to support EPW labor work projects, between EPW battalions. Ensures transportation is available to move supplies for a camp consisting of three MP Battalions (EPW/CI), including ration distribution, prisoner transport and prisoner details. Serves as a liaison officer/contact administrator for U.S. allied military, or host nation motor and rail assets. Coordinates with Area Support Groups for CSS services beyond the capabilities of EPW Battalions. Maintains liaison with tactical units/escort guard companies concerning transfer of EPWs. Coordinates with the brigade for daily transportation requirements for movement of EPW and their personal property.

D. Supply Officer. Coordinates the planning and direction of logistics operations to ensure the timely procurement of construction and maintenance material, general supplies, subsistence, Class VI comfort items, repair parts, and fuel and services from military and civilian sources to support the three EPW/CI battalions. Coordinates inspections from the EPW BDE of supply operations and records to ensure the receipt and storage of EPW personal property is IAW regulations. Coordinates requisitions for religious and recreational materials. Coordinates with local QM units for sufficient water supply for the camp and laundry and clothing exchange.

E. Field Medical Assistant. Plans and coordinates staff functions pertaining to health services plans and operations. Coordinates patient evacuation and treatment, medical administration, supply, training and maintenance. Evaluates the environmental health and sanitation measures to prevent and control disease in the EPW camp. Coordinates preventive medicine support from area medical units. Coordinates the utilization of retained persons to support the EPW population. Ensures medical facilities of the battalion operate IAW established regulations/policies.

F. Facilities/Contract Construction Management Engineer. Coordinates for the construction and maintenance of facilities to intern Enemy Prisoner of War/Civilian Internee (EPW/CI), utilizing available EPW and local sources of material to the maximum extent possible. Ensures construction standards satisfy security requirements. Coordinates with area combat engineers for water supply distribution to the internment facilities, disposal of garbage/sewage, forklifts/tractors, refrigeration containers, etc. Determines availability of necessary materials, tools and equipment requirements for EPW work projects. Coordinates with Engineer power plant operation/ maintenance teams, firefighting teams. Advises staff on Repairs and Utilities (R&S) section.

G. Legal Liaison Officer. Provides a coordination link to the EPW Brigade commander on legal problems concerning military law, international law and laws of the country concerned in conduct of EPW/CI operations.

H. Operations NCO. Assists Senior EPW/CI Officer in planning, coordinating and supervising the operational activities that support the unit mission. Supervises and reviews preparation of statistical data and reports concerning accountability of EPWs in the EPW camps. Inspects unit activities and facilities. Coordinates training for defense of the EPW camp, including NBC training. Also acts as the Detachment Sergeant.

I. Liaison NCO. Assists staff officers. Maintains liaison with enlisted personnel at battalion and attached escort guard and guard companies. Supervises personnel in the administrative functions of the detachment. Coordinates with Civil Affairs units for support as needed to ensure refugees and innocent civilians are not interned. Coordinates the work of interpreters for translation and operational support at the processing points in the compound.

J. Administrative Specialist and Administrative Clerk. Prepare correspondence, reports, and statistical presentations pertaining to the liaison operations of the detachment. Maintains files and records as required. Operate switchboard and vehicles as required.

K. Vehicle Driver. Vehicle driver for the Senior EPW/CI officer. Acts as courier for the detachment, when required.

Al Qaeda Training Manual Lesson Eighteen, Prisons and Detention Centers

UK/BM-176 TO UK/BM-180 TRANSLATION

The al Qaeda manual presented here was made available by the FBI which distributed the manual on their website: *www.fbi.gov*. The object of bin Laden is to establish a "Caliphate according to the prophet's path." To accomplish this objective he must induce others to engage in acts and would bring about a world economic collapse and social upheaval that would bring about the deaths of hundreds of millions. To contain this mad man the best weapon is the truth. The Disaster Center Lesson Eighteen PRISONS AND DETENTION CENTERS IF AN INDICTMENT IS ISSUED AND THE TRIAL BEGINS, THE BROTHER HAS TO PAY ATTENTION TO THE FOLLOWING:

1. At the beginning of the trial, once more the brothers must insist on proving that torture was inflicted on them by State Security [investigators] before the judge.
2. Complain [to the court] of mistreatment while in prison.
3. Make arrangements for the brother's defense with the attorney, whether he was retained by the brother's family or court-appointed.

4. The brother has to do his best to know the names of the state security officers, who participated in his torture and mention their names to the judge. [These names may be obtained from brothers who had to deal with those officers in previous cases.]

5. Some brothers may tell and may be lured by the state security investigators to testify against the brothers [i.e. affirmation witness], either by not keeping them together in the same prison during the trials, or by letting them talk to the media. In this case, they have to be treated gently, and should be offered good advice, good treatment, and pray that God may guide them.

6. During the trial, the court has to be notified of any mistreatment of the brothers inside the prison.

7. It is possible to resort to a hunger strike, but it is a tactic that can either succeed or fail.

8. Take advantage of visits to communicate with brothers outside prison and exchange information that may be helpful to them in their work outside prison [according to what occurred during the investigations]. The importance of mastering the art of hiding messages is self evident here.

- When the brothers are transported from and to the prison [on their way to the court] they should shout Islamic slogans out loud from inside the prison cars to impress upon the people and their family the need to support Islam.

- Inside the prison, the brother should not accept any work that may belittle or demean him or his brothers, such as the cleaning of the prison bathrooms or hallways.

- The brothers should create an Islamic program for themselves inside the prison, as well as recreational and educational ones, etc.

- The brother in prison should be a role model in selflessness. Brothers should also pay attention to each others needs and should help each other and unite vis a vis the prison officers.

- The brothers must take advantage of their presence in prison for obeying and worshipping [God] and memorizing the Qora 'an, etc. This is in addition to all guidelines and procedures that were contained in the lesson on interrogation and investigation. Lastly, each of us has to understand that we don't achieve victory against our enemies through these actions and security procedures. Rather, victory is achieved by obeying Almighty and Glorious

God and because of their many sins. Every brother has to be careful so as not to commit sins and every one of us has to do his best in obeying Almighty God, Who said in his Holy Book: "We will, without doubt. Help Our messengers and those who believe (both) in this world's life and the one Day when the Witnesses will stand forth." May God guide us.

Dedication

To this pure Muslim youth, the believer, the mujahid (fighter) for God's sake. I present this modest effort as a contribution from me to pave the way that will lead to Almighty God and to establish a caliphate along the lines of the prophet.

The prophet, peace be upon him, said according to what was related by Imam Ahmed: "Let the prophecy that God wants be in you, yet God may remove it if He so wills, and then there will be a Caliphate according to the prophet's path [instruction], if God so wills it. He will also remove that [the Caliphate] if He so wills, and you will have a disobedient king if God so wills it. Once again, if God so wills, He will remove him [the disobedient king], and you will have an oppressive lung. [Finally], if God so wills, He will remove him [the oppressive king], and you will have a Caliphate according to the prophet's path [instruction]. He then became silent."

THE IMPORTANCE OF TEAM WORK:

1. Team work is the only translation of God's command, as well as that of the prophet, to unite and not to disunite. Almighty God says, "And hold fast, all together, by the Rope which Allah (stretches out for you), and be not divided among yourselves." In "Sahih Muslim," it was reported by Abu Horairah, may Allah look kindly upon him, that the prophet, may Allah's peace and greetings be upon him, said: "Allah approves three [things] for you and disapproves three [things]: He approves that you worship him, that you do not disbelieve in Him, and that you hold fast, all together, by the Rope which Allah, and be not divided among yourselves. He disapproves of three: gossip, asking too much [for help], and squandering money."

2. Abandoning "team work" for individual and haphazard work means disobeying that orders of God and the prophet and falling victim to disunity.

3. Team work is-conducive to cooperation in righteousness and piety.

4. Upholding religion, which God has ordered us by His saying, "Uphold religion," will necessarily require an all out confrontation against all our enemies, who want to recreate darkness. In addition, it is imperative to stand against darkness in all arenas: the media, education, [religious] guidance, and counseling, as well as others. This will make it necessary for us to move on numerous fields so as to enable the Islamic movement to confront ignorance and achieve victory against it in the battle to uphold religion. All these vital goals cannot be adequately achieved without organized team work. Therefore, team work becomes a necessity, in accordance with the fundamental rule, "Duty cannot be accomplished without it, and it is a requirement." This way, team work is achieved through mustering and organizing the ranks, while putting the Amir (the Prince) before them, and the right man in the right place, making plans for action, organizing work, and obtaining facets of power.

Glossary

1LT: First Lieutenant. Army grade of O-2

AIT: Advance Individual Training. Individual job specific Army skill training

AK-47: Standard issue Soviet-block automatic/semi-automatic rifle

APC: Armored personnel carrier

Banana rat: Hutia, a large, docile Cuban rodent measuring up to two feet in length and weighing up to 15 pounds

BDE: Brigade

bivouac: military encampment

BLD: Brigade Liaison Detachment

C2: Command and Control

CamelBak: Plastic bladder a soldier wears on his/her back and drinks through a drinking (bite) tube

cammo: Camouflage

CAPT: Captain. Navy grade of O-6 rank; Army, Air Force, and Marine rank of O-3, abbreviated CPT

CDR: Commander. Navy grade of O-5, equivalent to Army, Air Force, and Marine rank of Lieutenant Colonel (LTC, O-5)

CI: Civilian Internee

CIF: Central Issuing Facility. Supply depot where mobilizing soldiers receive personal supply items, such as uniforms, boots, protective gear, etc.

CO: Commanding Officer

COL: Colonel. Army grade of O-6, a.k.a. "bird-colonel" due to the rank insignia of an eagle

Corpsman: Navy medic

CoS: Chief of Staff

CP: Command Post

CPT: Captain. Navy grade of O-6 rank (Navy abbreviation: CAPT); Army, Air Force, and Marine rank of O-3

CQ: In Charge of Quarters. Person in charge of administrative and emergency issues, usually during an overnight watch as others sleep

Cuban rock iguana: Black iguana indigenous to southeastern Cuba

CXR: Camp X-Ray. Army phonetic for "Camp X"

CXRMF: Camp X-Ray Medical Facility

FAS: First Aid Station. U.S. personnel medical facility, Freedom Heights and Camp America

EPW: Enemy Prisoner of War

FH: Fleet Hospital. Mobile, sectioned hospital consisting of lined, air conditioned tents and connex-type medical facilities joined by vestibules

GEN: General. Proper address of all general officers, but also specific to a Brigadier (one star) General

Gitmo: Guantanamo Bay, Cuba, also, the rock, the island, GTMO

GWOT: Global War on Terrorism

helo: Short for "helicopter"

hooch: Army dwelling. Could be a tent, could be a condo, or anything in-between that is used as a domicile while on deployment. In Abu Ghraib prison, it was a former prison cell

IAW: In Accordance With

ICRC: International Committee of the Red Cross

IDC: Independent Duty Corpsman

I/R: Internment/Resettlement

JAS: Joint Aid Station, Windward Loop

Jerk House: Open air restaurant run by Jamaicans, famous for its "jerk" spiced pulled pork and chicken, Johnny Cakes and Red Stripe Jamaican beer

JTF: Joint Task Force. Multiple military branches forming a single command structure and mission

Kevlar: Military helmet

Litter: Military stretcher used to transport the sick and wounded

LT: Lieutenant. Proper address of either First or Second Lieutenant in the Army, Air Force or Marines in the grade of O-1 or O-2; Navy "Lieutenant" is grade of O-3

LTC: Lieutenant Colonel. Grade of O-5 in the Army. Also proper address for lieutenant colonels is "Colonel"; Navy equivalent is "Commander"

LTCDR: Lieutenant Commander. Navy grade of O-4 and addressed as "Commander"; Army, Air Force, and Marine equivalent is rank of Major (MAJ), grade O-4

M-16: Standard issue military automatic/semi-automatic rifle

MAJ: Major. Army grade of O-4; Navy equivalent is Lieutenant Commander (LTCDR)

MP: Military Police

MRE: Meal-Ready-to-Eat—military combat ration worth about 1,500 calories each if all contents are consumed

MSG: Master Sergeant, Army grade of E-8; Navy equivalent is Senior Chief Petty Officer

NAV HOSP GTMO: Fixed, hard building hospital—not part of JTF 160 detainee care mission

NCOIC: Non-Commissioned Officer In Charge

NX: Navy Exchange. Shopping center/mall

OER: Officer Evaluation Report, or job performance review

OIC: Officer In Charge

OP CON: Operational control; to control a person, group, place, or action

OPS: Operations

OPSEC: Operational Security

PAO: Public Affairs Officer, or public relations representative

Pink Palace: Former dental clinic, World War II era two story building painted pale Caribbean pink—turned Joint Detainee Operations Group Headquarters, on top of McCalla Hill, Gitmo, Cuba

POW: Prisoner of War

PREV MED: Preventive Medicine. Also PVTMED

Puzzle Palace: Two-story Joint Task Force headquarters building several hundred yards northeast of the Pink Palace on McCalla Hill

Rick's: Officer's club at Gitmo

SS: *Schutzstaffel,* or "Defense echelon," Adolf Hitler's personal guard, or special security force

Sally port: Enclosed gateway separating holding areas and open areas in a prison camp

Seabees: Members of the construction battalions of the U.S. Navy, established in December, 1941, to build landing facilities, airfields, etc., in combat areas; Army equivalent are Combat Engineers. Motto: "We Build, We Fight!" And not necessarily in that order

SGT: Sergeant, Army grade of E-5; Navy equivalent Petty Officer Second Class

SIT REP: Situation Report

SOP: Standard Operating Procedures

SPC: Specialist. Army grade of E-4

SPRINT: U. S. Navy Special Psychiatric Rapid Intervention Team

SRP: Soldier Readiness Processing

UCMJ: Uniform Code of Military Justice. Statutes that govern behavior of military personnel

WL: Windward Loop. Street where many command group soldiers, sailors, airmen, Marine Corpsmen, and Coast Guard personnel lived in condominiums

Wehrmacht: German Army forces of World War II

Author's Bio Notes

Montgomery J. Granger is a three-time mobilized U.S. Army Reserve Major (Ret.), who was called into his Reserve Center in Uniondale (Long Island), New York, on 9/11, in response to the attacks on the World Trade Center's Twin Towers, the Pentagon, and Flight 93, which crashed at Shanksville, Pennsylvania. He answered his country's call to duty next in January 2002 for a mission to help run the military detention facility at the U.S. Naval Station at Guantanamo Bay, Cuba. He was called up again just six months after returning from duty at Gitmo, but this time remained stateside at the U.S. Army Reserve Training Center at Fort Dix, New Jersey. After nearly six months at Fort Dix, MAJ Granger returned to civilian life for about a year when he was involuntarily transferred to another Reserve Army unit that was deploying to Iraq in the fall of 2004. Major Granger served 14 months of active duty on his third deployment and served in Baghdad, Abu Ghraib, Camp Bucca, and Ashraf, Iraq, as Medical Service officer for military detention facility operations. He is married and is the father of five children, and lives on Long Island, New York. He is also the author of "Theodore," a personal narrative published in the 2006 Random House wartime anthology "Operation Homecoming: Iraq, Afghanistan and the Home Front in the Words of U.S. Troops and Their Families," where he wrote about his fear and anxiety over having left his family in 2002, and especially two-day-old Theodore, and what reaction there was upon his return. Operation Homecoming was sponsored in part by the National Endowment for the Arts, and edited by Andrew Carroll, editor of the New York Times bestselling book, *War Letters*.

Granger was born in Illinois, raised and schooled in Rubidoux, California, and attended undergraduate school at the University of Alabama in Tuscaloosa where he earned a Bachelor of Science degree in education. He earned a master's degree in curriculum and teaching from Teachers College—Columbia University, where he met his wife. He also attended the State University of New York at Stony Brook, where he earned professional credits to obtain a New York State School District Administrators' license. He is an accomplished coach and teacher of health and physical education, having taught in Alabama, California, New York City, and Long Island, before becoming a director of Health, Physical Education and Athletics. He was most recently Director of Health, Physical Education and Athletics, and then District Administrator for Operations for the Comsewogue school district in Port Jefferson Station, N.Y., and is now a Director of Health, Physical Education and Athletics, and Director of Facilities for the Sag Harbor Union Free School District in Long Island.

Granger is the author of many writings and musing as yet unpublished, but hopefully soon to be shared with a waiting world.